ABOUT THIS PUBLICATION

FOR SERVICE ASSISTANCE

Customer Service Department
1.704.898.0770

North Carolina General Statues is published by The Muliti-Media Group of Greater Charlotte in Charlotte, North Carolina. Copyright 2015 by the Multi-Media Group of Greater Charlotte. This book or parts thereof may not be reproduced in any form, stored in a retrieval system, or transmitted in any form by any means—electronic, mechanical, photocopy, recording or otherwise—without prior written permission of the publisher, except as provided by United States of America copyright law.

The records required by U.S. Code 2257(a) through (c) and the pertinent regulations 28 C.F.R. Cli. 1, Part 75 with respect to this publication and all materials associated with such records are maintained by The Multi-Media Group of Greater Charlotte, Publisher and available for review by Attorney General.

www.visionbooks.org

Copyright © 2015 by MMGGC
All rights reserved!

TID: 5108184
ISBN (10) digit: 1503246809
ISBN (13) digit: 978-1503246805

123-4-56789-01239-Paperback
123-4-56789-01239-Hardback

First Edition

090520140547

Printed in the United States of America

2015 EDITION

North Carolina Criminal Law

And Procedure-Pamphlet # 87

Printed In conjunction with the
Administration of the Courts

North Carolina Criminal Law and Procedure
Pamphlet Reference Guide

Chapters	Pamphlet
Chapter 1 Civil Procedure	1
Chapter 1 Civil Procedure (Continue)	2
Chapter 1A Rules of Civil Procedure	2
Chapter 1B Contribution.	2
Chapter 1C Enforcement of Judgments.	2
Chapter 1D Punitive Damages.	2
Chapter 1E Eastern Band of Cherokee Indians.	2
Chapter 1F North Carolina Uniform Interstate Depositions and Discovery Act.	2
Chapter 2 - Clerk of Superior Court [Repealed and Transferred.]	3
Chapter 3 - Commissioners of Affidavits and Deeds [Repealed.]	3
Chapter 4 - Common Law	3
Chapter 5 - Contempt [Repealed.]	3
Chapter 5A - Contempt	3
Chapter 6 - Liability for Court Costs	3
Chapter 7 - Courts [Repealed and Transferred.]	3
Chapter 7A – Judicial Department	3
Chapter 7A – Continuation (Judicial Department)	4
Chapter 7A – Continuation (Judicial Department)	5
Chapter 7B - Juvenile Code	5
Chapter 8 - Evidence	6
Chapter 8A - Interpreters for Deaf Persons [Recodified.]	6
Chapter 8B - Interpreters for Deaf Persons	6
Chapter 8C - Evidence Code	6
Chapter 9 - Jurors	6
Chapter 10 - Notaries [Repealed.]	6
Chapter 10A - Notaries [Recodified.]	6
Chapter 10B - Notaries	6
Chapter 11 - Oaths	6
Chapter 12 - Statutory Construction	6
Chapter 13 - Citizenship Restored	6
Chapter 14 - Criminal Law	7
Chapter 14 –Criminal Law (Continuation)	8
Chapter 15 - Criminal Procedure	9
Chapter 15A - Criminal Procedure Act (Continuation)	10
Chapter 15A - Criminal Procedure Act (Continuation)	11
Chapter 15B - Victims Compensation	11
Chapter 15C - Address Confidentiality Program	11
Chapter 16 - Gaming Contracts and Futures	11
Chapter 17 - Habeas Corpus	11

Chapter 17A - Law-Enforcement Officers [Recodified.]	11
Chapter 17B - North Carolina Criminal Justice Education and Training System [Recodified.] Chapter 17C - North Carolina Criminal Justice Education and Training Standards Commission	11
	11
Chapter 17D - North Carolina Justice Academy	11
Chapter 17E - North Carolina Sheriffs' Education and Training Standards Commission	11
Chapter 18 - Regulation of Intoxicating Liquors [Repealed.]	12
Chapter 18A - Regulation of Intoxicating Liquors [Repealed.]	12
Chapter 18B - Regulation of Alcoholic Beverages	12
Chapter 18C - North Carolina State Lottery	12
Chapter 19 - Offenses against Public Morals	12
Chapter 19A - Protection of Animals	12
Chapter 20 - Motor Vehicles	13
Chapter 20 - Motor Vehicles (Continuation)	14
Chapter 20 - Motor Vehicles (Continuation)	15
Chapter 20 - Motor Vehicles (Continuation)	16
Chapter 21 - Bills of Lading	17
Chapter 22 - Contracts Requiring Writing	17
Chapter 22A - Signatures	17
Chapter 22B - Contracts Against Public Policy	17
Chapter 22C - Payments to Subcontractors	17
Chapter 23 - Debtor and Creditor	17
Chapter 24 – Interest	17
Chapter 25 – Uniform Commercial Code	18
Chapter 25 – Uniform Commercial Code (Continuation)	19
Chapter 25A – Retail Installment Sales Act	20
Chapter 25B - Credit	20
Chapter 25C - Sales of Artwork	20
Chapter 26 - Suretyship	20
Chapter 27 - Warehouse Receipts [Repealed.]	20
Chapter 28 - Administration [Repealed.]	20
Chapter 28A - Administration of Decedents' Estates	20
Chapter 28B - Estates of Absentees in Military Service	20
Chapter 28C - Estates of Missing Persons	20
Chapter 29 - Intestate Succession	21
Chapter 30 - Surviving Spouses	21
Chapter 31 - Wills	21
Chapter 31A - Acts Barring Property Rights	21
Chapter 31B - Renunciation of Property and Renunciation of Fiduciary Powers Act	21
Chapter 31C - Uniform Disposition of Community Property Rights at Death Act	21
Chapter 32 - Fiduciaries	21
Chapter 32A - Powers of Attorney	21
Chapter 33 - Guardian and Ward [Repealed and Recodified.]	21

Chapter 33A - North Carolina Uniform Transfers to Minors Act	21
Chapter 33B - North Carolina Uniform Custodial Trust Act	21
Chapter 34 - Veterans' Guardianship Act	22
Chapter 35 - Sterilization Procedures	22
Chapter 35A - Incompetency and Guardianship	22
Chapter 36 - Trusts and Trustees [Repealed.]	22
Chapter 36A - Trusts and Trustees	22
Chapter 36B - Uniform Management of Institutional Funds Act [Repealed.]	22
Chapter 36C - North Carolina Uniform Trust Code	22
Chapter 36D - North Carolina Community Third Party Trusts, Pooled Trusts	23
Chapter 36E - Uniform Prudent Management of Institutional Funds Act	23
Chapter 37 - Allocation of Principal and Income [Repealed.]	23
Chapter 37A - Uniform Principal and Income Act	23
Chapter 38 - Boundaries	23
Chapter 38A - Landowner Liability	23
Chapter 39 - Conveyances	23
Chapter 39A - Transfer Fee Covenants Prohibited	23
Chapter 40 - Eminent Domain [Repealed.]	23
Chapter 40A - Eminent Domain	23
Chapter 41 - Estates	23
Chapter 41A - State Fair Housing Act	23
Chapter 42 - Landlord and Tenant	23
Chapter 42A - Vacation Rental Act	23
Chapter 43 - Land Registration	23
Chapter 44 - Liens	24
Chapter 44A - Statutory Liens and Charges	24
Chapter 45 - Mortgages and Deeds of Trust	24
Chapter 45A - Good Funds Settlement Act	24
Chapter 46 - Partition	24
Chapter 47 - Probate and Registration	25
Chapter 47A - Unit Ownership	25
Chapter 47B - Real Property Marketable Title Act	25
Chapter 47C - North Carolina Condominium Act	25
Chapter 47D - Notice of Settlement Act [Expired.]	25
Chapter 47E - Residential Property Disclosure Act	25
Chapter 47F - North Carolina Planned Community Act	25
Chapter 47G - Option to Purchase Contracts	25
Chapter 47H - Contracts for Deed	25
Chapter 48 - Adoptions	26
Chapter 48A - Minors	26
Chapter 49 - Bastardy	26
Chapter 49A - Rights of Children	26
Chapter 50 - Divorce and Alimony	26
Chapter 50A - Uniform Child-Custody Jurisdiction and	

Enforcement Act	26
Chapter 50B - Domestic Violence	26
Chapter 50C - Civil No-Contact Orders	26
Chapter 51 - Marriage	26
Chapter 52 - Powers and Liabilities of Married Persons	27
Chapter 52A - Uniform Reciprocal Enforcement of Support Act [Repealed.]	27
Chapter 52B - Uniform Premarital Agreement Act	27
Chapter 52C - Uniform Interstate Family Support Act	27
Chapter 53 - Banks	27
Chapter 53A - Business Development Corporations and North Carolina Capital Resource Corporations	28
Chapter 53B - Financial Privacy Act	28
Chapter 54 - Cooperative Organizations	28
Chapter 54A - Capital Stock Savings and Loan Associations [Repealed.]	28
Chapter 54B - Savings and Loan Associations	29
Chapter 54C - Savings Banks	29
Chapter 55 - North Carolina Business Corporation Act	30
Chapter 55A - North Carolina Nonprofit Corporation Act	31
Chapter 55B - Professional Corporation Act	31
Chapter 55C - Foreign Trade Zones	31
Chapter 55D - Filings, Names, and Registered Agents for Corporations, Nonprofit Corporations, and Partnerships	31
Chapter 56 - Electric, Telegraph and Power Companies [Repealed.]	31
Chapter 57 - Hospital, Medical and Dental Service Corporations [Recodified.]	31
Chapter 57A - Health Maintenance Organization Act [Recodified.]	31
Chapter 57B - Health Maintenance Organization Act [Recodified.]	31
Chapter 57C - North Carolina Limited Liability Company Act.	31
Chapter 58 - Insurance.	32
Chapter 58 - Insurance (Continuation)	33
Chapter 58 - Insurance (Continuation)	34
Chapter 58 - Insurance (Continuation)	35
Chapter 58 - Insurance (Continuation)	36
Chapter 58 - Insurance (Continuation)	37
Chapter 58 - Insurance (Continuation)	38
Chapter 58A - North Carolina Health Insurance Trust Commission [Recodified.]	38
Chapter 59 - Partnership.	39
Chapter 59B - Uniform Unincorporated Nonprofit Association Act.	39
Chapter 60 - Railroads and Other Carriers [Repealed and Transferred.]	39
Chapter 61 - Religious Societies	39
Chapter 62 - Public Utilities	39

Chapter 62 - Public Utilities (Continuation)	40
Chapter 62A - Public Safety Telephone Service And Wireless Telephone Service	40
Chapter 63 - Aeronautics	40
Chapter 63A - North Carolina Global TransPark Authority	40
Chapter 64 - Aliens	40
Chapter 65 – Cemeteries	40
Chapter 66 - Commerce and Business	41
Chapter 67 - Dogs	41
Chapter 68 - Fences and Stock Law	41
Chapter 69 - Fire Protection	41
Chapter 70 - Indian Antiquities, Archaeological Resources and Unmarked Human Skeletal Remains Protection	42
Chapter 71 - Indians [Repealed.]	42
Chapter 71A - Indians	42
Chapter 72 - Inns, Hotels and Restaurants	42
Chapter 73 - Mills	42
Chapter 74 - Mines and Quarries	42
Chapter 74A - Company Police [Repealed.]	42
Chapter 74B - Private Protective Services Act [Repealed.]	42
Chapter 74C - Private Protective Services	42
Chapter 74D - Alarm Systems	42
Chapter 74E - Company Police Act	42
Chapter 74F - Locksmith Licensing Act	42
Chapter 74G - Campus Police Act	42
Chapter 75 - Monopolies, Trusts and Consumer Protection	42
Chapter 75A - Boating and Water Safety	43
Chapter 75B - Discrimination in Business	43
Chapter 75C - Motion Picture Fair Competition Act	43
Chapter 75D - Racketeer Influenced and Corrupt Organizations	43
Chapter 75E - Unlawful Activities in Connection With Certain Corporate Transactions	43
Chapter 76 - Navigation	43
Chapter 76A - Navigation and Pilotage Commissions	43
Chapter 77 - Rivers, Creeks, and Coastal Waters	43
Chapter 78 - Securities Law [Repealed.]	43
Chapter 78A - North Carolina Securities Act	43
Chapter 78B - Tender Offer Disclosure Act [Repealed.]	43
Chapter 78C - Investment Advisers	43
Chapter 78D - Commodities Act	43
Chapter 79 - Strays [Repealed.]	43
Chapter 80 - Trademarks, Brands, etc.	44
Chapter 81 - Weights and Measures [Recodified.]	44
Chapter 81A - Weights and Measures Act of 1975.	44
Chapter 82 - Wrecks [Repealed.]	44
Chapter 83 - Architects [Recodified.]	44

Chapter 83A - Architects	44
Chapter 84 - Attorneys-at-Law	44
Chapter 84A - Foreign Legal Consultants	44
Chapter 85 - Auctions and Auctioneers [Repealed.]	44
Chapter 85A - Bail Bondsmen and Runners [Recodified]	44
Chapter 85B - Auctions and Auctioneers	44
Chapter 85C - Bail Bondsmen and Runners [Recodified.]	44
Chapter 86 - Barbers [Recodified.]	44
Chapter 86A - Barbers	44
Chapter 87 - Contractors	44
Chapter 88 - Cosmetic Art [Repealed.]	44
Chapter 88A - Electrolysis Practice Act	44
Chapter 88B - Cosmetic Art	45
Chapter 89 - Engineering and Land Surveying [Recodified.]	45
Chapter 89A - Landscape Architects	45
Chapter 89B - Foresters	45
Chapter 89C - Engineering and Land Surveying	45
Chapter 89D - Landscape Contractors	45
Chapter 89E - Geologists Licensing Act	45
Chapter 89F - North Carolina Soil Scientist Licensing Act	45
Chapter 89G - Irrigation Contractors	45
Chapter 90 - Medicine and Allied Occupations	45
Chapter 90 - Medicine and Allied Occupations (Continuation)	46
Chapter 90 - Medicine and Allied Occupations (Continuation)	47
Chapter 90 - Medicine and Allied Occupations (Continuation)	48
Chapter 90A - Sanitarians and Water and Wastewater Treatment Facility Operators	48
Chapter 90B - Social Worker Certification and Licensure Act	48
Chapter 90C - North Carolina Recreational Therapy Licensure Act	48
Chapter 90D - Interpreters and Transliterators	48
Chapter 91 - Pawnbrokers [Repealed.]	48
Chapter 91A - Pawnbrokers Modernization Act of 1989	48
Chapter 92 - Photographers [Deleted.]	48
Chapter 93 - Certified Public Accountants	48
Chapter 93A - Real Estate License Law	49
Chapter 93B - Occupational Licensing Boards	49
Chapter 93C - Watchmakers [Repealed.]	49
Chapter 93D - North Carolina State Hearing Aid Dealers and Fitters Board.	49
Chapter 93E - North Carolina Appraisers Act	49
Chapter 94 - Apprenticeship	49
Chapter 95 - Department of Labor and Labor Regulations	49
Chapter 95 - Department of Labor and Labor Regulations (Continuation)	50
Chapter 96 - Employment Security	50
Chapter 97 - Workers' Compensation Act	50
Chapter 97 - Workers' Compensation Act (Continuation)	51

Chapter 98 - Burnt and Lost Records	51
Chapter 99 - Libel and Slander	51
Chapter 99A - Civil Remedies for Criminal Actions	51
Chapter 99B - Products Liability	51
Chapter 99C - Actions Relating to Winter Sports Safety and Accidents	51
Chapter 99D - Civil Rights	51
Chapter 99E - Special Liability Provisions	51
Chapter 100 - Monuments, Memorials and Parks	51
Chapter 101 - Names of Persons	51
Chapter 102 - Official Survey Base	51
Chapter 103 - Sundays, Holidays and Special Days	51
Chapter 104 - United States Lands	51
Chapter 104A - Degrees of Kinship	51
Chapter 104B - Hurricanes or Other Acts of Nature	51
Chapter 104C - Atomic Energy, Radioactivity and Ionizing Radiation [Repealed and Recodified.]	51
Chapter 104D - Southern States Energy Compact	51
Chapter 104E - North Carolina Radiation Protection Act	51
Chapter 104F - Southeast Interstate Low-Level Radioactive Waste Management Compact [Repealed]	51
Chapter 104G - North Carolina Low-Level Radioactive Waste Management Authority Act of 1987 [Repealed]	51
Chapter 105 - Taxation	51
Chapter 105 - Taxation (Continuation)	52
Chapter 105 - Taxation (Continuation)	53
Chapter 105 - Taxation (Continuation)	54
Chapter 105A - Setoff Debt Collection Act	55
Chapter 105B - Defaulted Student Loan Recovery Act	55
Chapter 106 - Agriculture	55
Chapter 106 - Agriculture (Continue)	56
Chapter 106 - Agriculture (Continue)	57
Chapter 107 - Agricultural Development Districts [Repealed.]	57
Chapter 108 - Social Services [Repealed and Recodified.]	57
Chapter 108A - Social Services	57
Chapter 108B - Community Action Programs	58
Chapter 108C Medicaid and Health Choice Provider Requirements.	58
Chapter 108D Medicaid Managed Care for Behavioral Health Services.	58
Chapter 109 - Bonds [Recodified.]	58
Chapter 110 - Child Welfare	58
Chapter 111 - Aid to the Blind	58
Chapter 112 - Confederate Homes and Pensions [Repealed.]	58
Chapter 113 - Conservation and Development	58
Chapter 113 - Conservation and Development (Continuation)	59

Chapter 113A - Pollution Control and Environment	59
Chapter 113A - Pollution Control and Environment (Continuation)	60
Chapter 113B - North Carolina Energy Policy Act of 1975	60
Chapter 114 - Department of Justice	60
Chapter 115 - Elementary and Secondary Education [Repealed.]	60
Chapter 115A - Community Colleges, Technical Institutes, and Industrial Education Centers [Repealed.]	60
Chapter 115B - Tuition and Fee Waivers	60
Chapter 115C - Elementary and Secondary Education	60
Chapter 115C - Elementary and Secondary Education (Continuation)	61
Chapter 115C - Elementary and Secondary Education (Continuation)	62
Chapter 115C - Elementary and Secondary Education (Continuation)	63
Chapter 115D - Community Colleges	63
Chapter 115E - Private Educational Facilities Finance Act [Recodified]	63
Chapter 116 - Higher Education	63
Chapter 116 - Higher Education (Continuation)	63
Chapter 116A - Escheats and Abandoned Property [Repealed.]	64
Chapter 116B - Escheats and Abandoned Property	64
Chapter 116C - Continuum of Education Programs	64
Chapter 116D - Higher Education Bonds	64
Chapter 116E - Education Longitudinal Data System	64
Chapter 117 - Electrification	64
Chapter 118 - Firemen's and Rescue Squad Workers' Relief and Pension Funds [Recodified]	64
Chapter 118A - Firemen's Death Benefit Act [Repealed.]	64
Chapter 118B - Members of a Rescue Squad Death Benefit Act [Repealed.]	64
Chapter 119 - Gasoline and Oil Inspection and Regulation	64
Chapter 120 - General Assembly	65
Chapter 120 - General Assembly (Continuation)	66
Chapter 120 - General Assembly (Continuation)	67
Chapter 120C - Lobbying	67
Chapter 121 - Archives and History	67
Chapter 122 - Hospitals for the Mentally Disordered [Repealed.]	67
Chapter 122A - North Carolina Housing Finance Agency	67
Chapter 122B - North Carolina Agricultural Facilities Finance Act [Repealed.]	67
Chapter 122C - Mental Health, Developmental Disabilities, and Substance Abuse Act of 1985	67
Chapter 122C - Mental Health, Developmental Disabilities, and Substance Abuse Act of 1985 (Continuation)	68

Chapter 122D - North Carolina Agricultural Finance Act	68
Chapter 122E - North Carolina Housing Trust and Oil Overcharge Act	68
Chapter 123 - Impeachment	69
Chapter 123A - Industrial Development [Repealed.]	69
Chapter 124 - Internal Improvements	69
Chapter 125 - Libraries	69
Chapter 126 - State Personnel System	69
Chapter 127 - Militia [Repealed.]	69
Chapter 127A - Militia	69
Chapter 127B - Military Affairs	69
Chapter 127C - Advisory Commission on Military Affairs	69
Chapter 128 - Offices and Public Officers	69
Chapter 128 - Offices and Public Officers (Continuation)	70
Chapter 129 - Public Buildings and Grounds	70
Chapter 130 - Public Health [Repealed.]	70
Chapter 130A - Public Health	70
Chapter 130A - Public Health (Continuation)	71
Chapter 130A - Public Health (Continuation)	72
Chapter 130B - Hazardous Waste Management Commission [Repealed.]	72
Chapter 131 - Public Hospitals [Repealed.]	72
Chapter 131A - Health Care Facilities Finance Act	72
Chapter 131B - Licensing of Ambulatory Surgical Facilities [Repealed.]	72
Chapter 131C - Charitable Solicitation Licensure Act [Repealed.]	72
Chapter 131D - Inspection and Licensing of Facilities	72
Chapter 131E - Health Care Facilities and Services	72
Chapter 131E - Health Care Facilities and Services (Continuation)	73
Chapter 131F - Solicitation of Contributions	73
Chapter 132 - Public Records	73
Chapter 133 - Public Works	74
Chapter 134 - Youth Development [Recodified.]	74
Chapter 134A - Youth Services [Repealed.]	74
Chapter 135 - Retirement System for Teachers and State Employees; Social Security; Health Insurance Program for Children	74
Chapter 135 - Retirement System for Teachers and State Employees; Social Security; Health Insurance Program for Children	75
Chapter 136 - Transportation	75
Chapter 136 - Transportation (Continuation)	76
Chapter 137 - Rural Rehabilitation [Repealed.]	76
Chapter 138 - Salaries, Fees and Allowances	76
Chapter 138A - State Government Ethics Act	76

Chapter 139 - Soil and Water Conservation Districts	76
Chapter 140 - State Art Museum; Symphony and Art Societies	76
Chapter 140A - State Awards System	76
Chapter 141 - State Boundaries	76
Chapter 142 - State Debt	76
Chapter 143 - State Departments, Institutions, and Commissions	77
Chapter 143 - State Departments, Institutions, and Commissions (Continuation)	78
Chapter 143 - State Departments, Institutions, and Commissions (Continuation)	79
Chapter 143 - State Departments, Institutions, and Commissions (Continuation)	80
Chapter 143A - State Government Reorganization	80
Chapter 143B - Executive Organization Act of 1973	80
Chapter 143B - Executive Organization Act of 1973 (Continuation)	81
Chapter 143B - Executive Organization Act of 1973 (Continuation)	82
Chapter 143C - State Budget Act	83
Chapter 143D - The State Governmental Accountability and Internal Control Act	83
Chapter 144 - State Flag, Official Governmental Flags, Motto, and Colors	83
Chapter 145 - State Symbols and Other Official Adoptions.	83
Chapter 146 - State Lands	83
Chapter 147 - State Officers	83
Chapter 148 - State Prison System	84
Chapter 149 - State Song and Toast	84
Chapter 150 - Uniform Revocation of Licenses [Repealed.]	84
Chapter 150A - Administrative Procedure Act [Recodified.]	84
Chapter 150B - Administrative Procedure Act	84
Chapter 151 - Constables [Repealed.]	84
Chapter 152 - Coroners	84
Chapter 152A - County Medical Examiner [Repealed.]	84
Chapter 153 - Counties and County Commissioners [Repealed.]	84
Chapter 153A - Counties	84
Chapter 153A - Counties (Continuation)	85
Chapter 153B - Mountain Resources Planning Act	85
Chapter 153C - Uwharrie Regional Resources Act	85
Chapter 154 - County Surveyor [Repealed.]	85
Chapter 155 - County Treasurer [Repealed.]	85
Chapter 156 - Drainage	85

Chapter 156 – Drainage (Continuation)	86
Chapter 157 - Housing Authorities and Projects	86
Chapter 157A - Historic Properties Commissions [Transferred.]	86
Chapter 158 - Local Development	86
Chapter 159 - Local Government Finance	86
Chapter 159 - Local Government Finance (Continuation)	87
Chapter 159A - Pollution Abatement and Industrial Facilities Financing Act [Unconstitutional.]	87
Chapter 159B - Joint Municipal Electric Power and Energy Act	87
Chapter 159C - Industrial and Pollution Control Facilities Financing Act	87
Chapter 159D - The North Carolina Capital Facilities Financing Act	87
Chapter 159E - Registered Public Obligations Act	87
Chapter 159F - North Carolina Energy Development Authority [Repealed.]	87
Chapter 159G - Water Infrastructure	87
Chapter 159H - [Reserved.]	87
Chapter 159I - Solid Waste Management Loan Program and Local Government Special Obligation Bonds	87
Chapter 160 - Municipal Corporations [Repealed And Transferred.]	87
Chapter 160A - Cities and Towns	88
Chapter 160A - Cities and Towns (Continuation)	89
Chapter 160B - Consolidated City-County Act	89
Chapter 160C - Baseball Park Districts [Repealed.]	90
Chapter 161 - Register of Deeds	90
Chapter 162 - Sheriff	90
Chapter 162A - Water and Sewer Systems	90
Chapter 162B Continuity of Local Government in Emergency.	90
Chapter 163 Elections and Election Laws.	90
Chapter 163 Elections and Election Laws. (Continuation)	91
Chapter 164 Concerning the General Statutes of North Carolina.	92
Chapter 165 Veterans.	92
Chapter 166 Civil Preparedness Agencies [Repealed.]	92
Chapter 166A North Carolina Emergency Management Act.	92
Chapter 167 State Civil Air Patrol [Repealed.]	92
Chapter 168 Persons with Disabilities.	92
Chapter 168A Persons With Disabilities Protection Act.	92

§ 159-108. Agreements with property owners.

(a) Authorization. - A unit of local government that issues project development financing debt instruments may enter into agreements with the owners of real property in the development financing district for which the instruments were issued under which the owners agree to a minimum value at which their property will be assessed for taxation. Such an agreement may extend for the life of the development financing district or for a shorter period agreed to by the parties. The agreement may vary the agreed-upon minimum assessed value from year to year.

(b) Filing and Recording Agreement. - The unit shall file a copy of any agreement entered into pursuant to this section with the tax assessor for the county in which the development financing district is located. In addition, the unit shall cause the agreement to be recorded in the office of the register of deeds of that county, and the register of deeds shall index the agreement in the grantor's index under the name of the property owner. Once the agreement has been recorded in the office of the register of deeds, as required by this subsection, it is binding, according to its terms and for its duration, on any subsequent owner of the property.

(c) Minimum Assessment of Property. - An agreement entered into pursuant to this section establishes a minimum assessment of the real property subject to the agreement. If the county tax assessor determines that the real property has a true value less than the minimum established by the agreement, the assessor shall nevertheless assess the property at the minimum set out in the agreement. If the assessor, however, determines that the real property has a true value greater than the minimum established by the agreement, the assessor shall assess the property at the true value.

(d) Effect of Reappraisal. - If an agreement entered into pursuant to this section continues in effect after a reappraisal of property conducted pursuant to G.S. 105-286, the minimum assessment established in the agreement shall be adjusted as provided in this subsection. After the issuing unit of local government has adopted its budget ordinance and levied taxes for the fiscal year that begins next after the effective date of the reappraisal, it shall certify to the county tax assessor the total rate of ad valorem taxes levied by the unit and applicable to the property subject to the agreement. It shall also certify to the assessor the total rate of ad valorem taxes levied by the unit and applicable to the property in the immediately preceding fiscal year. The assessor shall determine the total amount of ad valorem taxes levied by the unit on the property in the immediately preceding fiscal year, based on the tax rate certified by the issuing unit. The assessor shall then determine a value of the property that would provide the same total amount of ad valorem taxes based on the tax rate certified for the fiscal year beginning next after the effective date of the reappraisal. The value so determined is the new minimum assessment for the property subject to the agreement.

(e) Agreement Effective Regardless of Improvements. - An agreement entered into pursuant to this section remains in effect according to its terms regardless of whether the improvements anticipated in the development financing plan are completed or whether those improvements continue to exist during the duration of the agreement. However, if any part of the property subject to the agreement is acquired by a public agency, the agreement is automatically modified by removing the acquired property from the agreement and reducing the minimum assessment accordingly. (2003-403, s. 2.)

§ 159-109. Special covenants.

A project development financing debt instrument order or a trust agreement securing project development financing debt instruments may contain covenants regarding:

(1) The pledge of all or any part of the taxes received or to be received on the incremental valuation in the development financing district during the life of the debt instruments.

(2) Rates, fees, rentals, tolls, or other charges to be established, maintained, and collected, and the use and disposal of revenues, gifts, grants, and funds received or to be received.

(3) The setting aside of debt service reserves and the regulation and disposition of these reserves.

(4) The custody, collection, securing, investment, and payment of any moneys held for the payment of project development financing debt instruments.

(5) Limitations or restrictions on the purposes to which the proceeds of sale of project development financing debt instruments may be applied.

(6) Limitations or restrictions on the issuance of additional project development financing debt instruments or notes for the same development financing district, the terms upon which additional project development financing debt instruments or notes may be issued or secured, or the refunding of outstanding project development financing debt instruments or notes.

(7) The acquisition and disposal of property for project development financing debt instrument projects.

(8) Provision for insurance and for accounting reports, and the inspection and audit of accounting reports.

(9) The continuing operation and maintenance of projects financed with the proceeds of the project development financing debt instruments. (2003-403, s. 2.)

§ 159-110. Security of project development financing debt instruments.

Project development financing debt instruments are special obligations of the issuing unit. Moneys in the Revenue Increment Fund required by G.S. 159-107(c) are pledged to the payment of the instruments, in accordance with G.S. 159-107(f). Except as provided in G.S. 159-111, the unit may pledge the following additional sources of funds to the payment of the debt instruments, and no other sources: the proceeds from the sale of property in the development financing district; net revenues from any public facilities, other than portions of public utility systems, in the development financing district financed with the proceeds of the project development financing debt instruments; and, subject to G.S. 159-47, net revenues from any other public facilities, other than portions of public utility systems, in the development financing district constructed or improved pursuant to the development financing plan.

Except as provided in G.S. 159-111, the principal and interest on project development financing debt instruments do not constitute a legal or equitable pledge, charge, lien, or encumbrance upon any of the unit's property or upon any of its income, receipts, or revenues, except as may be provided pursuant to this section. Except as provided in G.S. 159-107 and G.S. 159-111, neither the credit nor the taxing power of the unit is pledged for the payment of the principal or interest of project development financing debt instruments, and no holder of project development financing debt instruments has the right to compel the exercise of the taxing power by the unit or the forfeiture of any of its property in connection with any default on the instruments. Unless the unit's taxing power has been pledged pursuant to G.S. 159-111, every project development financing debt instrument shall contain recitals sufficient to show the limited nature of the security for the instrument's payment and that it is not secured by the full faith and credit of the unit. (2003-403, s. 2.)

§ 159-111. Additional security for project development financing debt instruments.

(a)   In order to provide additional security for debt instruments issued pursuant to this Article, the issuing unit of local government may pledge its faith and credit for the payment of the principal of and interest on the debt instruments. Before such a pledge may be given, the unit shall follow the procedures and meet the requirements for approval of general obligation bonds under Article 4 of this Chapter. The unit shall also follow the procedures and meet the requirements of this Article. If debt instruments are issued pursuant to this Article and are also secured by a pledge of the issuing unit's faith and credit, the debt instruments are subject to G.S. 159-112 rather than G.S. 159-65.

(b)   In order to provide additional security for debt instruments issued pursuant to this Article, and in lieu of pledging its faith and credit for that purpose pursuant to subsection (a) of this section, a unit of local government may pledge or grant a security interest in any available sources of revenues of the unit, including special assessments against property within the development financing district made by the unit pursuant to Article 9 of Chapter 153A of the General Statutes or Article 10 of Chapter 160A of the General Statutes, as long as doing so does not constitute a pledge of the unit's taxing power. In addition, to the extent the generation of the revenues is within the power of the unit, the unit may enter into covenants to take action in order to generate the revenues, as long as the covenant does not constitute a pledge of the unit's taxing power. In addition, the unit may pledge, mortgage, or grant a security interest in all or a portion of the real and personal property being financed or improved with the proceeds of the project development financing debt instrument. Property subject to a mortgage, deed of trust, security interest, or similar lien pursuant to this subsection may be sold at foreclosure in any manner permitted by the instrument creating the encumbrance, without compliance with any other provision of law regarding the disposition of publicly owned property.

(c) No agreement or covenant may contain a nonsubstitution clause that restricts the right of the issuing unit of local government to replace or provide a substitute for any project financed pursuant to this subsection.

(d) The obligation of a unit of local government with respect to the sources of payment shall be specifically identified in the proceedings of the governing body authorizing the unit to issue the debt instruments. The sources of payment so specifically identified and then held or thereafter received by the unit or any fiduciary of the unit are immediately subject to the lien of the proceedings without any physical delivery of the sources or further act. The lien is valid and binding as against all parties having claims of any kind against a unit without regard to whether the parties have notice of the lien. The proceedings or any other document or action by which the lien on a source of payment is created need not be filed or recorded in any manner other than as provided in this Article.

(e) A unit of local government that issues project development financing debt instruments may agree in the proceedings relating to an issue of project development financing debt instruments to any one or more of the following:

(1) That in preparing its budget for any fiscal year its finance officer shall include in the proposed budget an appropriation for the amount due on such debt instruments during the next budget year.

(2) In the event any portion of a reserve fund relating to such debt instruments is less than any reserve requirement relating thereto, including as a result of a use of the reserve fund for the payment of amounts due on such debt instrument, that in preparing its budget for any fiscal year its finance officer shall include in the proposed budget an appropriation for the amount required to restore such reserve fund to its required level during the next budget year.

(3) That if there is any surplus in any year in any fund or account of such unit of local government, it will consider appropriating such surplus for one or both of the uses set forth in subdivision (1) or (2) of this subsection.

In every instance, the unit of local government shall expressly state that its agreement under this provision is subject to a decision by its governing body to make such appropriation and that such an agreement does not create an obligation on such a governing body to make such appropriation.

(f) A unit of local government that enters into an increment agreement for the purposes described in G.S. 159-107(d)(2) may include in such increment agreement any one or more of the following:

(1) That in preparing its budget for any fiscal year its finance officer shall include in the proposed budget an appropriation for that portion of the amount due on such debt instruments during the next budget year which represents the expected percentage of such amount that would come from the taxes levied by such unit of local government.

(2) In the event any portion of a reserve fund relating to such debt instruments is less than any reserve requirement relating thereto, including as a result of a use of the reserve fund for the payment of amounts due on such debt instrument, that in preparing its budget for any fiscal year its finance officer shall include in the proposed budget an appropriation for some portion or all of the amount required to restore such reserve fund to its required level during the next budget year.

(3) That if there is any surplus in any year in any fund or account of such unit of local government, it will consider appropriating such surplus for one or both of the uses set forth in subdivision (1) or (2) of this subsection.

In every instance, the unit of local government shall expressly state that its agreement under this provision is subject to a decision by its governing body to make such appropriation and that such an agreement does not create an obligation on such a governing body to make such appropriation. (2003-403, s. 2; 2005-238, s. 6; 2009-525, s. 3.)

§ 159-112. Limitations on details of debt instruments.

In fixing the details of project development financing debt instruments, the governing body of the issuing unit of local government is subject to these restrictions and directions:

(1) The maturity date shall not exceed the shorter of (i) the longest of the various maximum periods of usefulness for the projects to be financed with debt instrument proceeds, as prescribed by the Local Government Commission pursuant to G.S. 159-122, or (ii) the end of the thirtieth year after the effective date of the development financing district.

(2) The first payment of principal shall be payable not more than seven years after the date of the debt instruments.

(3) Any debt instrument may be made payable on demand or tender for purchase as provided in G.S. 159-79, and any debt instrument may be made subject to redemption prior to maturity, with or without premium, on such notice, at such times, and with such redemption provisions as may be stated. Interest on the debt instruments shall cease when the instruments have been validly called for redemption and provision has been made for the payment of the principal of the instruments, any redemption, any premium, and the interest on the instruments accrued to the date of redemption.

(4) The debt instruments may bear interest at such rates payable semiannually or otherwise, may be in such denominations, and may be payable in such kind of money and in such place or places within or without this State as the issuing unit may determine. (2003-403, s. 2.)

§ 159-113. Annual report.

In July of each year, each unit of local government with outstanding project development financing debt instruments shall make a report to any other unit, and to any special district as defined in G.S. 159-7, in which the development financing district for which the instruments were issued is located. This report shall set out the base valuation for the development financing district, the current valuation for the district, the amount of remaining project development financing debt for the district, and the unit's estimate of when the debt will be retired. The unit of local government may meet this requirement by reporting this information in its annual financial statements required by G.S. 159-34. (2003-403, s. 2.)

§ 159-114: Reserved for future codification purposes.

§§ 159-115 through 159-119: Reserved for future codification purposes.

Article 7.

Issuance and Sale of Bonds.

§ 159-120. Definitions.

As used in this Article, unless the context clearly requires another meaning, the words "unit" or "issuing unit" mean "unit of local government" as defined in G.S. 159-44 or G.S. 159-102, "municipality" as defined in G.S. 159-81, and the State of North Carolina, and the words "governing body," when used with respect to the State of North Carolina, mean the Council of State. (1973, c. 494, s. 30; 1981 (Reg. Sess., 1982), c. 1276, s. 3; 1983, c. 554, s. 17; 2003-403, s. 6.)

§ 159-121. Coupon or registered bonds to be issued.

Bonds may be issued as (i) coupon bonds payable to bearer, (ii) coupon bonds registrable as to principal only or as to both principal and interest, or (iii) bonds without coupons registered as to both principal and interest. Each issuing unit may appoint or designate a bond registrar who shall be charged with the duty of attending to the registration and the registration of transfer of bonds. (1917, c. 138, s. 29; 1919, c. 178, s. 3(29); C.S., s. 2955; 1921, c. 8, s. 1; Ex. Sess. 1921, c. 106, s. 1; 1927, c. 81, s. 36; 1971, c. 780, s. 1; 1973, c. 494, s. 22.)

§ 159-122. Maturities of bonds.

(a)   (For effective date, see note) Except as provided in this subsection, the last installment of each bond issue shall mature not later than the date of expiration of the period of usefulness of the capital project to be financed by the bond issue, computed from the date of the bonds. The last installment of a refunding bond issue issued pursuant to G.S. 159-48(a)(4) or (5) shall mature not later than either (i) the shortest period, but not more than 40 years, in which the debt to be refunded can be finally paid without making it unduly burdensome on the taxpayers of the issuing unit, as determined by the Commission, computed from the date of the bonds, or (ii) the end of the unexpired period of usefulness of the capital project financed by the debt to be refunded. The last installment of bonds issued pursuant to G.S. 159-48(a)(1), (2), (3), (6), or (7) shall mature not later than 10 years after the date of the bonds, as determined by the Commission. The last installment of bonds issued pursuant to G.S. 159-48(c)(5) shall mature not later than eight years after the date of the bonds, as determined by the Commission.

(a) (For effective date, see note) Except as provided in this subsection, the last installment of each bond issue shall mature not later than the date of expiration of the period of usefulness of the capital project to be financed by the bond issue, computed from the date of the bonds. The last installment of a refunding bond issue issued pursuant to G.S. 159-48(a)(4) or (6) shall mature not later than either (i) the shortest period, but not more than 40 years, in which the debt to be refunded can be finally paid without making it unduly burdensome on the taxpayers of the issuing unit, as determined by the Commission, computed from the date of the bonds, or (ii) the end of the unexpired period of usefulness of the capital project financed by the debt to be refunded. The last installment of bonds issued pursuant to G.S. 159-48(a)(1), (2), (3), (6), or (7) shall mature not later than 10 years after the date of the bonds, as determined by the Commission. The last installment of bonds issued pursuant to G.S. 159-48(c)(5) shall mature not later than eight years after the date of the bonds, as determined by the Commission. The last installment of project development financing debt instruments shall mature on the earlier of 30 years after the effective date of the development financing district for which the instruments are issued or the longest of the various maximum periods of usefulness for the projects to be financed with debt instrument proceeds, as prescribed by the Commission pursuant to this section.

(b) The Commission shall by regulation establish the maximum period of usefulness of the capital projects for which units of local government may issue bonds, but no capital project may be assigned a period of usefulness in excess of 40 years.

(c) The determination of the Commission as to the classification of the capital projects for which a particular bond issue is authorized, and the Commission's determination of the maximum period of usefulness of the project, as evidenced by the secretary's certificate, shall be conclusive in any action or proceeding involving the validity of the bonds. (1917, c. 138, s. 18; 1919, c. 178, s. 3(18); C.S., s. 2942; 1921, c. 8, s. 1; Ex. Sess. 1921, c. 106, s. 1; 1927, c. 81, s. 11; 1929, c. 170; c. 171, s. 2; 1931, c. 60, ss. 50, 56; cc. 188, 301; 1933, c. 259, ss. 1, 2; 1953, c. 1065, s. 1; 1957, c. 266, s. 2; 1967, c. 987, s. 3; c. 1001, s. 2; c. 1086, ss. 1, 2, 4, 5; 1969, cc. 475, 834; 1971, c. 780, s. 1; 1973, c. 494, s. 23; 1981 (Reg. Sess., 1982), c. 1276, s. 4; 2003-403, s. 7.)

§ 159-123. Sale of bonds by sealed bids; private sales.

(a) Bonds issued by units of local government shall be sold by the Local Government Commission after advertisement and upon sealed bids, except as otherwise authorized by subsection (b) of this section.

(b) The following classes of bonds may be sold at private sale:

(1) Bonds that a State or federal agency has previously agreed to purchase.

(2) Any bonds for which no legal bid is received within the time allowed for submission of bids.

(3) Revenue bonds, including any refunding bonds issued pursuant to G.S. 159-84, and special obligation bonds issued pursuant to Chapter 159I of the General Statutes.

(4) Refunding bonds issued pursuant to G.S. 159-78.

(5) Refunding bonds issued pursuant to G.S. 159-72 if the Local Government Commission determines that a private sale is in the best interest of the issuing unit.

(6) Bonds the ownership of which results in a tax credit to the owners thereof pursuant to the provisions of the federal income tax laws if the Local Government Commission determines that a private sale is in the best interest of the issuing unit.

(7) Project development financing debt instruments.

(8) General obligation bonds issued pursuant to the Local Government Bond Act that have been rated by a nationally recognized credit rating agency at a credit rating below "AA" (or comparable category if stated differently) or that are unrated and that are not described in subdivisions (1) through (7) of this subsection.

(9) Bonds that are part of an issue in which the interest payments on some or all of the bonds is intended to be subsidized by payments from the federal government pursuant to the provisions of the federal tax laws, if the Local Government Commission determines that a private sale is in the best interest of the issuing unit.

(c)   When the issuing unit wishes to have a private sale of bonds, the governing board of the issuing unit shall adopt and file with the Commission a resolution requesting that the bonds be sold at private sale without advertisement to any purchaser or purchasers thereof, at such prices as the Commission determines to be in the best interest of the issuing unit, subject to the approval of the governing board of the issuing unit or one or more persons designated by resolution of the governing board of the issuing unit to approve such prices. Upon receipt of a resolution requesting a private sale of bonds, the Commission may offer them to any purchaser or purchasers without advertisement, and may sell them at any price the Commission deems in the best interest of the issuing unit, subject to the approval of the governing board of the issuing unit or the person or persons designated by resolution of the governing board of the issuing unit to approve such prices. For purposes of this subsection, any resolution of the governing board of the issuing unit which designates a person or persons to approve any price or prices shall also establish a minimum purchase price and a maximum interest rate or maximum interest cost and such other provisions relating to approval as it may determine. Notwithstanding any provisions of this Chapter to the contrary, general obligation bonds issued pursuant to Article 4 of this Chapter may be sold at private sale at not less than ninety-eight percent (98%) of the face value of the bonds plus one hundred percent (100%) of accrued interest.

(d)   This section shall not apply to funding or refunding bonds when the governing board of the issuing unit and the holders of the debt to be funded or refunded have agreed to exchange the original obligations for new ones at the same or an adjusted rate of interest. This section also shall not apply to debt instruments that the State has previously agreed to purchase pursuant to Chapter 159G of the General Statutes.

(e)   The issuing unit shall have the authority, subject to approval by the Commission, to select and retain the financial consultants, underwriters and bond attorneys to be associated with the bond issue. If the issuing unit shall affirmatively find that the underwriter, financial consultant or bond attorney selected and retained has adequately provided, in similar financial transactions, services of a nature and sophistication comparable to those required for the issuance and sale of the bonds in question and possesses the expertise necessary to perform the services required, approval of a financial consultant, underwriter or bond attorney shall not be withheld by the Commission solely for the reason that the underwriter, financial consultant or bond attorney has not had prior experience in the issuance and sale of a particular type, class or size of bond issue for which the underwriter, financial consultant or bond attorney is retained.

(f) The Commission shall not reject an application for approval of a bond issue because of the issuing units' selection of financial consultants, underwriters or bond attorneys so long as the selection is made in accordance with G.S. 159-123(e). Nothing herein shall limit or otherwise modify the role or powers of the Commission and its staff to review, approve, sell or participate in the sale of bonds pursuant to this Article. (1931, c. 60, ss. 17, 19; c. 296, s. 1; 1933, c. 258, s. 1; 1969, c. 943; 1971, c. 780, s. 1; 1977, c. 201, s. 4; 1985, c. 723, s. 1; 1987, c. 585, s. 3; c. 796, s. 4; 1989, c. 756, s. 5; 1991 (Reg. Sess., 1992), c. 1007, s. 43; 2000-69, s. 2; 2003-403, s. 8; 2009-140, s. 5; 2010-125, s. 1.)

§ 159-124. Date of sale; notice of sale and blank proposal.

The date of sale shall be fixed by the secretary in consultation with the issuing unit. Prior to the sale date, the secretary shall take such steps as are most likely, in his opinion, to give notice of the sale to all potential bidders within or without this State or the United States of America, taking into consideration the size and nature of the issue.

The secretary shall maintain a mailing list for notices of sale and blank proposals, and shall place thereon any person, firm, or corporation so requesting. Failure to send copies of notices and blank proposals to persons, firms, or corporations on the mailing list shall in no way affect the legality of the bonds.

The secretary shall prepare a notice of sale and blank proposal for bids for each bond issue required to be sold by sealed bids. The notice and blank proposal may be combined with such fiscal information as the secretary deems appropriate, and shall contain:

(1) A statement that the bonds are to be sold upon sealed bids without auction.

(2) The aggregate principal amount of the issue.

(3) The time and place of sale, the time within which bids must be received, the place to which bids must be delivered, and the time and place at which bids will be opened, which place or places may be within or without this State or the United States of America.

(4) Instructions for entering bids.

(5) Instructions as to the amount of bid deposit required, the form in which it is to be made, and the effect of failure of the bidder to comply with the terms of his bid. (1931, c. 60, s. 17; c. 296, s. 1; 1933, c. 256, s. 1; 1969, c. 943; 1971, c. 780, s. 1; 1987, c. 585, ss. 4, 5.)

§ 159-125. Bid instructions; bid deposit.

(a) Except for revenue bonds and project development financing debt instruments, no bid for less than ninety-eight percent (98%) of the face value of the bonds plus one hundred percent (100%) of accrued interest may be entertained.

Different rates of interest may be bid for bonds maturing in different years, and different rates of interest may be bid for bonds maturing in the same year unless the Secretary of the Commission requires one interest rate per maturity in connection with the sale of the bonds. This subsection applies to public sale of bonds only.

(b) The Secretary of the Commission may require that bids be accompanied by a bid deposit in an amount prescribed by the Secretary of the Commission or may determine that no bid deposit is required. If required, the bid deposit shall be made in a form approved by the Secretary of the Commission, and shall secure the issuing unit against loss resulting from the bidder's failure to comply with the terms of the bid.

(c) When a State or federal agency has agreed to purchase the bonds at a stated rate of interest unless more favorable bids are received, bids may be entertained from other purchasers for less than all of the bonds. (1931, c. 60, ss. 17, 19; c. 296, s. 1; 1933, c. 258, s. 1; 1969, c. 943; 1971, c. 780, s. 1; 1981 (Reg. Sess., 1982), c. 1276, s. 6; 1987, c. 585, s. 6; 2003-403, s. 9; 2005-238, s. 7.)

§ 159-126. Rejection of bids.

No legal bid may be rejected unless all bids are rejected. All bids shall be rejected upon objection to award by an authorized representative of the issuing unit. If bids have been rejected, another notice of sale shall be given and further bids invited. (1931, ch. 60, s. 18; 1935, c. 356, s. 1; 1939, c. 231, s. 3; 1971, c. 780, s. 1.)

§ 159-127. Award of bonds.

All bids received pursuant to a public sale shall be opened in public on a date and at a time and place to be specified in the notice of sale. Bonds sold at public sale shall be awarded to the bidder offering to purchase the bonds at the lowest interest cost to the issuing unit calculated in the manner established by the Secretary of the Commission in the notice of sale. (1931, c. 60, s. 18; 1935, c. 356, s. 1; 1939, c. 231, s. 3; 1971, c. 780, s. 1; 2005-238, s. 8.)

§ 159-128. Makeup and formal execution of bonds; temporary bonds.

The governing board of the issuing unit shall determine the form and manner of execution of the bonds, including any interest coupons to be attached thereto. The board may also provide for the authentication of the bonds by a trustee or fiscal agent. The board may authorize the use of facsimile signatures and seals on the bonds and coupons, if any, but at least one manual signature (which may be the signature of the representative of the Commission to the Commission's certificate) must appear on each bond that is represented by an instrument. Delivery of bonds executed in accordance with the board's determination shall be valid notwithstanding any change in officers or in the seal of the issuing unit occurring after the original execution of the bonds.

Before definitive bonds are prepared, the unit may issue interim receipts or temporary bonds, with or without coupons, exchangeable for definitive bonds when they have been executed and are available for delivery. (1917, c. 138, s. 28; 1919, c. 178, s. 3(28); C.S., s. 2954; 1921, c. 8, s. 1; Ex. Sess. 1921, c. 106, s. 1; 1927, c. 81, s. 35; 1969, c. 29; 1971, c. 780, s. 1; 1983, c. 322, s. 4.)

§ 159-129. Obligations of units certified by Commission.

Each bond or bond anticipation note that is represented by an instrument shall bear on its face or reverse a certificate signed by the secretary of the Commission or an assistant designated by the secretary that the issuance of the bond or note has been approved under the provisions of The Local Government Bond Acts, the Local Government Revenue Bond Act, or the North Carolina Project Development Financing Act. This signature may be a manual or facsimile signature as the Commission may determine. Each bond or bond anticipation note that is not represented by an instrument shall be evidenced by a writing relating to such obligation, which writing shall identify such obligation or the issue of which it is part, bear this certificate, and be on file with the Commission. The certificate shall be conclusive evidence that the requirements of this Subchapter have been observed, and no bond or note without the Commission's certificate or with respect to which a writing bearing this certificate has not been filed with the Commission shall be valid. (1931, c. 60, s. 22; c. 296, s. 2; 1971, c. 780, s. 1; 1973, c. 494, s. 24; 1981 (Reg. Sess., 1982), c. 1276, s. 7; 1983, c. 322, s. 5; 2003-403, s. 10.)

§ 159-130. Record of issues kept.

The secretary shall make a record of all bonds and notes issued under this Subchapter, showing the name of the issuing unit, the amount, date, the time fixed for payment of principal and interest, the rate of interest, the place at which the principal and interest will be payable, the denominations, the purpose of issuance, the name of the board in which is vested the authority and power to levy taxes or raise other revenues for the payment of the principal and interest thereof, and a reference to the law under which the bonds or notes were issued. The clerk of the issuing unit shall file with the secretary copies of all proceedings of the board in authorizing the bonds or notes, his certificate that they are correctly recorded in a bound book of the minutes and proceedings of the board, and a notation of the pages or other identification of the exact portion of the book in which the records appear. (1931, c. 60, s. 23; 1971, c. 780, s. 1; 1973, c. 494, s. 25.)

§ 159-131. Contract for services to be approved by Commission.

Any contract or agreement made by any unit with any person, firm, or corporation for services to be rendered in drafting forms of proceedings for a proposed bond issue or a proposed issue of notes shall be void unless approved by the Commission. Before giving its certificate to bonds or notes, the Commission shall satisfy itself by such evidence as it may deem sufficient, that no unapproved contract is in effect. This section shall not apply to contracts and agreements with attorneys-at-law licensed to practice before the courts of the State within which they have their residence or regular place of business so long as the contracts or agreements involve only legal services. (1931, c. 60, s. 24; 1971, c. 780, s. 1; 1973, c. 494, s. 26.)

§ 159-132. State Treasurer to deliver bonds and remit proceeds.

When the bonds are executed, they shall be delivered to the State Treasurer who shall deliver them to the order of the purchaser and collect the purchase price or proceeds. The Treasurer shall then pay from the proceeds any notes issued in anticipation of the sale of the bonds, deduct from the proceeds the Commission's expense in connection with the issue, and remit the net proceeds to the official depository of the unit after assurance that the deposit will be adequately secured as required by law. The proceeds of funding or refunding bonds may be deposited at the place of payment of the indebtedness to be refunded or funded for use solely in the payment of such indebtedness. The proceeds of revenue bonds shall be remitted to the trustee or other depository specified in the trust agreement or resolution securing them. Unless otherwise provided in the trust agreement or resolution securing the debt instruments, the proceeds of project development financing debt instruments shall be remitted in the manner provided by this section for the remission of the proceeds of general obligation bonds. (1931, c. 60, s. 25; 1935, c. 356, s. 2; 1971, c. 780, s. 1; 1981 (Reg. Sess., 1982), c. 1276, s. 8; 2003-403, s. 11.)

§ 159-133. Suit to enforce contract of sale.

The Commission may enforce in any court of competent jurisdiction any contract or agreement made by the Commission for the sale of any bonds or notes of a unit. (1931, c. 60, s. 26; 1971, c. 780, s. 1; 1973, c. 494, s. 27.)

§ 159-134. Fiscal agents.

An issuing unit may employ a bank or trust company either within or without this State as fiscal agent for the payment of installments of principal and interest on the bonds, and for the destruction of paid or cancelled bonds and coupons, and may pay reasonable fees for this service not in excess of maximum rates to be fixed by regulation of the Commission. If an issuing unit employs another person as such fiscal agent or any other person for other services pursuant to the Registered Public Obligations Act of North Carolina, then it may pay reasonable fees for such services not in excess of maximum rates to be fixed by regulation of the Commission. (1971, c. 780, s. 1; 1983, c. 322, s. 6.)

§ 159-135. Application of proceeds.

After payment of any notes issued in anticipation of the sale of the bonds and after payment of the cost of preparing, marketing, and issuing the bonds, the proceeds of the sale of a bond issue shall be applied only to the purposes for which the issue was authorized. Any excess amount which for any reason is not needed for any such purpose shall be applied either (i) toward the purchase and retirement of bonds of that issue at not more than their face value and accrued interest, or (ii) toward payment of the earliest maturing installments of that issue, or (iii) in accordance with any trust agreement or resolution securing the bonds. (1917, c. 138, s. 31; 1919, c. 178, s. 3(31); C.S., s. 2957; 1921, c. 8, s. 1; Ex. Sess. 1921, c. 106, s. 1; 1927, c. 81, s. 38; 1971, c. 780, s. 1; 1973, c. 494, s. 28.)

§ 159-136. Issuing unit to make and report debt service payments.

The finance officer of each unit having outstanding bonds or notes shall remit the funds necessary for the payment of maturing installments of principal and interest on the bonds or notes to the fiscal agent or agreed upon place of payment in sufficient time for the payment thereof, together with the agreed upon fiscal agency fees, and shall at the same time report the payment to the secretary on forms to be provided by the Commission. (1931, c. 60, s. 27; 1971, c. 780, s. 1.)

§ 159-137. Lost, stolen, defaced, or destroyed bonds or notes.

(a)   If lost, stolen, or completely destroyed, any bond, note, or coupon may be reissued in the same form and tenor upon the owner's furnishing to the satisfaction of the secretary and the issuing unit: (i) proof of ownership, (ii) proof of loss or destruction, (iii) a surety bond in twice the face amount of the bond or note and coupons, and (iv) payment of the cost of preparing and issuing the new bond, note, or coupons.

(b)   If defaced or partially destroyed, any bond, note, or coupon may be reissued in the same form and tenor to the bearer or registered holder, at his expense, upon surrender of the defaced or partially destroyed bond, note, or coupon and on such other conditions as the Commission may prescribe. The Commission may also provide for authentication of defaced or partially destroyed bonds, notes, or coupons instead of reissuing them.

(c)   Each new bond, note, or coupon issued under this section shall be signed by the officers of the issuing unit who are in office at the time, or by the State Treasurer if the unit no longer exists, and shall contain a recital to the effect that it is issued in exchange for or replacement of a certain bond, note, or coupon (describing it sufficiently to identify it) and is to be deemed a part of the same issue as the original bond, note, or coupon. (1935, c. 292, ss. 1, 2; 1939, c. 259; 1971, c. 780, s. 1.)

§ 159-138. Cancellation of bonds and notes.

Each bond or note and coupon shall be cancelled when (i) it is paid, or (ii) it is acquired by the issuing unit in any manner other than purchase for investment. A full report of the cancellation of all bonds, notes, and coupons shall be made to the secretary on forms provided by the Commission. (1931, c. 60, s. 27; 1939, c. 356; 1971, c. 780, s. 1.)

§ 159-139. Destruction of cancelled bonds, notes, and coupons.

(a)   All cancelled bonds, notes, and interest coupons of a unit may be destroyed in one of the following ways, in the discretion of the governing board:

(1) Method 1. - The finance officer shall make an entry in the official records of the unit, which may include the register for the bonds, notes, and coupons, showing:

a. With respect to bonds and notes, the purpose of issuance, the date of issue, serial numbers (if any), denomination, maturity date, and total principal amount.

b. With respect to coupons, the purpose of issue and date of the bonds to which the coupons appertain, the maturity date of the coupons and, as to each maturity date, the denomination, quantity, and total amount of coupons.

After this entry has been made, the paid bonds, notes, and coupons shall be destroyed or marked cancelled in the manner determined by the finance officer, who shall make an entry of the destruction or cancellation in the official records of the unit. Cancelled bonds, notes, or coupons shall not be destroyed until after one year from the date of payment.

(2) Method 2. - The governing board may contract with the bank, trust company or other person acting as fiscal agent for a bond issue for the destruction of bonds and interest coupons which have been cancelled by the fiscal agent. The contract shall require that the fiscal agent give the unit a written certificate of each destruction containing the same information required by Method 1 to be entered in the record of destroyed bonds and coupons. The certificates shall be filed among the permanent records of the finance officer's office. Cancelled bonds or coupons shall not be destroyed until one year from the date of payment.

(b) The provisions of G.S. 121-5 and G.S. 132-3 do not apply to paid bonds, notes, and coupons. The information required to be recorded prior to destruction under either Method 1 or Method 2 may as an alternative, be shown by photocopying, microfilming or other similar method of recording the information by directly reproducing the cancelled documents. (1941, cc. 203, 293; 1961, c. 663, ss. 1, 2; 1963, c. 1173, ss. 1, 2; 1971, c. 780, s. 1; 1973, c. 494, s. 29; 1983, c. 322, ss. 7, 8; 2005-238, s. 9.)

§ 159-140. Bonds or notes eligible for investment.

Subject to the provisions of G.S. 159-30, bonds or notes issued under the provisions of this Chapter are hereby made securities in which all public officers and public bodies of the State and its political subdivisions and agencies and all insurance companies, trust companies, investment companies, banks, savings banks, building and loan associations, savings and loan associations, credit unions, pension or retirement funds, other financial institutions engaged in business in the State, executors, administrators, trustees and other fiduciaries may properly and legally invest funds, including capital in their control or belonging to them. Such bonds or notes are hereby made securities which may properly and legally be deposited with and received by any State or municipal officer or any agency or politicial subdivision of the State for any purpose for which the deposit of bonds, notes or obligations of the State is now or may hereafter be authorized by law. (1977, c. 403.)

§ 159-141. Terms and conditions of sale.

Notwithstanding the foregoing, any bond of the State may be sold upon such terms and conditions, at such interest rate or rates, for such price and in such manner, either public or private, as the State Treasurer shall determine. (1983, c. 554, s. 18.)

§§ 159-142 through 159-147. Reserved for future codification purposes.

Article 8.

Financing Agreements and Other Financing Arrangements.

§ 159-148. Contracts subject to Article; exceptions.

(a) Except as provided in subsection (b) of this section, this Article applies to any contract, agreement, memorandum of understanding, and any other transaction having the force and effect of a contract (other than agreements made in connection with the issuance of revenue bonds, special obligation bonds issued pursuant to Chapter 159I of the General Statutes, or of general obligation bonds additionally secured by a pledge of revenues) made or entered into by a unit of local government (as defined by G.S. 159-7(b) or, in the case of a special obligation bond, as defined in Chapter 159I of the General Statutes), relating to the lease, acquisition, or construction of capital assets, which contract does all of the following:

(1) Extends for five or more years from the date of the contract, including periods that may be added to the original term through the exercise of options to renew or extend.

(2) Obligates the unit to pay sums of money to another, without regard to whether the payee is a party to the contract.

(3) Obligates the unit over the full term of the contract, including periods that may be added to the original term through the exercise of options to renew or extend:

a. For baseball park districts, to at least five hundred thousand dollars ($500,000).

b. For housing authorities, to at least five hundred thousand dollars ($500,000) or a sum equal to two thousand dollars ($2,000) per housing unit owned and under active management by the housing authority, whichever is less.

c. For other units, to at least five hundred thousand dollars ($500,000) or a sum equal to one-tenth of one percent (1/10 of 1%) of the assessed value of property subject to taxation by the contracting unit, whichever is less.

(4) Obligates the unit, expressly or by implication, to exercise its power to levy taxes either to make payments falling due under the contract, or to pay any judgment entered against the unit as a result of the unit's breach of the contract.

Contingent obligation shall be included in calculating the value of the contract. Several contracts that are all related to the same undertaking shall be deemed a single contract for the purposes of this Article. When several contracts are considered as a single contract, the term shall be that of the contract having the longest term, and the sums to fall due shall be the total of all sums to fall due under all single contracts in the group.

(b) This Article shall not apply to:

(1) Contracts between a unit of local government and the State of North Carolina or the United States of America (or any agency of either) entered into as a condition to the making of grants or loans to the unit of local government.

(2) Contracts for the purchase, lease, or lease with option to purchase of motor vehicles or voting machines.

(3) Loan agreements entered into by a unit of local government pursuant to the North Carolina Solid Waste Management Loan Program, Chapter 159I of the General Statutes. (1971, c. 780, s. 1; 1973, c. 494, s. 31; 1989, c. 756, s. 6; 1991, c. 11, s. 4; 1997-380, s. 4; 1998-222, s. 1; 2001-206, s. 2; 2001-414, s. 52.)

§ 159-149. Application to Local Government Commission for approval of contract.

A unit of local government may not enter into any contract subject to this Article unless it is approved by the Local Government Commission as evidenced by the secretary's certificate thereon. Any contract subject to this Article that does not bear the secretary's certificate thereon shall be void, and it shall be unlawful for any officer, employee, or agent of a unit of local government to make any payments of money thereunder. Before executing a contract subject to this Article, the governing board of the contracting unit shall file an application for Commission approval of the contract with the secretary of the Commission. The application shall state such facts and have attached to it such documents concerning the proposed contract and the financial condition of the contracting unit as the secretary may require. The Commission may prescribe the form of the application.

Before he accepts the application, the secretary may require the governing board or its representatives to attend a preliminary conference at which time the secretary and his deputies may informally discuss the proposed contract.

After an application in proper form and order has been filed, and after a preliminary conference if one is required, the secretary shall notify the unit in writing that the application has been filed and accepted for submission to the Commission. The secretary's statement shall be conclusive evidence that the unit has complied with this section. (1971, c. 780, s. 1.)

§ 159-150. Sworn statement of debt; debt limitation.

After or at the time an application is filed under G.S. 159-149, the finance officer, or some other officer designated by the board, shall prepare, swear to, and file with the secretary and for public inspection in the office of the clerk to the board a statement of debt in the same form prescribed in G.S. 159-55 for statements of debt filed in connection with general obligation bond issues. The sums to be included in gross debt and the deductions therefrom to arrive at net debt shall be the same as prescribed in G.S. 159-55, except that sums to fall due under contracts subject to this Article shall be treated as if they were evidenced by general obligation bonds of the unit.

No contract subject to this Article may be executed if the net debt of the contracting unit, after execution of the contract, would exceed eight percent (8%) of the assessed value of property subject to taxation by the contracting unit. (1971, c. 780, s. 1; 1991, c. 11, s. 5.)

§ 159-151. Approval of application by Commission.

(a)   In determining whether a proposed contract shall be approved, the Commission may consider:

(1)   Whether the undertaking is necessary or expedient.

(2)   The nature and amount of the outstanding debt of the contracting unit.

(3)   The unit's debt management procedures and policies.

(4)   The unit's tax and special assessments collection record.

(5)   The unit's compliance with the Local Government Budget and Fiscal Control Act.

(6)   Whether the unit is in default in any of its debt service obligations.

(7)   The unit's present tax rates, and the increase in tax rate, if any, necessary to raise the sums to fall due under the proposed contract.

(8)   The unit's appraised and assessed value of property subject to taxation.

(9) The ability of the unit to sustain the additional taxes necessary to perform the contract.

(10) If the proposed contract is for utility or public service enterprise, the probable net revenues of the undertaking to be financed and the extent to which the revenues of the utility or enterprise, after addition of the revenues of the undertaking to be financed, will be sufficient to meet the sums to fall due under the proposed contract.

(11) Whether the undertaking could be financed by a bond issue, and the reasons and justifications offered by the contracting unit for choosing this method of financing rather than a bond issue.

The Commission shall have authority to inquire into and to give consideration to any other matters that it may believe to have bearing on whether the contract should be approved.

(b) The Commission shall approve the application if, upon the information and evidence it receives, it finds and determines:

(1) That the proposed contract is necessary or expedient.

(2) That the contract, under the circumstances, is preferable to a bond issue for the same purpose.

(3) That the sums to fall due under the contract are adequate and not excessive for its proposed purpose.

(4) That the unit's debt management procedures and policies are good, or that reasonable assurances have been given that its debt will henceforth be managed in strict compliance with law.

(5) That the increase in taxes, if any, necessary to meet the sums to fall due under the contract will not be excessive.

(6) That the unit is not in default in any of its debt service obligations.

The Commission need not find all of these facts and conclusions if it concludes that (i) the proposed project is necessary and expedient, (ii) the proposed undertaking cannot be economically financed by a bond issue and (iii) the contract will not require an excessive increase in taxes.

If the Commission tentatively decides to deny the application because it cannot be supported from the information presented to it, it shall so notify the unit filing the information. If the unit so requests, the Commission shall hold a public hearing on the application at which time any interested persons shall be heard. The Commission may appoint a hearing officer to conduct the hearing and to present a summary of the testimony and his recommendation for the Commission's consideration. (1971, c. 780, s. 1; 1973, c. 494, s. 32.)

§ 159-152. Order approving or denying the application.

(a) After considering an application, and conducting a public hearing thereon if one is requested under G.S. 159-151, the Commission shall enter its order either approving or denying the application. An order approving an application shall not be regarded as an approval of the legality of the contract in any respect.

(b) If the Commission enters an order denying an application, the proceedings under this Article shall be at an end. (1971, c. 780, s. 1.)

§ 159-153. Approval of other financing arrangements.

(a) Commission Approval Required. - Except as provided in subsection (b) of this section, approval by the Commission in accordance with this section is required before a unit of local government, or any public body, agency, or similar entity created by any action of a unit of local government, may do any of the following:

(1) Incur indebtedness.

(2) Enter into any similar type of financing arrangement.

(3) Approve or otherwise participate in the incurrence of indebtedness or the entering into of a similar type of financing arrangement by another party on its behalf.

(a1) Nonprofit Water Corporation. - A loan from the Water Infrastructure Fund to a nonprofit water corporation, as defined in G.S. 159G-20, is subject to approval by the Commission under this section.

(a2) Investor-Owned Drinking Water Corporation. - A loan from the DWSRF, an account within the Water Infrastructure Fund, to an investor-owned drinking water corporation, as defined in G.S. 159G-20, is subject to approval by the Commission under this section.

(b) Exceptions. - Approval by the Commission in accordance with this section is not required in any of the following cases:

(1) Another law of this State already specifically requires Commission approval of the indebtedness or financing arrangement and the required approval is obtained in accordance with that law.

(2) The indebtedness or financing arrangement is a contract entered into by a unit of local government pursuant to G.S. 160A-20 and is not subject to review by the Commission pursuant to G.S. 160A-20(e).

(3) The indebtedness or financing arrangement is excepted from the review requirements of this Article because it does not meet the conditions of G.S. 159-148(a)(1) or (3) or because it is excluded pursuant to G.S. 159-148(b).

(c) Effect of Special Act. - No special, local, or private act shall be construed to create an exception from the review of the Commission required by this section unless the act explicitly excludes the review and approval of the Commission.

(d) Factors Considered. - The Commission may consider all of the following factors in determining whether to approve the incurrence of, entering into, approval of, or participation in any indebtedness or financing arrangement subject to approval pursuant to this section:

(1) Whether the undertaking is necessary or expedient.

(2) The nature and amount of the outstanding debt of the entity proposing to incur the indebtedness or enter the financing arrangement.

(3) Whether the entity proposing to operate the facilities financed by the indebtedness or financing arrangement and the entity obligating itself under the

indebtedness or financing arrangement have demonstrated or can demonstrate the financial responsibility and capability to fulfill their obligations with respect to the indebtedness or financing arrangement. In making this determination, the Commission may consider the operating entity's experience and financial position, the nature of the undertaking being financed, and any additional security such as insurance, guaranties, or property to be pledged to secure the indebtedness or financing arrangement.

(4)   Whether the proposed date and manner of sale of obligations will have an adverse effect upon any scheduled or anticipated sale of obligations by the State or any political subdivision or by any agency of either of them.

(5)   The local government unit's debt management procedures and policies.

(6)   The local government unit's compliance with the Local Government Budget and Fiscal Control Act.

(7)   Whether the local government unit is in default in any of its debt service obligations.

(e)   Documentation. - To facilitate the review of the proposed indebtedness or financing arrangement by the Commission, the Secretary may require the unit or other entity to obtain and submit any financial data and information about the proposed indebtedness or financing arrangement and security for it, including any proposed prospectus or offering circular, the proposed financing arrangement and security document, and annual and other financial reports and statements of the obligated entity. Applications and other documents required by the Commission must be in the form prescribed by the Commission.

(f)   Conditions for Approval. - If the Commission determines that all of the following conditions are met, the Commission shall approve the incurrence of the indebtedness, entering of the financing arrangement, or approval or other participation in the indebtedness or financing arrangement, by the unit of local government or the other entity referred to in subsection (a) of this section:

(1)   The amount of the indebtedness to be incurred or financed is not excessive for the purpose contemplated.

(2)   The entity that will operate the facilities financed by the indebtedness or financing arrangement and the entity obligating itself under the indebtedness or financing arrangement have demonstrated or can demonstrate the financial

responsibility and capability to fulfill their obligations with respect to the indebtedness or financing arrangement.

(3) The proposed date and manner of sale of obligations will not have an adverse effect upon any scheduled or anticipated sale of obligations by the State or any political subdivision or any agency of either of them. (1998-222, s. 2; 1999-213, s. 11; 2005-454, s. 10; 2011-145, s. 13.11A(e).)

§§ 159-154 through 159-159. Reserved for future codification purposes.

Article 9.

Bond Anticipation, Tax, Revenue and Grant Anticipation Notes.

Part 1. Bond Anticipation Notes.

§ 159-160. Definitions.

As used in this Part, the words "unit" or "issuing unit" means "unit of local government" as defined in G.S. 159-44 or G.S. 159-102, "municipality" as defined in G.S. 159-81, and the State of North Carolina. (1973, c. 494, s. 36; 1981 (Reg. Sess., 1982), c. 1276, s. 9; 1983, c. 554, s. 19; 2003-403, s. 12.)

§ 159-161. Bond anticipation notes.

At any time after a bond order has taken effect and with the approval of the Commission, the issuing unit may borrow money for the purposes for which the bonds are to be issued, in anticipation of the receipt of the proceeds of the sale of the bonds, and within the maximum authorized amount of the bond issue. General obligation bond anticipation notes shall be payable not later than seven years after the time the bond order takes effect and shall not be renewed or extended beyond such time, except that, if the issuance of bonds under the bond order is extended by an order of the board of the issuing unit which takes effect pursuant to G.S. 159-64, the bond anticipation notes may be renewed and extended and shall be payable not later than 10 years after the time the bond order takes effect and that, if the issuance of bonds under the bond order is prevented or prohibited by any order of any court, the bond anticipation notes may be renewed or extended by the length of time elapsing between the date of institution of the action or proceeding and the date of its final disposition. Any extension of the time for issuing bonds under a bond order granted by act of the General Assembly pursuant to G.S. 159-64 shall also extend the time for issuing and paying notes under this section for the same period of time. (1917, c. 138, ss. 13, 14; 1919, c. 178, s. 3(13), (14); C.S., ss. 2934, 2935, 1021, c. 8, s 1; Ex. Sess. 1921, c. 106, s. 1; 1927, c. 81, s. 39; 1931, c. 293; 1939, c. 231, s. 1; 1953, c. 693, ss. 2, 4; 1969, c. 687, s. 3; 1971, c. 780, s. 1; 1973, c. 494, s. 33; 1977, c. 404, s. 1; 1979, c. 444, s. 2.)

§ 159-162. Security of general obligation bond anticipation notes.

The faith and credit of the issuing unit are hereby pledged for the payment of each note issued in anticipation of the sale of general obligation bonds according to its terms, and the power and obligation of the issuing unit to levy taxes and raise other revenues for the prompt payment of such notes shall be unrestricted as to rate or amount, notwithstanding any other provisions of law. The proceeds of each general obligation bond issue are also hereby pledged for the payment of any notes issued in anticipation of the sale thereof, and any such notes shall be retired from the proceeds of the bonds as the first priority. In the discretion of the governing board, notes issued in anticipation of the sale of general obligation bonds may be paid from current revenues or other funds instead of from the bond proceeds, but if this is done, the bond order shall be amended to reduce the aggregate authorized principal amount by the amount of the bond anticipation notes and accrued interest thereon. Such an amendment need not be published and shall take effect upon its passage. (1971, c. 780, s. 1.)

§ 159-163. Security of revenue bond anticipation notes.

Notes issued in anticipation of the sale of revenue bonds are hereby declared special obligations of the issuing unit. Neither the credit nor the taxing power of the issuing unit may be pledged for the payment of notes issued in anticipation of the sale of revenue bonds, and no holder of a revenue bond anticipation note shall have the right to compel the exercise of the taxing power by the issuing unit or the forfeiture of any of its property in connection with any default thereon. Notes issued in anticipation of the sale of revenue bonds shall be secured, to the extent and as provided in the resolution authorizing the issuance of such notes, by a pledge, charge, and lien upon the proceeds of the revenue bonds in anticipation of the sale of which such notes are issued and upon the revenues securing such revenue bonds; provided, however, that such notes shall be payable as to both principal and interest from such revenues if not paid from the proceeds of such revenue bonds or otherwise paid. The provisions of G.S. 159-90(b) shall apply to revenue bond anticipation notes as well as to revenue bonds. (1971, c. 780, s. 1; 1979, c. 428; 1985, c. 265, s. 2.)

§ 159-163.1. Security of project development financing debt instrument anticipation notes.

Notes issued in anticipation of the sale of project development financing debt instruments are special obligations of the issuing unit. Except as provided in G.S. 159-107 and G.S. 159-110, neither the credit nor the taxing power of the issuing unit may be pledged for the payment of notes issued in anticipation of the sale of project development financing debt instruments. No holder of a project development financing debt instrument anticipation note has the right to compel the exercise of the taxing power by the issuing unit or the forfeiture of any of its property in connection with any default on the note. Notes issued in anticipation of the sale of project development financing debt instruments may be secured by the same pledges, charges, liens, covenants, and agreements made to secure the project development financing debt instruments. In addition, the proceeds of each project development financing debt instrument issue are pledged for the payment of any notes issued in anticipation of the sale of the instruments, and these notes shall be retired from the proceeds of the sale as the first priority. (2003-403, s. 13.)

§ 159-164. Form of notes to be issued.

Bond anticipation loans shall be evidenced by negotiable notes in bearer form or by certificated or uncertificated registered public obligations pursuant to the Registered Public Obligations Act. Such notes and certificated registered public obligations are hereby declared to be investment securities within the meaning of Article 8 of the Uniform Commercial Code as enacted in this State. Bond anticipation notes may be renewed or extended from time to time, but not beyond the time period allowed in G.S. 159-161. The governing board may authorize the issuance of bond anticipation notes by resolution which shall fix the maximum aggregate principal amount of the notes and may authorize any officer to fix, within the limitations prescribed by the resolution, the rate of interest, the place or places of payment, and the denomination or denominations of the notes. The notes shall be signed with the manual or facsimile signatures of officers designated by the governing board for that purpose, but at least one manual signature must appear on each note (which may be the signature of the representative of the Commission to the Commission's certificate). The resolution shall specify the form and manner of execution of the notes. (1917, c. 138, ss. 13, 14; 1919, c. 178, s. 3(13), (14); C.S., ss. 2934, 2935; 1921, c. 8, s. 1; Ex. Sess. 1921, c. 106, s. 1; 1927, c. 81, s. 39; 1931, c. 293; 1939, c. 231, s. 1; 1953, c. 693, ss. 2, 4; 1969, c. 687, s. 3; 1971, c. 780, s. 1; 1973, c. 494, s. 34; 1983, c. 322, s. 9.)

§ 159-165. Sale and delivery of bond anticipation notes.

(a) Bond anticipation notes of a municipality, including special obligation bond anticipation notes issued pursuant to Chapter 159I of the General Statutes, shall be sold by the Commission at public or private sale according to such procedures as the Commission may prescribe. Bond anticipation notes of the State shall be sold by the State Treasurer at public or private sale, upon such terms and conditions, and according to such procedures as the State Treasurer may prescribe.

(b) (See note) When the bond anticipation notes are executed, they shall be delivered to the State Treasurer who shall deliver them to the order of the purchaser and collect the purchase price or proceeds. The Treasurer shall then deduct from the proceeds the Commission's expense in connection with the issue, and remit the net proceeds to the official depository of the unit after assurance that the deposit will be adequately secured as required by law. The net proceeds of revenue bond anticipation notes or special obligation bond anticipation notes shall be remitted to the trustee or other depository specified in the trust agreement or resolution securing them. If the notes have been issued to renew outstanding notes, the Treasurer, in lieu of collecting the purchase price or proceeds, may provide for the exchange of the newly issued notes for the notes to be renewed.

(b) (For effective date, see note) When the bond anticipation notes are executed, they shall be delivered to the State Treasurer who shall deliver them to the order of the purchaser and collect the purchase price or proceeds. The

Treasurer shall then deduct from the proceeds the Commission's expense in connection with the issue, and remit the net proceeds to the official depository of the unit after assurance that the deposit will be adequately secured as required by law. The net proceeds of revenue bond anticipation notes, special obligation bond anticipation notes, or project development financing debt instrument anticipation notes shall be remitted to the trustee or other depository specified in the trust agreement or resolution securing them. If the notes have been issued to renew outstanding notes, the Treasurer, in lieu of collecting the purchase price or proceeds, may provide for the exchange of the newly issued notes for the notes to be renewed. (1917, c. 138, s. 14; 1919, c. 178, s. 3(14); C.S., s. 2935; 1921, c. 8, s. 1; Ex. Sess. 1921, c. 106, s. 1; 1927, c. 81, s. 39; 1931, c. 293; 1939, c. 231, s. 1; 1953, c. 693, s. 2; 1969, c. 687, s. 3; 1971, c. 780, s. 1; 1973, c. 494, s. 35; 1983, c. 554, s. 20; 1989, c. 756, s. 7; 2003-403, s. 14.)

§§ 159-166 through 159-167. Reserved for future codification purposes.

Part 2. Tax, Revenue and Grant Anticipation Notes.

§ 159-168. "Unit" defined.

For purposes of this Part, "unit," "unit of local government," or "issuing unit" mean a "unit of local government" as defined by G.S. 159-7(b) and a "public authority" as defined by G.S. 159-7(b). (1973, c. 494, s. 40; 1975, c. 674, s. 2.)

§ 159-169. Tax anticipation notes.

(a) A unit of local government having the power to levy taxes is authorized to borrow money for the purpose of paying appropriations made for the current fiscal year in anticipation of the collection of taxes due and payable within the fiscal year, and to issue its negotiable notes in evidence thereof. A tax anticipation note shall mature not later than 30 days after the close of the fiscal year in which it is issued, and may not be renewed beyond that time.

(b) No tax anticipation loan shall be made if the amount thereof, together with the amount of tax anticipation notes authorized or outstanding on the date the loan is authorized, would exceed fifty percent (50%) of the amount of taxes uncollected as of the date of the proposed loan authorization, as certified in writing to the governing board by the chief financial officer of the issuing unit.

Each tax anticipation note shall bear on its face or reverse the following certificate signed by the finance officer: "This note and all other tax anticipation notes of (issuing unit) authorized or outstanding as of (date) amount to fifty percent (50%) or less of the amount of taxes for the current fiscal year uncollected as of the above date." No tax anticipation note shall be valid without this certificate.

(c) The faith and credit of the issuing unit are hereby pledged for the payment of each tax anticipation note issued under this section according to its terms, and the power and obligation of the issuing unit to levy taxes and raise other revenues for the prompt payment of such notes shall be unrestricted as to rate or amount, notwithstanding any other provisions of law. (1917, c. 138, s. 12; 1919, c. 178, s. 3(12); 1921, c. 8, s. 1; Ex. Sess. 1921, c. 106, s. 1; 1927, c. 81, s. 4; 1971, c. 780, s. 1; 1973, c. 494, s. 37.)

§ 159-170. Revenue anticipation notes.

(a) Authorization; Term. - A unit of local government or a nonprofit corporation or association operating or leasing a public hospital as defined in G.S. 159-39, is authorized to borrow money for the purpose of paying appropriations made or expenses budgeted or incurred for the current fiscal year in anticipation of the receipt of revenues, other than taxes, estimated in its budget to be realized or collected in cash during the fiscal year, and to issue its negotiable notes in evidence thereof. A nonprofit corporation or association operating or leasing a public hospital may only borrow money pursuant to this section if it is legally entitled to collect and pledge such revenues to the payment of the noted as provided in this section. A revenue anticipation note shall mature not later than 30 days after the close of the fiscal year in which it is issued, and may not be renewed beyond that time.

(b) Limit on Amount; Disclosure. - No revenue anticipation loan shall be made if the amount thereof, together with the amount of all revenue anticipation notes authorized or outstanding on the date the loan is authorized, would exceed eighty percent (80%) of the revenues of the issuing unit or the nonprofit corporation or association operating or leasing a public hospital, other than taxes, estimated in its budget to be realized or collected in cash during the fiscal year. Each revenue anticipation note shall bear on its face a statement to the effect that it is payable solely from budgeted nontax revenues of the issuing unit or the nonprofit corporation or association operating or leasing a public hospital and that the faith and credit of the issuing unit or, in the case of revenue anticipation notes issued by a nonprofit corporation or association operating or leasing a public hospital, the local government unit that owns the public hospital are not pledged for the payment of the note. Each note shall also bear on its face or reverse the following certificate signed by the finance officer: "This note and all other revenue anticipation notes of (issuer) authorized or outstanding as of (date) amount to eighty percent (80%) or less of the budgeted nontax revenues for the current fiscal year as of the above date." No revenue anticipation note shall be valid without this certificate.

(c) Faith and Credit Not Pledged. - Revenue anticipation notes issued under this section shall be special obligations of the issuing unit or the nonprofit corporation or association operating or leasing a public hospital. Neither the credit nor the taxing power of the issuing unit or, in the case of revenue anticipation notes issued by a nonprofit corporation or association operating or leasing a public hospital, the local government unit that owns the public hospital may be pledged for the payment of revenue anticipation notes. No holder of a revenue anticipation note shall have the right to compel the exercise of the taxing power by the issuing unit or, in the case of revenue anticipation notes issued by a nonprofit corporation or association operating or leasing a public hospital, the local government unit that owns the public hospital or the forfeiture of any of its property in connection with any default thereon.

(d) Any revenue anticipation notes issued by a nonprofit corporation or association operating or leasing a public hospital pursuant to this section are subject to the approval of the city, county, hospital district, or hospital authority which owns the hospital. Approval of the city, county, hospital district, or hospital authority may be withheld only under one or more of the following circumstances:

(1) The contract would cause the city, county, hospital district, or hospital authority to breach or violate any covenant in an existing financing instrument entered into by such entity.

(2) The contract would restrict the ability of the city, county, hospital district, or hospital authority to incur anticipated bank eligible indebtedness under federal tax laws.

(3) The entering into of the contract would have a material adverse impact on the credit ratings of the city, county, hospital district, or hospital authority or otherwise materially interfere with an anticipated financing by such entity. (1917,

c. 138, s. 12; 1919, c. 178, s. 3(12); 1921, c. 8, s. 1; Fx. Sess. 1921, c. 106, s. 1; 1927, c. 81, s. 4; 1971, c. 780, s. 1; 1973, c. 494, s. 38; 1999-386, s. 3.)

§ 159-171. Grant anticipation notes.

(a)   A unit of local government is authorized to borrow money for the purpose of paying appropriations made for a capital project in anticipation of the receipt of moneys from grant commitments for such capital project from the State or the United States or any agencies of either, and to issue its negotiable notes in evidence thereof. Grant anticipation notes shall mature not later than 12 months after the estimated completion date of such capital project as determined by the governing body of the unit of local government and may be renewed from time to time, but no renewal shall mature later than 12 months after the estimated completion date of such capital project.

(b)   No grant anticipation note may be issued if the amount thereof, together with the amount of all other notes authorized or issued in anticipation of the same grant commitment, shall exceed ninety percent (90%) of the unpaid amount of said grant commitment. Each note shall bear on its face a statement to the effect that it is payable solely from moneys received from a described grant and that the faith and credit of the issuing unit are not pledged for the payment thereof, and on its face or reverse the following certificate signed by the finance officer: "This note and all other grant anticipation notes of (issuing unit) authorized or outstanding as of (date) and issued or to be issued in anticipation of (describe grant commitment) amount to ninety percent (90%) or less of the unpaid amount of said grant commitment." No grant anticipation note shall be valid without this certificate.

(c)   Grant anticipation notes issued under this section shall be special obligations of the issuing unit. Neither the credit nor the taxing power of the issuing unit may be pledged for the payment of grant anticipation notes, and no holder of such notes shall have the right to compel the exercise of the taxing power by the issuing unit or the forfeiture of any of its property in connection with any default thereon. (1975, c. 674, s. 1.)

§ 159-172. Authorization and issuance of notes.

(a) Notes issued under this Part shall be authorized by resolution of the governing board of the issuing unit. The resolution shall fix the maximum aggregate principal amount of notes to be issued thereunder, and may authorize any officer to fix, within the limitations prescribed by the resolution, the rate of interest, the place or places of payment, and the denomination or denominations of the notes. Notes that are represented by instruments shall be signed with the manual or facsimile signatures of the officers designated by the government board for that purpose, but at least one manual signature (which may be the signature of the representative of the Commission to the Commission's certificate) must appear on each note that is represented by an instrument. Several notes may be issued under one authorization so long as the aggregate principal amount of notes outstanding at any one time does not exceed the limits of the authorization.

(b) Before any notes may be issued pursuant to this Part, they must be approved by the Commission. In determining whether to approve the issuance of notes, the Commission may consider (i) the reasonableness of the budget estimates of the taxes or other revenues in anticipation of which the tax or revenue anticipation notes are to be issued, (ii) the firm and binding character of the grant commitment in anticipation of which the grant anticipation notes are to be issued, (iii) whether the amount of the notes, together with the amount of other authorized or outstanding notes issued or to be issued in anticipation of the same taxes or other revenues or grant commitments, exceeds the limitations prescribed in G.S. 159-169, 159-170 or 159-171 as the case may be, and (iv) any other matters that the Commission considers to have a bearing on whether the issue should be approved. The Commission shall approve the issuance of the notes if, upon the information and evidence it receives, it finds and determines that (i) the issue is necessary and expedient, (ii) the budget estimates of the taxes or other revenues are reasonable or the grant commitment is firm and binding, and (iii) the amount of the notes, together with the amounts of other authorized or outstanding notes issued or to be issued in anticipation of the same taxes or other revenues or grant commitments do not exceed the appropriate limitations prescribed by this Part. An order approving an issue shall not be regarded as an approval of the legality of the notes in any respect.

(c) Notes issued under this Part shall be sold by the Commission at public or private sale according to such procedures as the Commission may prescribe. Each such note that is represented by an instrument shall bear on its face or reverse a certificate signed by the secretary of the Commission or an assistant designated by him that the issuance of the note has been approved under the provisions of The Local Government Finance Act. Such signature may be a manual or facsimile signature as the Commission may determine. Each note that is not represented by an instrument shall be evidenced by a writing relating to such note, which writing shall identify such note or the issue of which it is a part, bear such certificate and be on file with the Commission. The certificate shall be conclusive evidence that the requirements of this Part have been observed, and no note without the Commission's certificate or with respect to which a writing bearing such certificate has not been filed with the Commission shall be valid.

(d) When the notes are executed, they shall be delivered to the State Treasurer who shall deliver them to the order of the purchaser and collect the purchase price or proceeds. The Treasurer shall also collect from their purchaser the purchase price or proceeds of notes that are not represented by instruments. The Treasurer shall then deduct from the proceeds the Commission's expense in connection with the issue, and remit the net proceeds to the official depository of the unit after assurance that the deposit will be adequately secured as required by law. If the notes have been issued to renew outstanding notes, the Treasurer, in lieu of collecting the purchase price or proceeds, may provide for the exchange of the newly issued notes for the notes to be renewed. (1917, c. 138, s. 14; 1919, c. 178, s. 3(14); C.S., s. 2935; 1921, c. 8, s. 1; Ex. Sess. 1921, c. 106, s. 1; 1927, c. 81, s. 4; 1931, c. 293; 1939, c. 231, s. 1; 1971, c. 780, s. 1; 1973, c. 494, s. 39; 1975, c. 674, ss. 3-5; 1983, c. 322, ss. 10-12.)

§§ 159-173 through 159-175. Reserved for future codification purposes.

Article 9A.

Borrowing by Cities for Competitive Purposes.

§ 159-175.10. Additional requirements for review of city financing application; communications service.

The Commission shall apply additional requirements to an application for financing by a city or a joint agency under Part 1 of Article 20 of Chapter 160A of the General Statutes for the construction, operation, expansion, or repair of a communications system or other infrastructure for the purpose of offering communications service, as that term is defined in G.S. 160A-340(3), that is or will be competitive with communications service offered by a private communications service provider. This section does not apply to the repair, rebuilding, replacement, or improvement of an existing communications network, or equipment relating thereto, but does apply to the expansion of such existing network. The additional requirements are the following:

(1)   Prior to submitting an application to the Commission, a city or joint agency shall comply with the provisions of G.S. 160A-340.3 requiring at least two public hearings on the proposed communications service project and notice of the hearings to private communications service providers who have requested notice.

(2)   At the same time the application is submitted to the Commission, the city or joint agency shall serve a copy of the application on each person that provides competitive communications service within the city's jurisdictional boundaries or in areas adjacent to the city. No hearing on the application shall be heard by the Commission until at least 60 days after the application is submitted to the Commission.

(3)   Upon the request of a communications service provider, the Commission shall accept written and oral comments from competitive private communications service providers in connection with any hearing or other review of the application.

(4)   In considering the probable net revenues of the proposed communications service project, the Commission shall consider and make written findings on the reasonableness of the city or joint agency's revenue projections in light of the current and projected competitive environment for the services to be provided, taking into consideration the potential impact of technological innovation and change on the proposed service offerings and the level of demonstrated community support for the project.

(5)   The city or joint agency making the application to the Commission shall bear the burden of persuasion with respect to subdivisions (1) through (4) of this section. (2011-84, s. 3; 2012-194, s. 36.)

Article 10.

Assistance for Defaulting Units in Refinancing Debt.

§ 159-176. Commission to aid defaulting units in developing refinancing plans.

If a unit of local government or municipality (as defined in G.S. 159-44 or 159-81) fails to pay any installment of principal or interest on its outstanding debt on or before the due date (whether the debt is evidenced by general obligation bonds, revenue bonds, bond anticipation notes, tax anticipation notes, or revenue anticipation notes) and remains in default for 90 days, the Commission may take such action as it deems advisable to investigate the unit's or municipality's fiscal affairs, consult with its governing board, and negotiate with its creditors in order to assist the unit or municipality in working out a plan for refinancing, adjusting, or compromising the debt. When a plan is developed that the Commission finds to be fair and equitable and reasonably within the ability of the unit or municipality to meet, the Commission shall enter an order finding that it is fair, equitable, and within the ability of the unit or municipality to meet. The Commission shall then advise the governing board to take the necessary steps to implement it. If the governing board declines or refuses to do so within 90 days after receiving the Commission's advice, the Commission may enter an order directing the governing board to implement the plan. When this order is entered, the members of the governing board and all officers and employees of the unit or municipality shall be under an affirmative duty to do all things necessary to implement the plan. The Commission may apply to the appropriate division of the General Court of Justice for a court order to the governing board and other officers and employees of the unit or municipality to enforce the Commission's order. (1935, c. 124, ss. 1, 2; 1971, c. 780, s. 1; 1973, c. 494, s. 41; 1981 (Reg. Sess., 1982), c. 1276, s. 12.)

§ 159-176. (For effective date, see note) Commission to aid defaulting units in developing refinancing plans.

If a unit of local government or municipality (as defined in G.S. 159-44, 159-81, or 159-102) fails to pay any installment of principal or interest on its outstanding debt on or before the due date (whether the debt is evidenced by general obligation bonds, revenue bonds, project development financing debt instruments, bond anticipation notes, tax anticipation notes, or revenue anticipation notes) and remains in default for 90 days, the Commission may take such action as it deems advisable to investigate the unit's or municipality's fiscal affairs, consult with its governing board, and negotiate with its creditors in order to assist the unit or municipality in working out a plan for refinancing, adjusting, or compromising the debt. When a plan is developed that the Commission finds to be fair and equitable and reasonably within the ability of the unit or municipality to meet, the Commission shall enter an order finding that it is fair, equitable, and within the ability of the unit or municipality to meet. The Commission shall then advise the governing board to take the necessary steps to implement it. If the governing board declines or refuses to do so within 90 days after receiving the Commission's advice, the Commission may enter an order directing the governing board to implement the plan. When this order is entered, the members of the governing board and all officers and employees of the unit or municipality shall be under an affirmative duty to do all things necessary to implement the plan. The Commission may apply to the appropriate division of the General Court of Justice for a court order to the governing board and other officers and employees of the unit or municipality to enforce the Commission's order. (1935, c. 124, ss. 1, 2; 1971, c. 780, s. 1; 1973, c. 494, s. 41; 1981 (Reg. Sess., 1982), c. 1276, s. 12; 2003-403, s. 15.)

§ 159-177. Power to require reports and approve budgets.

When a refinancing plan has been put into effect pursuant to G.S. 159-176, the Commission shall have authority to require any periodic reports on the unit's or municipality's financial affairs (in addition to those otherwise required by law) that the secretary deems necessary, and to approve or reject the unit's or municipality's annual budget ordinance. The governing board of the unit or municipality shall obtain the approval of the secretary before adopting the annual budget ordinance. If the Commission recommends modifications in the budget, the governing board shall be under an affirmative duty to make the modifications before adopting the budget ordinance. (1935, c. 124, ss. 3, 4; 1971, c. 780, s. 1; 1973, c. 494, ss. 41, 42.)

§ 159-178. Duration of Commission's powers.

The power and authority granted to the Commission in this Article shall continue with respect to a defaulting unit of local government or municipality until the Commission is satisfied that the unit or municipality has performed or will perform the duties required of it in the refinancing plan, and until agreements made with the unit's or municipality's creditors have been performed in accordance with the plan. (1935, c. 124, s. 5; 1971, c. 780, s. 1; 1973, c. 494, s. 41, 1975, c. 10, s. 62.)

§§ 159-179 through 159-180. Reserved for future codification purposes.

Article 11.

Enforcement of Chapter.

§ 159-181. Enforcement of Chapter.

(a)   If any finance officer, governing board member, or other officer or employee of any local government or public authority (as local government and public authority are defined in G.S. 159-7(b)) shall approve any claim or bill knowing it to be fraudulent, erroneous, or otherwise invalid, or make any written statement, give any certificate, issue any report, or utter any other document required by this Chapter, knowing that any portion of it is false, or shall willfully fail or refuse to perform any duty imposed upon him by this Chapter, he is guilty of a Class 3 misdemeanor and upon conviction shall only be fined not more than one thousand dollars ($1,000) and forfeits his office, and shall be personally liable in a civil action for all damages suffered thereby by the unit or authority or the holders of any of its obligations.

(b)   If any person embezzles any funds belonging to any local government or public authority, or appropriates to his own use any personal property having a value of more than fifty dollars ($50.00) belonging to any local government or public authority, in addition to the crimes and punishment otherwise provided by law, upon conviction he forfeits his office or position and is forever thereafter barred from holding any office or place of trust or profit under the State of North Carolina or any political subdivisions thereof until the disability is removed in the manner provided for restoration of citizenship in Chapter 13 of the General Statutes.

(c)   The Local Government Commission shall have authority to impound the books and records of any unit of local government or public authority and assume full control of all its financial affairs (i) when the unit or authority defaults on any debt service payment or, in the opinion of the Commission, will default on a future debt service payment if the financial policies and practices of the unit or authority are not improved, or (ii) when the unit or authority persists, after notice and warning from the Commission, in willfully or negligently failing or refusing to comply with the provisions of this Chapter. When the Commission takes action under this section, the Commission is vested with all of the powers of the governing board as to the levy of taxes, expenditure of money, adoption of budgets, and all other financial powers conferred upon the governing board by law. This subsection (c) does not apply to contractual obligations undertaken by a unit of local government in a debt instrument issued pursuant to Chapter 159G of the General Statutes unless such debt instrument is secured by a pledge of the faith and credit of the unit of local government.

(d)   The Local Government Commission shall have authority to impound the books and records associated with the water and/or sewer enterprise system of any unit of local government or public authority, assume full control of all its affairs, or take any lesser actions deemed necessary by the Commission when, for three consecutive fiscal years, the audited financial statements of the unit or public authority demonstrate that the unit or public authority meets any one of the following three criteria: (i) the enterprise system experienced negative working capital; (ii) the enterprise system experienced a quick ratio of less than 1.0; or (iii) the unit or public authority experienced a net loss of revenue from operations in the enterprise system using the modified accrual budgetary basis of accounting. Before the Commission assumes full control of an enterprise system as described in this subsection, it must find that the impact of items (i) through (iii) threatens the financial stability of the unit or public authority, and that the unit or public authority has failed to make corrective changes in its operation of the enterprise system after having received notice and warning from the Commission. The notice and warning may occur prior to the expiration of the three-year period. When the Commission takes action under this section, the Commission is vested with the powers of the governing board as the Commission shall deem necessary, which may include all powers of the governing board as to the operation of the enterprise system, including, but not limited to, setting rates, negotiating contracts, collecting payments that are due, suspending service to nonpaying customers, resolving disputes with third parties, and transferring the ownership of the enterprise system. For purposes of this subsection, the term "working capital" means current assets, such as cash, inventory, and accounts receivable, less current liabilities, determined in accordance with generally accepted accounting principles, and the phrase "quick ratio of less than 1.0" means that the ratio of liquid assets, cash and receivables, to current liabilities is less than 1.0. (1971, c. 780, s. 1; 1973, c.

494, s. 43; 1987, c. 790, s. 5; 1993, c. 539, s. 108; 1994, Ex. Sess., c. 24, s. 14(c); 2013-150, s. 1.)

§ 159-182. Offending officers and employees removed from office.

If an officer or employee of a local government or public authority persists, after notice and warning from the Commission, in failing or refusing to comply with any provision of this Chapter, he forfeits his office or employment. The Commission may enter an order suspending the offender from further performance of his office or employment after first giving him notice and an opportunity to be heard in his own defense, pending the outcome of quo warranto proceedings. Upon suspending a local officer or employee under this section, the Commission shall report the circumstances to the Attorney General who shall initiate quo warranto proceedings against the officer or employee in the General Court of Justice. If an officer or employee persists in performing any official act in violation of an order of the Commission suspending him from performance of his duties, the Commission may apply to the General Court of Justice for a restraining order and injunction. (1931, c. 60, s. 45; 1971, c. 780, s. 1; 1973, c. 494, s. 44.)

§§ 159-183 through 159-187. Reserved for future codification purposes.

Article 12.

Borrowing by Development Authorities Created by General Assembly.

§ 159-188. Borrowing authority.

A development authority created as a body corporate and politic by an act of the General Assembly, and having as its purpose to stimulate, foster, coordinate, plan, improve and encourage economic development in order to relieve poverty, dependency, chronic unemployment, underemployment and to promote the improvement and development of the economy of a county of the State, and whose members are appointed by the board of commissioners of such county, shall have authority to borrow money from an agency or instrumentality of the United States government and to execute and deliver obligations for the repayment thereof and to encumber its property for the purpose of securing any such obligation and to execute and deliver such mortgages, deeds of trust and other instruments as are necessary or proper for such purpose; provided, that such obligations shall be repayable only from the revenues of such authority.

Insofar as the provisions of this section are not consistent with the provisions of any other section or law, public or private, the provisions of this section shall be controlling. (1979, c. 512, ss. 1, 2.)

§§ 159-189 through 159-192: Reserved for future codification purposes. (2003-388, s. 4.)

Article 13.

Interest Rate Swap Agreements for Governmental Units.

§ 159-193. Definitions.

The following definitions apply in this Article:

(1) Governmental unit. - Any of the following:

a. A unit of local government as defined in G.S. 159-44.

b. A municipality as defined in G.S. 159-81.

c. A joint agency as defined in G.S. 159B-3.

d. Any department, agency, board, commission, or authority of the State that is authorized by law to issue bonds.

e. The State Treasurer in connection with the issuance, incurrence, carrying, or securing of obligations for or on behalf of the State pursuant to an act of the General Assembly.

(2) Obligations. - Any of the following:

a. Bonds, notes, bond anticipation notes, or other evidences of indebtedness issued by a governmental unit.

b. Lease purchase or installment financing agreements entered into by a governmental unit.

(3) Swap agreement. - Any of the following:

a. An agreement, including terms and conditions incorporated by reference in the agreement, that is a rate swap agreement, basis swap, forward rate agreement, interest rate option, rate cap agreement, rate floor agreement, rate collar agreement, or other similar agreement, including any option to enter into or terminate any of the foregoing.

b. Any combination of the agreements described in sub-subdivision a. of this subdivision.

c. A master agreement for any of the agreements described in sub-subdivisions a. and b. of this subdivision, together with all supplements.

d. One or more transactions entered into pursuant to a master agreement. (2003-388, s. 4; 2005-403, s. 4.)

§ 159-194. Swap agreements.

(a) Subject to the provisions of this Article, a governmental unit may from time to time purchase, enter into, modify, amend, or terminate one or more swap agreements that it determines are necessary or desirable in connection with the issuance, incurrence, carrying, or securing of obligations. This authorization also includes the authority to enter into modifications or reversals of a swap agreement previously entered into by the governmental unit and the authority to enter into a swap agreement that modifies the interest rate payment calculation method under a swap agreement previously entered into to another interest rate calculation method or that reverses, in whole or in part, the effect of a prior swap agreement on the governmental unit's interest rate cost or risk. A swap agreement entered into by a governmental unit may contain any provisions, including provisions regarding payments, term, termination payments, security, default, and remedies, and may be with any parties, that the governmental unit determines are necessary or desirable.

(b) No governmental unit shall enter into a swap agreement pursuant to this Article other than for the primary purpose of managing interest rate risk on or interest rate costs of its obligations. A swap agreement may provide that the payments thereunder are based upon a fixed or variable interest rate calculation method. A governmental unit shall not engage in the business of acting as a dealer in swap agreements. A swap agreement may be entered into in connection with specific obligations of the governmental unit, which may consist of multiple series or issues of obligations as specified by the governmental unit. The swap agreement may be entered into at a time before, at the same time as, or after, the obligations are issued or incurred by the governmental unit. Each swap agreement may be entered for a notional amount up to, but not exceeding, the principal amount of the obligations with respect to which the swap agreement is entered. A swap agreement may have a term as long as, or less than, the term of the obligations with respect to which the swap agreement is entered.

(c)   In connection with entering into a swap agreement, a governmental unit may enter into credit enhancement agreements to secure the obligations of the governmental unit under the swap agreement, with any payment, security, default, remedy, and other terms and conditions that the governmental unit determines, including entering into binding agreements to deliver collateral, either at the time the swap agreement is entered into or at future times under conditions set forth in the swap agreement. (2003-388, s. 4.)

§ 159-195. Nature of duties of a governmental unit under a swap agreement.

The duty of a governmental unit to make the payments required and to perform the other duties of the governmental unit under a swap agreement shall constitute a continuing contractual obligation of the governmental unit, enforceable in accordance with applicable law for the enforcement of contractual obligations of that governmental unit. A governmental unit may limit its duties under a swap agreement to designated property or a designated source of revenues or receipts of the governmental unit, such as the revenues of a specified utility or other public service enterprise system of the governmental unit. If a governmental unit enters into a swap agreement in connection with obligations that are secured by a designated form of security, then, subject to the terms of the bond order or resolution, trust indenture or trust agreement, installment contract or lease purchase agreement, or similar instrument pursuant to which the obligations are issued or incurred, the governmental unit may pledge, mortgage, or grant a security interest in the revenues of the utility or other public service enterprise system, program, receipts, property, or similar arrangement securing the obligations to secure the payment and performance of its duties under the swap agreement. Any pledge of assets, revenues, or receipts to secure the duties of a governmental unit under a swap agreement shall become effective in the same manner and to the same extent as a pledge of those assets, revenues, or receipts to secure the obligations with respect to which the swap agreement is entered. (2003-388, s. 4.)

§ 159-196. Approval by Commission.

(a) Approval Required. - If either of the following conditions is met, a governmental unit shall not enter into a swap agreement unless the Commission first approves the governmental unit's entering into the swap agreement:

(1) The unit is a unit of local government as defined in G.S. 159-44, a municipality as defined in G.S. 159-81, or a joint agency as defined in G.S. 159B-3.

(2) The sale, issuance, or incurrence of the obligations with respect to which the swap agreement is entered into is subject to the approval of the Commission.

(b) Factors. - The Commission may consider all of the following factors in determining whether to approve the swap agreement:

(1) The nature and amount of the outstanding debt of the governmental unit proposing to enter the swap agreement.

(2) The governmental unit's debt management procedures and policies.

(3) To the extent applicable, the governmental unit's compliance with the Local Government Budget and Fiscal Control Act.

(4) Whether the governmental unit is in default in any of its debt service obligations.

(5) The credit rating of the governmental unit.

(c) Amendments. - If a swap agreement is subject to approval by the Commission pursuant to this section and is approved, then the governmental unit shall not enter into any amendment to the swap agreement that terminates or changes the time period covered by the swap agreement, changes the interest rate calculation method under the swap agreement, or changes the notional amounts covered by the swap agreement without the prior approval of the Secretary of the Commission.

(d) Approval Not Required. - A swap agreement is not subject to approval by the Commission except as provided in this section. This section does not require the approval of the Commission of a swap agreement entered into by a private entity receiving the benefit of financing through the issuance of obligations by a governmental unit. (2003-388, s. 4.)

§ 159-197. Additional method.

This Article provides an additional and alternative method for the doing of the things authorized by it and is supplemental to powers conferred by other laws. This Article does not derogate any existing powers. (2003-388, s. 4.)

§ 159-198. Severability.

If any provision of this Article or its application is held invalid, the invalidity does not affect other provisions or applications of this Article that can be given effect without the invalid provisions or application, and to this end the provisions of this Article are severable. (2003-388, s. 4.)

§ 159-199. Validation of preexisting swap agreements.

All proceedings taken by the governing bodies of governmental units in connection with the authorization of swap agreements and all swap agreements entered into by governmental units before the effective date of this Article are ratified. (2003-388, s. 4.)

§ 159-200. Liberal construction.

This Article, being necessary for the prosperity and welfare of the State and its inhabitants, shall be liberally construed to effect its purposes. (2003-388, s. 4.)

§§ 159-201 through 159-209: Reserved for future codification purposes.

Article 14.

Borrowing by Airport Authorities.

§ 159-210. Borrowing authority.

Whenever an airport authority is authorized by general or local act to erect and construct improvements and facilities and to lease these improvements and facilities, the authority may borrow money for use in making and paying for these improvements and facilities, secured by and on the credit only of the lease agreements in respect to these improvements and facilities, and to pledge and assign the leases and lease agreements as security for the authorized loans. The airport authority's power to borrow money under this section is subject to the approval of the Commission. To the extent this section conflicts with any local act, then this section shall control. (2005-342, s. 4.)

Chapter 159A.

Pollution Abatement and Industrial Facilities Financing Act.

§§ 159A-1 through 159A-25. Unconstitutional.

Chapter 159B.

Joint Municipal Electric Power and Energy Act

Article 1.

Short Title, Legislative Findings and Definitions.

§ 159B-1. Short title.

This Chapter may be cited as the "Joint Municipal Electric Power and Energy Act." (1975, c. 186, s. 1.)

§ 159B-2. Legislative findings and purposes.

The General Assembly hereby finds and determines that:

A critical situation exists with respect to the present and future supply of electric power and energy in the State of North Carolina;

The public utilities operating in the State have sustained greatly increased capital and operating costs;

Such public utilities have found it necessary to postpone or curtail construction of planned generation and transmission facilities serving the consumers of electricity in the State, increasing the ultimate cost of such facilities to the public utilities, and that such postponements and curtailments will have an adverse effect on the provision of adequate and reliable electric service in the State;

The above conditions have occurred despite substantial increases in electric rates;

In the absence of further material increases in electric rates, additional postponements and curtailments in the construction of additional generation and transmission facilities may occur, thereby impairing those utilities' ability to continue to provide an adequate and reliable source of electric power and energy in the State;

Seventy-two municipalities in the State have for many years owned and operated systems for the distribution of electric power and energy to customers in their respective service areas and are empowered severally to engage in the generation and transmission of electric power and energy;

Such municipalities owning electric distribution systems have an obligation to provide their inhabitants and customers an adequate, reliable and economical source of electric power and energy in the future;

In order to achieve the economies and efficiencies made possible by the proper planning, financing, sizing and location of facilities for the generation and transmission of electric power and energy which are not practical for any municipality acting alone, and to insure an adequate, reliable and economical supply of electric power and energy to the people of the State, it is desirable for the State of North Carolina to authorize municipal electric systems to jointly plan, finance, develop, own and operate electric generation and transmission facilities appropriate to their needs in order to provide for their present and future power requirements for all uses without supplanting or displacing the service at retail of other electric suppliers operating in the State, and

The joint planning, financing, development, ownership and operation of electric generation and transmission facilities by municipalities which own electric distribution systems and the issuance of revenue bonds for such purposes as provided in this Chapter is for a public use and for public and municipal purposes and is a means of achieving economies, adequacy and reliability in the generation of electric power and energy and in the meeting of future needs of the State and its inhabitants.

In addition to the authority granted municipalities to jointly plan, finance, develop, own and operate electric generation and transmission facilities by Article 2 of this Chapter and the other powers granted in said Article 2, and in addition and supplemental to powers otherwise conferred on municipalities by the laws of this State for interlocal cooperation, it is desirable for the State of North Carolina to authorize municipalities and joint agencies to form joint municipal assistance agencies which shall be empowered to provide aid and assistance to municipalities in the construction, ownership, maintenance, expansion and operation of their electric systems, and to empower joint agencies authorized herein to provide aid and assistance to municipalities or joint municipal assistance agencies in the development and implementation of integrated resource planning, including, but not limited to, the evaluation of resources, generating facilities, alternative energy resources, conservation and load management programs, transmission and distribution facilities, and purchase power options, and in the development, construction and operation of supply-side and demand-side resources, in addition to exercising such other powers as hereinafter provided to joint municipal assistance agencies and joint agencies. In order to provide maximum economies and efficiencies to municipalities and the consuming public in the generation and transmission of electric power and energy contemplated by Article 2 of this Chapter, it is also desirable that the joint municipal assistance agencies authorized herein be empowered to act as provided in Article 3 of this Chapter and that such agency or agencies be empowered to act for and on behalf of any one or more municipalities or joint agencies, as requested, with respect to the construction, ownership, maintenance, expansion and operation of their electric systems; and that the joint agencies authorized herein be empowered to act as provided in Article 2 of this Chapter and that such joint agencies be empowered to act for and on behalf of any one or more municipalities or joint municipal assistance agencies, in each case as requested, with respect to the integrated resource planning and development, construction, and operation of supply-side and demand-side options described above. (1975, c. 186, s. 1; 1983, c. 609, s. 2; 1991 (Reg. Sess., 1992), c. 888, s. 1; 1995, c. 412, s. 1.)

§ 159B-3. Definitions.

The following terms whenever used or referred to in this Chapter shall have the following respective meanings unless a different meaning clearly appears from the context:

(1)   "Bonds" shall mean revenue bonds, notes and other evidences of indebtedness of a joint agency or municipality issued under the provisions of this Chapter and shall include refunding bonds.

(2)   "Cost" or "cost of a project" shall mean, but shall not be limited to, the cost of acquisition, construction, reconstruction, improvement, enlargement, betterment or extension of any project, including the cost of studies, plans, specifications, surveys, and estimates of costs and revenues relating thereto; the cost of land, land rights, rights-of-way and easements, water rights, fees, permits, approvals, licenses, certificates, franchises, and the preparation of applications for and securing the same; administrative, legal, engineering and inspection expenses; financing fees, expenses and costs; working capital; initial fuel costs; interest on the bonds during the period of construction and for such reasonable period thereafter as may be determined by the issuing municipality or joint agency (provided that a period of three years shall be deemed to be reasonable for bonds issued to finance a generating unit expected to be operated to supply base load); establishment of reserves; and all other expenditures of the issuing municipality or joint agency incidental, necessary or convenient to the acquisition, construction, reconstruction, improvement, enlargement, betterment or extension of any project and the placing of the same in operation. The term shall also mean the capital cost of fuel for any project.

(2a)   "Electric system" shall mean any electric power generation, transmission or distribution system.

(3)   "Governing board" shall mean the legislative body, council, board of commissioners, board of trustees, or other body charged by law with governing the municipality, joint agency, or joint municipal assistance agency, including any executive committee created pursuant to G.S. 159B-10.

(4) "Joint agency" shall mean a public body and body corporate and politic organized in accordance with the provisions of Article 2 of this Chapter.

(4a) "Joint municipal assistance agency" shall mean a public body and body corporate and politic organized in accordance with the provisions of Article 3 of this Chapter.

(5) "Municipality" shall mean a city, town or other unit of municipal government created under the laws of the State, or any board, agency, or commission thereof, owning a system or facilities for the generation, transmission or distribution of electric power and energy for public and private uses.

(6) "Project" shall mean any system or facilities for the generation, transmission and transformation, or any of them, of electric power and energy by any means whatsoever including, but not limited to, any one or more electric generating units situated at a particular site, or any interest in the foregoing, whether an undivided interest as a tenant in common or otherwise. Project does not mean an administrative office building or office or facilities related to the administrative office building or office.

(7) "State" shall mean the State of North Carolina. (1975, c. 186, s. 1; 1977, c. 708, s. 2; 1983, c. 609, ss. 3-6; 1985, c. 266, s. 1; 1989, c. 329; 1991, c. 513, s. 1; 1995, c. 412, s. 2.)

Article 2.

Joint Agencies; Municipalities.

§ 159B-4. Authority of municipalities to jointly cooperate.

In addition and supplemental to the powers otherwise conferred on municipalities by the laws of the State, and in order to accomplish the purposes of this Chapter and to obtain a supply of electric power and energy for the present and future needs of its inhabitants and customers, a municipality may jointly or severally plan, finance, develop, construct, reconstruct, acquire, improve, enlarge, better, own, operate and maintain a project situated within or without the State with one or more other municipalities or joint agencies created pursuant to this Chapter or, in the case of projects for the generation and transmission of electric power and energy, jointly with any persons, firms, associations or corporations, public or private, engaged in the generation, transmission or distribution of electric power and energy for resale within this State or any state contiguous to the State, and may make such plans and enter into such contracts in connection therewith, not inconsistent with the provisions of this Chapter, as are necessary or appropriate.

Prior to acquiring any generation project the governing board shall determine the needs of the municipality for power and energy based upon engineering studies and reports, and shall not acquire a project in excess of that amount of capacity and the energy associated therewith required to provide for its projected needs for power and energy from and after the date the project is estimated to be placed in normal continuous operation and for such reasonable period of time thereafter as shall be determined by the governing board and approved by the North Carolina Utilities Commission in a proceeding instituted pursuant to G.S. 159B-24. In determining the future power requirements of a municipality, there shall be taken into account the following:

(1) The economies and efficiencies to be achieved in constructing on a large scale facilities for the generation of electric power and energy;

(2) The municipality's needs for reserve and peaking capacity and to meet obligations under pooling and reserve sharing agreements reasonably related to its needs for power and energy to which it is or may become a party;

(3) The estimated useful life of such project;

(4) The estimated time necessary for the planning, development, acquisition or construction of such project and the length of time required in advance to obtain, acquire or construct additional power supply; and

(5) The reliability and availability of existing or alternative power supply sources and the cost of such existing or alternative power supply sources.

A determination by such governing board approved by the North Carolina Utilities Commission based upon appropriate findings of the foregoing matters shall be conclusive as to the quantity of the interest which a municipality may acquire in a generation project unless a party to the proceeding aggrieved by the determination of said Commission shall file notice of appeal pursuant to Article 5 of Chapter 62 of the General Statutes of North Carolina.

Nothing herein contained shall prevent a municipality or municipalities from undertaking studies to determine whether there is a need for a project or whether such project is feasible. (1975, c. 186, s. 1; 1977, c. 385, s. 2; 1983, c. 574, s. 1; 1995, c. 412, s. 3.)

§ 159B-5. Joint ownership of a project; provisions of the contract or agreement with respect thereto.

Each municipality shall own a project in proportion to the amount of the money furnished or the value of property or other consideration supplied by it for the planning, development, acquisition or construction thereof, and shall be entitled to a percentage share of the output and capacity therefrom equal to such ownership proportion in such project.

Each municipality shall be severally liable for its own acts and not jointly or severally liable for the acts, omissions or obligations of others, and no money or property or other consideration supplied by any municipality shall be credited or otherwise applied to the account of any other municipality, nor shall the share of any municipality in a project be charged directly or indirectly with any debt or obligation of any other municipality or be subject to any lien as a result thereof. The acquisition of a project shall include, but shall not be limited to, the purchase or lease of an existing, completed project and the purchase of a project under construction. A municipality participating in the joint or several planning, financing, construction, reconstruction, acquisition, improvement, enlargement, betterment, ownership, operation or maintenance of any project under this Chapter may furnish money derived solely from the proceeds of bonds or from the ownership and operation of its electric system, or both, and provide property, both real and personal, services and other considerations.

Any contracts entered into by municipalities with respect to ownership in a project shall contain such terms, conditions and provisions, not inconsistent with the provisions hereof, as the governing boards of the municipalities shall deem to be in the interests of the municipalities. Any such contracts shall be ratified by resolution of the governing board of each municipality spread upon its minutes. Any such contracts shall include, but shall not be limited to, the following:

(1)   The purpose or purposes of the contract;

(2)   The duration of the contract;

(3)   The manner of appointing or employing the personnel necessary in connection with the project;

(4)   The method of financing the project, including the apportionment of costs and revenues;

(5)   Provisions specifying the ownership interests of the parties in real property used or useful in connection with the project, and the procedures for the disposition of such property when the contract expires, is terminated or when the project, for any reason, is abandoned, decommissioned or dismantled;

(6)   Provisions relating to alienation and prohibiting partition of a municipality's interest in a project, which provisions shall not be subject to any provision of law restricting covenants against alienation or partition;

(7)   Provisions for the construction of a project, which may include the determination that one participating municipality or any person, firm or corporation may construct the project as agent for all the parties;

(8)   Provisions for the operation and maintenance of a project, which may include the determination that one participating municipality or any person, firm or corporation may operate and maintain the project as agent for all the parties;

(9)   Provisions for the creation of a committee of representatives of the participating municipalities with such powers of supervision of the construction and operation of the project as the contract, not inconsistent with the provisions of this Chapter, may provide;

(10)   Provisions that if one or more of the municipalities shall default in the performance or discharge of its or their obligations with respect to the project, the other party or parties may assume, pro rata or otherwise, the obligations of such defaulting party or parties and may succeed to such rights and interests of the defaulting party or parties in the project as may be agreed upon in the contract;

(11)   Methods for amending the contract;

(12)   Methods for terminating the contract; and

(13)   Any other necessary or proper matter.

For the purpose of paying its respective share of the cost of a project or projects, a municipality may issue its bonds as provided in this Chapter, and, notwithstanding the provisions of any other law to the contrary, may secure the payment of the principal of, premium, if any, and interest on such bonds by a lien and charge on all, or any portion of, the revenue derived or to be derived from the ownership and operation of its system or facilities for the generation, transmission, or distribution of electric power or energy or its interests in any project or projects, or a combination of such revenues. Provided that all bonds issued under the provisions of this Chapter shall be authorized and issued by the governing board of a city, town, or other unit of municipal government created under the laws of the State.

In connection with any project undertaken pursuant to this Chapter, a municipality shall have all of the rights and powers granted to a joint agency by subdivisions (12) and (13) of G.S. 159B-11.

Notwithstanding the provisions of any other law to the contrary, any contracts with respect to the sale or purchase of capacity, output, power or energy from a project may extend for a period not exceeding 50 years from the date a project is estimated to be placed in normal continuous operation; and the execution and effectiveness thereof shall not be subject to any authorizations or approvals by the State or any agency, commission or instrumentality or political subdivision thereof except as in this Chapter specifically required and provided. (1975, c. 186, s. 1; 1983, c. 574, ss. 2-2.6.)

§ 159B-5.1. Joint ownership with other public or private entities engaged in generation, transmission or distribution of electric power for resale.

Municipalities and joint agencies may jointly or severally own, operate and maintain projects with any person, firm, association or corporation, public or private, engaged in the generation, transmission or distribution of electric power and energy for resale within this State or any state contiguous to this State. Any municipality or joint agency shall have for such purposes all powers conferred upon them by the provisions of this Chapter including the power to issue revenue bonds pursuant to the provisions of this Chapter to finance its share of the cost of any such project. The definitions and all other terms and provisions of this Chapter shall be construed so as to include such undivided ownership interest in order to fully effectuate the power and authority conferred by the foregoing provisions of this section. (1977, c. 708, s. 3.)

§ 159B-6. Sale of capacity and output by a municipality.

Capacity or output derived by a municipality from its ownership share of a project not then required by such municipality for its own use and for the use of its consumers may be sold or exchanged by such municipality, for such consideration and for such period and upon such other terms and conditions as may be determined by the parties, to any municipality owning electric distribution facilities in this State, to any electric membership corporation or public utility authorized to do business in this State, or to any state, federal or municipal agency which owns electric generation, transmission or distribution facilities. Provided, however, that the foregoing limitations shall not apply to the temporary sale of excess capacity and energy without the State in cases of emergency or when required to fulfill obligations under any pooling or reserve-sharing agreements reasonably related to its needs for power and energy. Provided further, however, that sales of excess capacity or output of a project to electric membership corporations, public utilities, and other persons the interest on whose securities and other obligations is not exempt from taxation by the federal government shall not be made in such amounts, for such periods of time, and under such terms and conditions as will cause the interest on bonds issued to finance the cost of a project to become taxable by the federal government. (1975, c. 186, s. 1.)

§ 159B-7. Licenses, permits, certificates and approvals.

Municipalities proposing to jointly plan, finance, develop, own and operate a project are hereby authorized, either jointly or separately, to apply to the appropriate agencies of the State, the United States, or any state thereof, and to any other proper agency for such licenses, permits, certificates or approvals as may be necessary, and to construct, maintain and operate projects in accordance with such licenses, permits, certificates or approvals and to obtain, hold and use such licenses, permits, certificates and approvals in the same manner as any other operating unit of any other person. (1975, c. 186, s. 1.)

§ 159B-8: Repealed by Session Laws 1995, c. 412, s. 4.

§ 159B-9 Creation of a joint agency; board of commissioners.

(a) The governing boards of two or more municipalities may by resolution or ordinance determine that it is in the best interests of the municipalities in accomplishing the purposes of this Chapter to create a joint agency as prescribed herein for the purpose of undertaking the planning, financing, development, acquisition, construction, reconstruction, improvement, enlargement, betterment, operation and maintenance of a project or projects as an alternative or supplemental method of obtaining the benefits and assuming the responsibilities of ownership in a project.

In determining whether or not creation of a joint agency for such purpose is in the best interests of the municipalities, the governing boards shall take into consideration, but shall not be limited to, the following:

(1) Whether or not a separate entity may be able to finance the cost of projects in a more efficient and economical manner;

(2) Whether or not better financial market acceptance may result if one entity is responsible for issuing all of the bonds required for a project or projects in a timely and orderly manner and with a uniform credit rating instead of multiple entities issuing separate issues of bonds;

(3) Whether or not savings and other advantages may be obtained by providing a separate entity responsible for the acquisition, construction, ownership and operation of a project or projects; and

(4) Whether or not the existence of such a separate entity will foster the continuation of joint planning and undertaking of projects, and the resulting economies and efficiencies to be derived from such joint planning and undertaking.

If each governing board shall determine that it is in the best interest of the municipality to create a joint agency to provide power and energy to the municipality as provided in this Chapter, each shall adopt a resolution or ordinance so finding (which need not prescribe in detail the basis for the determination), and which shall set forth the names of the municipalities which are proposed to be initial members of the joint agency. The governing board of the municipality shall thereupon by ordinance or resolution appoint one commissioner of the joint agency who may, at the discretion of the governing board, be an officer or employee of the municipality.

Any two or more commissioners so named may file with the Secretary of State an application signed by them setting forth (i) the names of all the proposed member municipalities; (ii) the name and official residence of each of the commissioners so far as known to them; (iii) a certified copy of the appointment evidencing their right to office; (iv) a statement that each governing board of each respective municipality appointing a commissioner has made the aforesaid determination; (v) the desire that a joint agency be organized as a public body and a body corporate and politic under this Chapter; and (vi) the name which is proposed for the joint agency.

The application shall be subscribed and sworn to by such commissioners before an officer or officers authorized by the laws of the State to administer and certify oaths.

The Secretary of State shall examine the application and, if he finds that the name proposed for the joint agency is not identical with that of any other corporation of this State or of any agency or instrumentality thereof, or so nearly similar as to lead to confusion and uncertainty, he shall receive and file it and shall record it in an appropriate book of record in his office.

When the application has been made, filed and recorded as herein provided, the joint agency shall constitute a public body and a body corporate and politic under the name proposed in the application. The Secretary of State shall make and issue to the commissioners executing the application a certificate of incorporation pursuant to this Chapter under the seal of the State, and shall record the same with the application. The certificate shall set forth the names of the member municipalities.

In any suit, action or proceeding involving the validity or enforcement of, or relating to, any contract of the joint agency, the joint agency, in the absence of establishing fraud in the premises, shall be conclusively deemed to have been established in accordance with the provisions of this Chapter upon proof of the issuance of the aforesaid certificate by the Secretary of State. A copy of such certificate, duly certified by the Secretary of State, shall be admissible in evidence in any such suit, action or proceeding, and shall be conclusive proof of the filing and contents thereof.

Notice of the issuance of such certificate shall be given to all of the proposed member municipalities by the Secretary of State. If a commissioner of any such municipality has not signed the application to the Secretary of State and such municipality does not notify the Secretary of State of the appointment of a commissioner within 40 days after receipt of such notice, such municipality shall be deemed to have elected not to be a member of the joint agency. As soon as practicable after the expiration of such 40-day period, the Secretary of State shall issue a new certificate of incorporation, if necessary, setting forth the names of those municipalities which have elected to become members of the joint agency. The failure of any proposed member to become a member shall not affect the validity of the corporate existence of the joint agency.

(b) After the creation of a joint agency, any other municipality may become a member thereof upon application to such joint agency after the adoption of a resolution or ordinance by the governing board of the municipality setting forth the determination and finding prescribed in paragraph (a) of this G.S. 159B-9, and authorizing said municipality to participate, and with the unanimous consent of the members of the joint agency evidenced by the resolutions of their respective governing bodies. Any municipality may withdraw from a joint agency, provided, however, that all contractual rights acquired and obligations incurred while a municipality was a member shall remain in full force and effect.

(c) The powers of a joint agency shall be exercised by or under the authority of, and the business and affairs of a joint agency shall be managed under the direction of, its board of commissioners. However, all or a portion of those powers and the management of all or any part of the business and affairs of a joint agency may be exercised by an executive committee created pursuant to G.S. 159B-10. The board of commissioners shall consist of commissioners appointed by the respective governing boards of the municipalities which are members of the joint agency. Each commissioner shall have not less than one vote and may have in addition thereto such additional votes as the governing boards of a majority of the municipalities which are members of the agency shall determine. Each commissioner shall serve at the pleasure of the governing board by which the commissioner was appointed. Each appointed commissioner before entering upon his duties shall take and subscribe to an oath before some person authorized by law to administer oaths to execute the duties of his office faithfully and impartially, and a record of each such oath shall be filed with the governing board of the appointing municipality and spread upon its minutes. The governing board of each of the municipalities may appoint up to two alternate commissioners to act in lieu of its appointed commissioner when the appointed commissioner is unable for any reason to attend meetings of the board of commissioners or any committee thereof, and the governing board shall designate them as first or second alternate commissioner. Each alternate commissioner shall serve at the pleasure of the governing body by which that commissioner was appointed and shall take, subscribe to and file an oath in the same manner as prescribed for regularly appointed commissioners. Such alternate commissioner when acting in lieu of the regularly appointed commissioner shall be deemed to be the commissioner of such municipality, and shall have the rights, powers and authority of the regularly appointed commissioner, including any committee function of said commissioner, other than such commissioner's position as an officer pursuant to paragraph (d) of this G.S. 159B-9. A certificate entered into the minutes of the board of commissioners of a joint agency by the clerk or other custodian of the minutes and records of the governing body of a municipality, appointing commissioners and alternate commissioners and reciting their appointments, shall constitute conclusive evidence of their appointment. The offices of commissioner, alternate commissioner, or officer of a joint agency are hereby declared to be offices which may be held by the holders of any office, place of trust or profit in addition to and concurrently with those offices permitted by G.S. 128-1.1 and other offices permitted by other General Statute.

(d)   The board of commissioners of the joint agency shall annually elect one of the commissioners as chairman, another as vice-chairman, and another person or persons, who may but need not be commissioners, as treasurer, secretary, and, if desired, assistant secretary and assistant treasurer. The office of treasurer or assistant treasurer may be held by the secretary or assistant secretary. The board of commissioners may also appoint such additional officers as it deems necessary. The secretary or any assistant secretary of the joint agency shall keep a record of the proceedings of the joint agency, and the secretary shall be the custodian of all records, books, documents and papers filed with the joint agency, the minute book or journal of the joint agency and its official seal. Either the secretary or the assistant secretary of the joint agency may cause copies to be made of all minutes and other records and documents of the joint agency and may give certificates under the official seal of the joint agency to the effect that such copies are true copies, and all persons dealing with the joint agency may rely upon such certificates.

(e)   A majority of the commissioners of a joint agency then in office shall constitute a quorum. A vacancy in the board of commissioners of the joint agency shall not impair the right of a quorum to exercise all the rights and perform all the duties of the joint agency. Any action taken by the joint agency under the provisions of this Chapter may be authorized by resolution at any regular or special meeting, and each such resolution may take effect immediately and need not be published or posted. A majority of the votes which the commissioners present are entitled to cast shall be necessary and sufficient to take any action or to pass any resolution, provided that such commissioners present are entitled to cast a majority of the votes of all commissioners of the board.

(f)   No commissioner of a joint agency shall receive any compensation for the performance of his duties hereunder, provided, however, that each commissioner may be paid his necessary expenses incurred while engaged in the performance of such duties. (1975, c. 186, s. 1; 1977, c. 385, ss. 3, 4; 1979, c. 102; 1983, c. 574, s. 3; 1985, c. 243, s. 1; 1995, c. 412, s. 5.)

§ 159B-10. Executive committee, composition; powers and duties; terms.

(a)   The board of commissioners of a joint agency may create an executive committee by resolution. The board may provide for the composition and terms of office of, and the method of filling vacancies on, the executive committee. The executive committee may include representatives of the joint agency, representatives of any other joint agency, and any other persons. The executive committee of a joint agency may simultaneously act as the executive committee of any other joint agency or agencies, or joint municipal assistance agency or agencies, if so provided by all such entities, and also may simultaneously act as the sole governing board of any joint municipal assistance agency created by two or more joint agencies pursuant to G.S. 159B-45 if so provided by all such joint agencies. An executive committee acting as the sole governing board of a joint municipal assistance agency shall not be subject to the limitations on the powers and authority of executive committees set forth in subsection (b) of this section.

(b)   Except as limited by resolution of the board of commissioners creating an executive committee and except as otherwise provided in this subsection, an executive committee shall have and shall exercise all of the powers and authority of the board of commissioners creating the executive committee. However, the executive committee shall not have the power or authority to (i) amend any resolution of the board of commissioners of the joint agency relating to the creation of the executive committee or providing for its powers or authority; or (ii) adopt or amend a budget. Any rate for a joint agency adopted by an executive committee may be rejected, within 30 days following the adoption of the rate, by a vote of two-thirds in number of the commissioners representing the joint agency members affected by the rate. In the event that any rate is rejected in this manner, the executive committee shall, within 10 days following the action on the part of the commissioners, adopt a second rate for that joint agency, which may be the same rate as previously adopted. This second rate may be rejected, within 10 days following the adoption of the rate, by a vote of two-thirds in number of the commissioners representing the joint agency members affected by the rate. If a second rate adopted by the executive committee is rejected in this manner, the board of commissioners of the affected joint agency shall, acting by weighted vote, adopt a rate for the joint agency which is sufficient at least to comply with the requirements of G.S. 159B-17(b). No such rate adopted by the executive committee shall become effective so long as it is subject to rejection by commissioners of a joint agency as provided for in this subsection. However, if the executive committee determines that the establishment of a rate is required within 50 days to enable a joint agency to satisfy the requirements of G.S. 159B-17(b), the rate adopted by the executive committee shall be effective until changed by the executive committee or board of commissioners in accordance with this subsection.

(c)   Each member of the executive committee shall have one vote and shall serve at the pleasure of the governing board by which the member was appointed. Before performing duties as a member, each member shall take and subscribe to an oath before some person authorized by law to administer oaths to execute the duties of the office faithfully and impartially, and a record of each oath shall be filed with the governing board appointing the member and spread upon its minutes. The office of a member of an executive committee may be held by the holders of any office, place of trust or profit in addition to and concurrently with those offices permitted by G.S. 128-1.1 and other offices permitted by law.

(d)   The executive committee shall annually elect from its membership a chair and vice-chair, and shall elect another person or persons, who need not be members, to serve as secretary and, if desired, assistant secretary. The secretary or any assistant secretary of the executive committee shall keep a record of the proceedings of the executive committee, and the secretary shall be the custodian of all records, books, documents, and papers filed with the executive committee, as well as the minute book or journal of the executive committee. Either the secretary or the assistant secretary of the executive committee may cause copies to be made of all minutes and other records and documents of the executive committee and may give certificates of the executive committee to the effect that the copies are true copies, and all persons dealing with the executive committee may rely upon those certificates.

(e)   A majority of the members of an executive committee then serving shall constitute a quorum. A vacancy on the executive committee shall not impair the right of a quorum to exercise all the rights and perform all the duties of the executive committee. Any action taken by the executive committee under the provisions of this Chapter may be authorized by resolution at any regular or special meeting, and each such resolution may take effect immediately and need not be published or posted. A vote of the majority of the members present shall be necessary and sufficient to take any action or to pass any resolution, provided that those members present are entitled to cast a majority of the votes of all members of the executive committee.

(f)   Members of the executive committee, and of any subcommittee created by the executive committee, may receive compensation and be paid expenses for the performance of their duties as determined by the board or boards of commissioners creating that executive committee. However, for any member of an executive committee who is an employee of a municipality, a payment in lieu of any compensation shall be made to the municipality for distribution to the executive committee member in the manner and amount, if any, it deems appropriate. An executive committee for more than one entity may be referred to as a board of directors of any or each of those entities. (1975, c. 186, s. 1; 1977, c. 385, s. 5; 1995, c. 412, s. 6.)

§ 159B-11. General powers of joint agencies; prerequisites to undertaking projects.

Each joint agency shall have all of the rights and powers necessary or convenient to carry out and effectuate the purposes and provisions of this Chapter, including, but without limiting the generality of the foregoing, the rights and powers:

(1)   To adopt bylaws for the regulation of the affairs and the conduct of its business, and to prescribe rules, regulations and policies in connection with the performance of its functions and duties;

(2)   To adopt an official seal and alter the same at pleasure;

(3)   To acquire and maintain an administrative office building or office at such place or places as it may determine, which building or office may be used or owned alone or together with any other joint agency or agencies, joint

municipal assistance agency, municipalities, corporations, associations or persons under such terms and provisions for sharing costs and otherwise as may be determined;

(4) To sue and be sued in its own name, and to plead and be impleaded;

(5) To receive, administer and comply with the conditions and requirements respecting any gift, grant or donation of any property or money;

(6) To acquire by purchase, lease, gift, or otherwise, or to obtain options for the acquisition of, any property, real or personal, improved or unimproved, including an interest in land less than the fee thereof;

(7) To sell, lease, exchange, transfer or otherwise dispose of, or to grant options for any such purposes with respect to, any real or personal property or interest therein;

(8) To pledge, assign, mortgage or otherwise grant a security interest in any real or personal property or interest therein, including the right and power to pledge, assign or otherwise grant a security interest in any money, rents, charges or other revenues and any proceeds derived by the joint agency from the sales of property, insurance or condemnation awards;

(9) To issue bonds of the joint agency for the purpose of providing funds for any of its corporate purposes;

(10) To study, plan, finance, construct, reconstruct, acquire, improve, enlarge, extend, better, own, operate and maintain one or more projects, either individually or jointly with one or more municipalities in this State or any state contiguous to this State owning electric distribution facilities or with any political subdivisions, agencies or instrumentalities of any state contiguous to this State or with other joint agencies created pursuant to this Chapter, and to pay all or any part of the costs thereof from the proceeds of bonds of the joint agency or from any other available funds of the joint agency; no provisions of law with respect to the acquisition, construction, or operation of property by other public bodies shall be applicable to any project as defined in this Chapter and as authorized by this subdivision unless the General Assembly shall specifically so state;

(11) To authorize the construction, operation or maintenance of any project or projects by any person, firm, association, or corporation, public or private;

(12) To acquire by private negotiated purchase or lease or otherwise an existing project, a project under construction, or other property, either individually or jointly, with one or more municipalities or joint agencies in this State or any state contiguous to this State owning electric distribution facilities or with any political subdivisions, agencies or instrumentalities of any state contiguous to this State or with other joint agencies created pursuant to this Chapter; to acquire by private negotiated purchase or lease or otherwise any facilities for the development, production, manufacture, procurement, handling, storage, fabrication, enrichment, processing or reprocessing of fuel of any kind or any facility or rights with respect to the supply of water, and to enter into agreements by private negotiation or otherwise, for a period not exceeding fifty (50) years, for the development, production, manufacture, procurement, handling, storage, fabrication, enrichment, processing or reprocessing of fuel of any kind or any facility or rights with respect to the supply of water; no provisions of law with respect to the acquisition, construction or operation of property by other public bodies shall be applicable to any agency created pursuant to this Chapter unless the legislature shall specifically so state;

(13) To dispose of by private negotiated sale or lease, or otherwise, an existing project or a project under construction, or to dispose of by private negotiated sale or lease, or otherwise any facilities for the development, production, manufacture, procurement, handling, storage, fabrication, enrichment, processing or reprocessing of fuel of any kind or any facility or rights with respect to the supply of water; no provisions of law with respect to the disposition of property by other public bodies shall be applicable to an agency created pursuant to this Chapter unless the legislature shall specifically so state;

(14) To fix, charge and collect rents, rates, fees and charges for electric power or energy and other services, facilities and commodities sold, furnished or supplied through any project or activity permitted in this Chapter;

(15) To generate, produce, transmit, deliver, exchange, purchase, sell for resale only, electric power or energy, and to enter into contracts for any or all such purposes;

(16) To negotiate and enter into contracts for the purchase, sale for resale only, exchange, interchange, wheeling, pooling, transmission or use of electric power and energy with any person, firm, association, or corporation, public or private;

(17)   To make and execute contracts and other instruments necessary or convenient in the exercise of the powers and functions of the joint agency under this Chapter, including contracts with persons, firms, associations, or corporations, public or private;

(18)   To apply to the appropriate agencies of the State, the United States or any state thereof, and to any other proper agency, for such permits, licenses, certificates or approvals as may be necessary, and to construct, maintain and operate projects and undertake other activities permitted in this Chapter in accordance with such licenses, permits, certificates or approvals, and to obtain, hold and use such licenses, permits, certificates and approvals in the same manner as any other person or operating unit of any other person;

(19)   To employ engineers, architects, attorneys, real estate counselors, appraisers, financial advisors and such other consultants and employees as may be required in the judgment of the joint agency and to fix and pay their compensation from funds available to the joint agency therefor and to select and retain subject to approval of the Local Government Commission the financial consultants, underwriters and bond attorneys to be associated with the issuance of any bonds and to pay for services rendered by underwriters, financial consultants or bond attorneys out of the proceeds of any such issue with regard to which the services were performed;

(19a)   To purchase power and energy, and services and facilities relating to the utilization of power and energy, from any source on behalf of its members and other customers and to furnish, sell, lease, exchange, transfer, or otherwise dispose of, or to grant options for any such purposes with respect to the same, to its members and other customers in such amounts, with such characteristics, for such periods of time and under such terms and conditions as the governing board of the joint agency shall determine;

(19b)   To provide aid and assistance to municipalities, and to act for or on behalf of any municipality, in any activity related to the development and implementation of integrated resource planning, including, but not limited to, the evaluation of resources, generating facilities, alternative energy resources, conservation and load management programs, transmission and distribution facilities, and purchased power options, and related to the development, construction and operation of supply-side and demand-side resources, and to do such other acts and things as provided in Article 3 of this Chapter as if the joint agency were a joint municipal assistance agency, and to carry out the powers granted in this Chapter in relation thereto; to provide aid and assistance to any joint municipal assistance agency in the exercise of its respective powers and functions; and

(20) To do all acts and things necessary, convenient or desirable to carry out the purposes, and to exercise the powers granted to the joint agency in this Chapter.

No joint agency shall undertake any project required to be financed, in whole or in part, with the proceeds of bonds without the approval of a majority of its members. Before undertaking any project, a joint agency shall, based upon engineering studies and reports, determine that such project is required to provide for the projected needs for power and energy of its members from and after the date the project is estimated to be placed in normal and continuous operation and for a reasonable period of time thereafter. Prior to or simultaneously with granting a certificate of public convenience and necessity for any such generation project the North Carolina Utilities Commission, in a proceeding instituted pursuant to G.S. 159B-24 of this Chapter, shall approve such determination. In determining the future power requirements of the members of a joint agency, there shall be taken into account the following:

(1) The economies and efficiencies to be achieved in constructing on a large scale facilities for the generation of electric power and energy;

(2) Needs of the joint agency for reserve and peaking capacity and to meet obligations under pooling and reserve-sharing agreements reasonably related to its needs for power and energy to which the joint agency is or may become a party;

(3) The estimated useful life of such project;

(4) The estimated time necessary for the planning, development, acquisition, or construction of such project and the length of time required in advance to obtain, acquire or construct additional power supply for the members of the joint agency;

(5) The reliability and availability of existing alternative power supply sources and the cost of such existing alternative power supply sources.

A determination by the joint agency approved by the North Carolina Utilities Commission based upon appropriate findings of the foregoing matters shall be conclusive as to the appropriateness of a project to provide the needs of the members of a joint agency for power and energy unless a party to the proceeding aggrieved by the determination of said Commission shall file notice of appeal pursuant to Article 5 of Chapter 62 of the General Statutes of North Carolina.

Nothing herein contained shall prevent a joint agency from undertaking studies to determine whether there is a need for a project or whether such project is feasible. (1975, c. 186, s. 1; 1977, c. 385, ss. 6-10; 1983, c. 574, ss. 4, 4.1; 1985, c. 212, s. 1; c. 723, s. 3; 1991 (Reg. Sess., 1992), c. 888, s. 2; 1993, c. 182, s. 1; 1995, c. 412, s. 7.)

§ 159B-12. Sale of capacity and output by a joint agency; other contracts with a joint agency.

Any municipality which is a member of the joint agency may contract to buy from the joint agency power and energy for its present or future requirements, including the capacity and output of one or more specified projects. As the creation of a joint agency is an alternative method whereby a municipality may obtain the benefits and assume the responsibilities of ownership in a project, any such contract may provide that the municipality so contracting shall be obligated to make the payments required by the contract whether or not a project is completed, operable or operating and notwithstanding the suspension, interruption, interference, reduction or curtailment of the output of a project or the power and energy contracted for, and that such payments under the contract shall not be subject to any reduction, whether by offset or otherwise, and shall not be conditioned upon the performance or nonperformance of the joint agency or any other member of the joint agency under the contract or any other instrument. Any contract with respect to the sale or purchase of capacity or output of a project entered into between a joint agency and its member municipalities may also provide that if one or more of such municipalities shall default in the payment of its or their obligations with respect to the purchase of said capacity or output, then in that event the remaining member municipalities which are purchasing capacity and output under the contract shall be required to accept and pay for and shall be entitled proportionately to and may use or otherwise dispose of the capacity or output which was to be purchased by the defaulting municipality. Notwithstanding the provisions of any other law to the contrary, any such contract with respect to the sale or purchase of capacity, output, power, or energy from a project may extend for a period not exceeding

50 years from the date a project is estimated to be placed in normal continuous operation.

Any municipality may contract with a joint agency, or may contract indirectly with a joint agency through a joint municipal assistance agency, to implement the provisions of G.S. 159B-11(19a) and (19b). Notwithstanding the provisions of any law to the contrary, including, but not limited to, the provisions of G.S. 159B-44(13), any contract between a joint agency and a municipality or a joint municipal assistance agency (or between a municipality and a joint municipal assistance agency) to implement the provisions of G.S. 159B-11(19b) may extend for a period not exceeding 30 years; provided, that any such contract in respect of a capital project to be used by or for the benefit of a municipality shall be subject to the prior approval of the Local Government Commission of North Carolina. In reviewing any such contract for approval, said Local Government Commission shall consider the municipality's debt management procedures and policies, whether the municipality is in default with respect to its debt service obligations and such other matters as said Local Government Commission may believe to have a bearing on whether the contract should be approved.

Notwithstanding the provisions of any law to the contrary, the execution and effectiveness of any contracts authorized by this section shall not be subject to any authorizations or approvals by the State or any agency, commission or instrumentality or political subdivision thereof except as in this Chapter specifically required and provided.

Payments by a municipality under any contract authorized by this section shall be made solely from the revenues derived from the ownership and operation of the electric system of said municipality and any obligation under such contract shall not constitute a legal or equitable pledge, charge, lien, or encumbrance upon any property of the municipality or upon any of its income, receipts, or revenues, except the revenues of its electric system, and neither the faith and credit nor the taxing power of the municipality are, or may be, pledged for the payment of any obligation under any such contract. A municipality or joint agency, pursuant to an agreement with a municipality, shall be obligated to fix, charge and collect rents, rates, fees and charges for electric power and energy and other services, activities permitted in this Chapter, facilities and commodities sold, furnished or supplied through the electric system of the municipality sufficient to provide revenues adequate to meet its obligations under any such contract and to pay any and all other amounts payable from or constituting a charge and lien upon such revenues, including amounts sufficient to pay the principal of and interest on general obligation bonds heretofore or hereafter issued by the municipality for purposes related to its electric system.

Payments by any joint municipal assistance agency to any joint agency under any contract or contracts authorized by this section, shall be made solely from the sources specified in such contract or contracts and no other, and any obligation under such contract shall not constitute a legal or equitable pledge, charge, lien, or encumbrance upon any property of the joint municipal assistance agency or upon any of its income, receipts, or revenues, or upon any property of any municipality with which the joint agency or joint municipal assistance agency contracts or upon any of such municipality's income, receipts, or revenues in each case except such sources so specified. A joint municipal assistance agency shall be obligated to fix, charge and collect rents, rates, fees, and charges for providing aid and assistance sufficient to provide revenues adequate to meet its obligations under such contract.

Any municipality which is a member of a joint agency may furnish the joint agency with money derived solely from the ownership and operation of its electric system or facilities and provide the joint agency with personnel, equipment and property, both real and personal. Any municipality may also provide any services to a joint agency.

Any member of a joint agency may contract for, advance or contribute funds derived solely from the ownership and operation of its electric system or facilities to a joint agency as may be agreed upon by the joint agency and the member, and the joint agency shall repay such advances or contributions from proceeds of bonds, from operating revenues or from any other funds of the joint agency, together with interest thereon as may be agreed upon by the member and the joint agency. (1975, c. 186, s. 1; 1983, c. 574, s. 5; 1991 (Reg. Sess., 1992), c. 888, s. 3; 1995, c. 412, s. 8.)

§ 159B-13. Sale of excess capacity and output by a joint agency.

A joint agency may sell or exchange the excess capacity or output of a project not then required by any of its members, for such consideration and for such period and upon such other terms and conditions as may be determined by the parties, to any person, firm, association, or corporation, public or private. (1975, c. 186, s. 1; 1977, c. 385, s. 11; 1995, c. 412, s. 9.)

§ 159B-14. Bonds of a joint agency.

A joint agency may issue bonds for the purpose of paying the cost of a project and secure both the principal of and interest on the bonds by a pledge of part or all of the revenues derived or to be derived from all or any of its projects, and any additions and betterments thereto or extensions thereof, or from the sale of power and energy and services and facilities related to the utilization of power and energy, or from other activities or facilities permitted in this Chapter, or from contributions or advances from its members. A joint agency may issue bonds that are not for the purpose of paying the cost of a project and secure the bonds solely by a pledge of revenues, solely by a security interest in real or personal property, or by both a pledge of revenues and a security interest in real or personal property. Bonds of a joint agency shall be authorized by a resolution adopted by its governing board and spread upon its minutes. (1975, c. 186, s. 1; 1983, c. 574, s. 6; 1991, c. 513, s. 2; 1995, c. 412, s. 10.)

§ 159B-15. Issuance of bonds.

(a) Each municipality and joint agency is hereby authorized to issue at one time or from time to time its bonds for the purpose of paying all or any part of the cost of any of the purposes herein authorized. The principal of, premium, if any, and the interest on bonds issued to pay the cost of a project shall be payable solely from revenues. Bonds that are not issued to pay the cost of a project shall be payable from revenues, from property pledged as security for the bonds, or from both.

The bonds of each issue shall bear interest at such rate or rates as may be determined or provided for by the Local Government Commission of North Carolina with the approval of the issuer. The bonds of each issue shall be dated and shall mature in such amounts and at such time or times, not exceeding 50 years from their respective date or dates, as may be determined by the governing board of the issuer, and may be made redeemable before maturity at such price or prices and under such terms and conditions as may be fixed by the governing board of the issuer prior to the issuance of the bonds. The governing board of the issuer shall determine the form and the manner of execution of the bonds, including any interest coupons to be attached thereto, and shall fix the denomination or denominations of the bonds and the place or places of payment of principal and interest, which may be at any bank or trust company within or without the State. In case any officer whose signature or a facsimile of whose signature shall appear on any bonds or coupons shall cease to be such officer before the delivery of such bond, such signature or such facsimile shall nevertheless be valid and sufficient for all purposes the same as if he had remained in office until such delivery. The governing board of the issuer may also provide for the authentication of the bonds by a trustee or fiscal agent appointed by the issuer, or by an authenticating agent of any such trustee or fiscal agent. The bonds may be issued in coupon or in fully registered form, or both, as the governing board of the issuer may determine, and provisions may be made for the registration of any coupon bonds as to principal alone and also as to both principal and interest, and for the reconversion into coupon bonds of any bonds registered as to both principal and interest, and for the interchange of registered and coupon bonds. At the election of a joint agency, any bonds issued and sold in accordance with the provisions of this Chapter may be purchased or otherwise acquired by the joint agency and held by it in lieu of cancellation, and subsequently resold.

(a1) Notwithstanding anything in this Chapter to the contrary, the Local Government Commission of North Carolina and the issuer (i) may authorize officers or employees of either or both thereof to fix principal amounts, maturity dates, interest rates or methods of fixing interest rates, interest payment dates, denominations, redemption rights of the issuer or holder, places of payment of principal and interest, and purchase prices of any bonds, to sell and deliver any bonds in whole or in part at one time or from time to time, and to fix other matters and procedures necessary to complete the transactions authorized, all subject to such limitations as may be prescribed by the Local Government Commission with the approval of the issuer, (ii) may approve insurance contracts, agreements for lines of credit, letters of credit, commitments to purchase bonds and any other transactions to provide security to assure, timely payment of bonds, (iii) may employ one or more persons or firms to assist in the sale of the bonds and appoint one or more banks, trust companies or any dealer in bonds, within or without the State, as depository for safekeeping and as agent for the delivery and payment of the bonds, and (iv) may provide for the payment of fees and expenses in connection with the foregoing either from the proceeds of the bonds or from other available funds.

(b) The proceeds of the bonds of each issue shall be used solely for the purposes for which such bonds have been issued, and shall be disbursed in such manner and under such restrictions, if any, as the governing board of the issuer may provide in the resolution authorizing the issuance of such bonds or in any trust agreement securing the same. The municipality or joint agency may issue interim receipts or temporary bonds, with or without coupons, exchangeable for definitive bonds when such bonds shall have been executed and are available for delivery. The municipality or joint agency may also provide for the replacement of any bonds which shall have become mutilated or shall have been destroyed or lost.

(c) Bonds may be issued under the provisions of this Chapter without obtaining, except as otherwise expressly provided in G.S. 159B-24 of this Chapter, the consent of the State or of any political subdivision, or of any agency, commission or instrumentality of either thereof, and without any other approvals, proceedings or the happening of any conditions or things other than those approvals, proceedings, conditions or things which are specifically required by this Chapter and the provisions of the resolution authorizing the issuance of such bonds or the trust agreement securing the same. (1975, c. 186, s. 1; 1983, c. 574, ss. 7, 7.1; 1985, c. 266, ss. 2, 3; 1991, c. 513, s. 3; 1995, c. 412, s. 11.)

§ 159B-16. Resolution or trust agreement.

In the discretion of the governing board of the issuer, any bonds issued under the provisions of this Chapter may be secured by a trust agreement by and between the issuer and a corporate trustee, which may be any trust company or bank having the powers of a trust company within or without the State. Such trust agreement or the resolution providing for the issuance of such bonds may contain such provisions for protecting and enforcing the rights and remedies of the bondholders and of the trustee as may be reasonable and proper and not in violation of law, and may restrict the individual right of action by bondholders. The trust agreement or the resolution providing for the issuance of such bonds may contain covenants including, but not limited to, the following:

(1) The pledge of all or any part of the revenues derived or to be derived from the project or projects to be financed by the bonds, or from the sale or other disposition of power and energy and services and facilities related to the utilization of power and energy, or from other services or activities permitted in this Chapter, or from contributions and advances from members of a joint agency, or from the electric system or other facilities of a municipality or a joint agency.

(2)   The rents, rates, fees and charges to be established, maintained, and collected, and the use and disposal of revenues, gifts, grants and funds received or to be received by the municipality or joint agency.

(3)   The setting aside of reserves and the investment, regulation and disposition thereof.

(4)   The custody, collection, securing, investment, and payment of any moneys held for the payment of bonds.

(5)   Limitations or restrictions on the purposes to which the proceeds of sale of bonds then or thereafter to be issued may be applied.

(6)   Limitations or restrictions on the issuance of additional bonds; the terms upon which additional bonds may be issued and secured; or the refunding of outstanding or other bonds.

(7)   The procedure, if any, by which the terms of any contract with bondholders may be amended, the percentage of bonds the bondholders of which must consent thereto, and the manner in which such consent may be given.

(8)   Events of default and the rights and liabilities arising thereupon, the terms and conditions upon which bonds issued under this Chapter shall become or may be declared due before maturity, and the terms and conditions upon which such declaration and its consequences may be waived.

(9)   The preparation and maintenance of a budget.

(10)   The retention or employment of consulting engineers, independent auditors, and other technical consultants.

(11)   Limitations on or the prohibition of free service to any person, firm or corporation, public or private.

(12)   The acquisition and disposal of property, provided that no project or part thereof shall be mortgaged by such trust agreement or resolution.

(13)   Provisions for insurance and for accounting reports and the inspection and audit thereof.

(14) The continuing operation and maintenanoo of the project or other facilities.

(15) For bonds that are not issued to pay the cost of a project, the pledge, assignment, mortgage, or grant of a security interest in any real or personal property or interest in real or personal property, including the pledge, assignment, or grant of a security interest in money, rents, charges, or other revenues or proceeds derived by the joint agency from the sale of property, from insurance, or from a condemnation award. In the event of default on a bond secured by a pledge, assignment, mortgage, or grant of a security interest, the rights of the bond holders and the liabilities arising from the default shall be limited, except to the extent provided in a pledge of revenues, to the specific property or interest in property pledged, assigned, or mortgaged or in which a security interest was granted to secure the bonds, and no claim for any deficiency shall be made nor any deficiency judgment entered as a result of the pledge, assignment, mortgage, or grant of a security interest in the property or the interest in property. (1975, c. 186, s. 1; 1983, c. 574, s. 8; 1991, c. 513, ss. 4, 5; 1995, c. 412, s. 12.)

§ 159B-16.1. Revenues - NCEMPA members.

(a) A municipality is hereby authorized to fix, charge and collect rents, rates, fees and charges for electric power and energy and other services, facilities and commodities sold, furnished or supplied through the facilities of its electric system or its interest in any joint project. Before it revises its rates, fees or charges as authorized under this subsection, a municipality shall hold a public hearing on the matter. A notice of the hearing shall be published at least once a week for two successive weeks in a newspaper having general circulation in the municipality. The notice shall state that the public hearing will be held in connection with the municipality's action to revise its rates, fees, or charges authorized in this section and state the amount of the proposed revision. At the hearing, any retail electric customer of the municipality may appear and be heard on the proposed revision to the rates, fees, or charges. The provisions of G.S. 160A-81 shall apply to any public hearing held under this subsection. The provisions of this subsection relating to a public hearing shall not apply to action required to be taken for a municipality by the Local Government Commission, in accordance with G.S. 159-181(c), or to action required to be taken by a municipality to revise its rates, fees or charges authorized in this subsection if the revision is required to be implemented immediately as a result of a catastrophic event or to avoid impairing the ability of the municipality to comply with applicable law or its contractual obligations relating to its outstanding bonds or other indebtedness. For so long as any bonds of a municipality are outstanding and unpaid, the rents, rates, fees and charges shall be so fixed as to provide revenues sufficient to pay all costs of and charges and expenses in connection with the proper operation and maintenance of its electric system, and its interest in any joint project, and all necessary repairs, replacements or renewals thereof, to pay when due the principal of, premium, if any, and interest on all bonds and other evidences of indebtedness payable from said revenues, to create and maintain reserves as may be required by any resolution or trust agreement authorizing and securing bonds, to pay when due the principal of, premium, if any, and interest on all general obligation bonds heretofore or hereafter issued to finance additions, improvements and betterments to its electric system, and to pay any and all amounts which the municipality may be obligated to pay from said revenues by law or contract.

(b) A joint agency is hereby authorized to fix, charge, and collect rents, rates, fees and charges for electric power and energy and other services, facilities and commodities sold, furnished or supplied through the facilities of its projects or otherwise as authorized by this Chapter. A joint agency may only take action to change the rates, fees, or charges authorized in this subsection in a public meeting. Notice of the public meeting shall be given to each municipality that is a member of the joint agency. A notice of the meeting shall be published at least once a week for two successive weeks in a newspaper having general circulation in each municipality that is a member of the joint agency. The notice shall state that the public meeting will be held in connection with the joint agency's action to revise its rates, fees, or charges authorized in this subsection and state the amount of the proposed revision. The provisions of this subsection relating to publication of a notice shall not apply to action required to be taken by a joint agency to revise its rates, fees or charges authorized in this subsection if the revision is required to be implemented immediately as a result of a catastrophic event or to avoid impairing the ability of the joint agency to comply with applicable law or its contractual obligations relating to its outstanding bonds or other indebtedness. For so long as any bonds of a joint agency are outstanding and unpaid, the rents, rates, fees and charges shall be so fixed as to provide revenues sufficient to pay all costs of and charges and expenses in connection with the proper operation and maintenance of its projects, and all necessary repairs, replacements or renewals thereof, to pay when due the principal of, premium, if any, and interest on all bonds and other evidences of indebtedness payable from said revenues, to create and maintain reserves as may be required by any resolution or trust agreement authorizing and securing bonds, and to pay any and all amounts which the joint agency may be obligated to pay from said revenues by law or contract.

(c) Any pledge of revenues, securities or other moneys made by a municipality, joint agency or joint municipal assistance agency pursuant to this Chapter shall be valid and binding from the date the pledge is made. The revenues, securities, and other moneys so pledged and then held or thereafter received by the municipality, joint agency or joint municipal assistance agency or any fiduciary shall immediately be subject to the lien of the pledge without any physical delivery thereof or further act, and the lien of the pledge shall be valid and binding as against all parties having claims of any kind in tort, contract, or otherwise against the municipality, joint agency or joint municipal assistance agency without regard to whether such parties have notice thereof. The resolution or trust agreement or any financing statement, continuation statement or other instrument by which a pledge of revenues, securities or other moneys is created need not be filed or recorded in any manner.

(d) This section applies only to all rates, fees, or charges for electric service provided by the North Carolina Eastern Municipal Power Agency (NCEMPA) or a member city or town of the NCEMPA on or after October 1, 2012. The following cities and towns are members of the North Carolina Eastern Municipal Power Agency: Apex, Ayden, Belhaven, Benson, Clayton, Edenton, Elizabeth City, Farmville, Fremont, Greenville, Hamilton, Hertford, Hobgood, Hookerton, Kinston, LaGrange, Laurinburg, Louisburg, Lumberton, New Bern, Pikeville, Red Springs, Robersonville, Rocky Mount, Scotland Neck, Selma, Smithfield, Southport, Tarboro, Wake Forest, Washington, and Wilson. (1975, c. 186, s. 1; 1983, c. 574, s. 9; 1985, c. 212, s. 2; 1991 (Reg. Sess., 1992), c. 888, s. 4; 1995, c. 412, s. 13; 2012-167, ss. 1, 3.)

§ 159B-17. Revenues - other municipalities.

(a) A municipality is hereby authorized to fix, charge and collect rents, rates, fees and charges for electric power and energy and other services, facilities and commodities sold, furnished or supplied through the facilities of its electric system or its interest in any joint project. For so long as any bonds of a municipality are outstanding and unpaid, the rents, rates, fees and charges shall be so fixed as to provide revenues sufficient to pay all costs of and charges and expenses in connection with the proper operation and maintenance of its electric system, and its interest in any joint project, and all necessary repairs, replacements or renewals thereof, to pay when due the principal of, premium, if any, and interest on all bonds and other evidences of indebtedness payable from said revenues, to create and maintain reserves as may be required by any resolution or trust agreement authorizing and securing bonds, to pay when due the principal of, premium, if any, and interest on all general obligation bonds heretofore or hereafter issued to finance additions, improvements and betterments to its electric system, and to pay any and all amounts which the municipality may be obligated to pay from said revenues by law or contract.

(b)   A joint agency is hereby authorized to fix, charge, and collect rents, rates, fees and charges for electric power and energy and other services, facilities and commodities sold, furnished or supplied through the facilities of its projects or otherwise as authorized by this Chapter. For so long as any bonds of a joint agency are outstanding and unpaid, the rents, rates, fees and charges shall be so fixed as to provide revenues sufficient to pay all costs of and charges and expenses in connection with the proper operation and maintenance of its projects, and all necessary repairs, replacements or renewals thereof, to pay when due the principal of, premium, if any, and interest on all bonds and other evidences of indebtedness payable from said revenues, to create and maintain reserves as may be required by any resolution or trust agreement authorizing and securing bonds, and to pay any and all amounts which the joint agency may be obligated to pay from said revenues by law or contract.

(c)   Any pledge of revenues, securities or other moneys made by a municipality, joint agency or joint municipal assistance agency pursuant to this Chapter shall be valid and binding from the date the pledge is made. The revenues, securities, and other moneys so pledged and then held or thereafter received by the municipality, joint agency or joint municipal assistance agency or any fiduciary shall immediately be subject to the lien of the pledge without any physical delivery thereof or further act, and the lien of the pledge shall be valid and binding as against all parties having claims of any kind in tort, contract, or otherwise against the municipality, joint agency or joint municipal assistance agency without regard to whether such parties have notice thereof. The resolution or trust agreement or any financing statement, continuation statement or other instrument by which a pledge of revenues, securities or other moneys is created need not be filed or recorded in any manner. (1975, c. 186, s. 1; 1983, c. 574, s. 9; 1985, c. 212, s. 2; 1991 (Reg. Sess., 1992), c. 888, s. 4; 1995, c. 412, s. 13; 2012-167, s. 1.)

§ 159B-18. Trust funds; Investment authority

(a) Notwithstanding any other provisions of law to the contrary, all moneys received pursuant to the authority of this Chapter, whether as proceeds from the sale of bonds or as revenues, shall be deemed to be trust funds to be held and applied solely as provided in this Chapter. The resolution authorizing the bonds of any issue or the trust agreement securing such bonds may provide that any of such moneys may be temporarily invested and reinvested pending the disbursements thereof in such securities and other investments as shall be provided in such resolution or trust agreement, and shall provide that any officer with whom, or any bank or trust company with which, such moneys shall be deposited shall hold and apply the same for the purposes hereof, subject to such regulation as this Chapter and such resolution or trust agreement may provide.

(b) Any moneys received pursuant to the authority of this Chapter and any other moneys available to a joint agency for investment may be invested:

(1) As provided in subsection (a) of this section;

(2) As provided in G.S. 159-30, except that:

a. A joint agency may also invest, in addition to the obligations enumerated in G.S. 159-30(c)(2), in bonds, debentures, notes, participation certificates, or other evidences of indebtedness issued, or the principal of and the interest on which are unconditionally guaranteed, whether directly or indirectly, by any agency or instrumentality of, or corporation wholly owned by, the United States of America.

b. For purposes of G.S. 159-30(c)(12), a joint agency may also enter into repurchase agreements with respect to, in addition to the obligations enumerated in G.S. 159-30(c)(12):

1. Obligations of the Federal Financing Bank, the Federal Farm Credit Bank, the Bank for Cooperatives, the Federal Intermediate Credit Bank, the Federal Land Banks, the Federal Home Loan Banks, the Federal Home Loan Mortgage Corporation, Fannie Mae, the Government National Mortgage Association, the Federal Housing Administration, the Farmers Home Administration, and the United States Postal Service;

2. Bonds, debentures, notes, participation certificates, or other evidences of indebtedness issued, or the principal of and the interest on which are unconditionally guaranteed, whether directly or indirectly, by any agency or instrumentality of, or corporation wholly owned by, the United States of America;

3. Mortgage-backed pass-through securities guaranteed by the Government National Mortgage Association, the Federal Home Loan Mortgage Corporation, or Fannie Mae;

4. Direct or indirect obligations which are collateralized by or represent beneficial ownership interests in mortgage-backed pass-through securities guaranteed by the Government National Mortgage Association, the Federal Home Loan Mortgage Corporation, Fannie Mae; and

5. Direct or indirect obligations, trust certificates, or other similar instruments which are both: (i) guaranteed by the Government National Mortgage Association, the Federal Home Loan Mortgage Corporation, or Fannie Mae; (ii) collateralized by or represent beneficial ownership interests in mortgage-backed pass-through securities which are guaranteed by the Government National Mortgage Association, the Federal Home Loan Mortgage Corporation, or Fannie Mae; including, but not limited to, Real Estate Mortgage Investment Conduit Certificates; and (iii) for purposes of the second proviso of G.S. 159-30(c)(12)a., the financial institution serving either as trustee or as fiscal agent for a joint agency holding the obligations subject to the repurchase agreement may also be the provider of the repurchase agreement if the obligations that are subject to the repurchase agreement are held in trust by the trustee or fiscal agent for the benefit of the joint agency;

(3) In mortgage-backed pass-through securities guaranteed by the Government National Mortgage Association, the Federal Home Loan Mortgage Corporation, or Fannie Mae;

(4) In direct or indirect obligations which are collateralized by or represent beneficial ownership interests in mortgage-backed pass-through securities guaranteed by the Government National Mortgage Association, the Federal Home Loan Mortgage Corporation, or Fannie Mae; and

(5) In direct or indirect obligations, trust certificates, or other similar instruments which are (i) guaranteed by the Government National Mortgage Association, the Federal Home Loan Mortgage Corporation, or Fannie Mae, and (ii) collateralized by or represent beneficial ownership interests in mortgage-

backed pass-through securities which are guaranteed by the Government National Mortgage Association, the Federal Home Loan Mortgage Corporation, or Fannie Mae, including, but not limited to, Real Estate Mortgage Investment Conduit Certificates. (1975, c. 186, s. 1; 1991 (Reg. Sess., 1992), c. 888, s. 5; 1993, c. 445, s. 1; 1995, c. 412, s. 14; 2001-487, s. 14(n).)

§ 159B-19. Remedies.

Any holder of bonds issued under the provisions of this Chapter or any of the coupons appertaining thereto, and the trustee under any trust agreements, except to the extent the rights herein given may be restricted by such trust agreement or the resolution authorizing the issuance of such bonds, may, either at law or in equity, by suit, action, mandamus or other proceeding, protect and enforce any and all rights under the laws of the State or granted hereunder, or, to the extent permitted by law, under such trust agreement or resolution authorizing the issuance of such bonds or under any agreement or other contract executed by the municipality or joint agency pursuant to this Chapter, and may enforce and compel the performance of all duties required by this Chapter or by such trust agreement or resolution to be performed by any joint agency or municipality or by any officer thereof, including the fixing, charging and collecting of rents, rates, fees and charges. (1975, c. 186, s. 1.)

§ 159B-20. Status of bonds under Uniform Commercial Code.

Whether or not the bonds and interest coupons appertaining thereto are of such form and character as to be investment securities under Article 8 of the Uniform Commercial Code as enacted in this State, all bonds and interest coupons appertaining thereto issued under this Chapter are hereby made investment securities within the meaning of and for all the purposes of Article 8 of the Uniform Commercial Code as enacted in this State, subject only to the provisions of the bonds pertaining to registration. (1975, c. 186, s. 1.)

§ 159B-21. Bonds eligible for investment.

Bonds issued by a municipality or joint agency under the provisions of this Chapter are hereby made securities in which all public officers and agencies of the State and all political subdivisions, all insurance companies, banking associations, investment companies, executors, administrators, trustees and other fiduciaries may properly and legally invest funds, including capital in their control or belonging to them. Such bonds are hereby made securities which may properly and legally be deposited with and received by any officer or agency of the State or any political subdivision for any purpose for which the deposit of bonds or obligations of the State or any political subdivision is now or may hereafter be authorized by law. (1975, c. 186, s. 1.)

§ 159B-22. Agreement of the State.

The State does hereby covenant and agree with the holders of any bonds that so long as any bonds of a municipality or joint agency are outstanding and unpaid the State will not limit or alter the rights vested in such municipality or joint agency to acquire, construct, reconstruct, improve, enlarge, better, extend, own, operate and maintain its electric system or any project or interest therein, as the case may be, or to establish, maintain, revise, charge, and collect the rents, rates, fees and charges referred to in this Chapter and to fulfill the terms of any agreements made with the holders of the bonds or in any way impair the rights and remedies of the bondholders, until the bonds, together with interest thereon, interest on any unpaid installment of interest, and all costs and expenses in connection with any action or proceedings by or on behalf of the bondholders, are fully paid, met and discharged. (1975, c. 186, s. 1.)

§ 159B-23. Limited liability.

(a) Bonds shall be special obligations of the municipality or joint agency issuing them. The principal of, premium, if any, and interest on the bonds shall not be payable from the general funds of the municipality or joint agency. Bonds issued to pay the cost of a project and, except as provided in this subsection, bonds that are not issued to pay the cost of a project shall not constitute a legal or equitable pledge, charge, lien, or encumbrance upon any of the municipality's or joint agency's property or upon any of its income, receipts, or revenues, except the funds pledged under the resolution authorizing the bonds or the trust agreement securing the bonds. Bonds that are not issued to pay the cost of a project and that are secured by a pledge, assignment, mortgage, or grant of a security interest in property shall constitute an encumbrance on the municipality's or joint agency's property as provided in the resolution authorizing the bonds or the trust agreement securing the bonds.

(b) Neither the faith and credit nor the taxing power of a municipality or of the State are, or may be, pledged for the payment of the principal of or interest on bonds, and no holder of bonds shall have the right to compel the exercise of the taxing power by the State or a municipality. No holder of bonds issued to pay the cost of a project shall have the right to compel the forfeiture of any of the municipality's or joint agency's property in connection with any default on the bonds. A holder of bonds that are not issued to pay the cost of a project and that are secured by a pledge, assignment, mortgage, or grant of a security interest in property may compel the forfeiture of the property to the extent allowed in the resolution authorizing the bonds or the trust agreement securing the bonds.

(c) Every bond issued to pay the cost of a project shall recite in substance that the principal of and interest on the bond is payable solely from the revenues pledged to its payment and that the municipality or joint agency is not obligated to pay the principal or interest except from these revenues. A bond that is not issued to pay the cost of a project shall recite in substance that the principal of and interest on the bond is payable and secured as provided in the resolution authorizing the bond or the trust agreement securing the bond. (1975, c. 186, s. 1; 1991, c. 513, s. 6.)

§ 159B-24. Approval and sale of bonds.

Prior to the acquisition or the commencement of construction of any project consisting of a system or facilities for the generation of power and energy which is to be financed by the issuance of bonds under the provisions of this Chapter, the participating municipalities or joint agency, as the case may be, shall first obtain a certificate of public convenience and necessity and, in the same proceeding, the approval required by G.S. 159B-4 hereof, in the case of the participating municipalities, or the approval required by G.S. 159B-11 hereof, in the case of a joint agency, from the North Carolina Utilities Commission under such rules, regulations and procedures as the Commission may prescribe.

No municipality or joint agency shall issue any bonds pursuant to this Chapter unless and until, and only to the extent that, the issuance of such bonds is approved by the Local Government Commission. A participating municipality or joint agency shall file with the secretary of the Local Government Commission an application for Commission approval of the issuance of the bonds upon such form as the said Commission may prescribe, which form shall provide for the submission of such information as the secretary may require concerning the proposed bond issue, the details thereof and the security therefor. Before he accepts the application, the secretary may require the governing board or its representatives to attend a preliminary conference at which time the secretary and his deputies may informally discuss the details of the proposed issue and the security therefor.

After an application in proper form has been filed, and after a preliminary conference if one is required, the secretary shall notify the municipality or joint agency in writing that the application has been filed and accepted for submission to the Commission. The secretary's statement shall be conclusive evidence that the municipality or joint agency, as the case may be, has complied with the requirements of this section with respect to the filing of an application for approval by the said Local Government Commission.

In determining whether a proposed bond issue shall be approved, the Commission may consider:

(1)   The municipality's or joint agency's debt management procedures and policies.

(2)   Whether the municipality or joint agency is in default with respect to any of its debt service obligations.

(3)   Whether, based upon feasibility reports submitted to it, the probable revenues of the project to be financed or the revenues of the municipality's electric system, as the case may be, will be sufficient to service the proposed bonds.

The Commission may inquire into and give consideration to any other matters that it may believe to have a bearing on whether the issue should be approved except matters which are expressly required by the provisions of this Chapter to be determined by the North Carolina Utilities Commission.

The Commission shall approve the application if, upon the information and evidence it receives, it finds and determines:

(1)   That, based upon engineering studies and feasibility reports submitted to it, the principal amount of the proposed bonds will be adequate and not excessive for the proposed purpose of the issue.

(2)   That the municipality's or joint agency's debt management procedures and policies are good, or that reasonable assurances have been given that its debt will henceforth be managed in strict compliance with law.

(3)   That the requirements of this Chapter with respect to the issuance of the bonds and the details thereof and security therefor have been, or will be, satisfied.

(4)   That the issuance of the proposed bonds will effectuate the purposes and policies of this Chapter.

After considering an application, the Local Government Commission shall enter its order either approving or denying the application. An order approving an issue shall not be regarded as an approval of the legality of the bonds in any respect.

If the Commission enters an order denying the application, the proceedings under this section shall be at an end.

At any time after the Commission approves an application for the issuance of bonds, the governing board of the issuer may adopt a bond resolution or enter into a trust agreement in accordance with the provisions of this Chapter, and may thereafter at one time, or from time to time, issue the bonds as provided herein.

Upon the filing with the Local Government Commission of a resolution of the issuer requesting that its bonds be sold, such bonds may be sold in such manner, either at public or private sale, and for such price as the Local Government Commission shall determine to be for the best interest of the issuer and effectuate best the purposes of this Chapter, provided that such sale shall be approved by the issuer.

Except as herein expressly provided, bonds may be issued and sold under the provisions of this Chapter without obtaining the approval or consent of any other department, division, commission, board, bureau or agency of the State, and without any other proceeding or the happening of any other condition or thing than those proceedings, conditions or things which are specifically required by this Chapter. (1975, c. 186, s. 1; 1995, c. 412, s. 15.)

§ 159B-25. Refunding bonds.

(a)   A municipality or joint agency is hereby authorized to provide by resolution for the issuance of refunding bonds of the municipality or joint agency for the purpose of refunding any bonds then outstanding which shall have been issued under the provisions of this Chapter, including the payment of any redemption premium thereon and any interest accrued or to accrue to the date of redemption of such bonds.

(b)   In addition to any refunding bonds that may be issued pursuant to subsection (a), a municipality or joint agency is hereby authorized to provide by resolution for the issuance of refunding bonds for the purpose of providing for the payment of any interest accrued or to accrue on any bonds which shall have been issued by the joint agency under the provisions of this Chapter; provided, however, that the refunding bonds are issued on or prior to June 30, 1992, and the latest maturity of the refunding bonds issued for a project is no later than the latest maturity of any other bonds issued by the municipality or joint agency, as the case may be, then outstanding for the same project; and provided further that the Local Government Commission shall conduct an evidentiary hearing and upon the evidence presented find and determine that:

(1)   The municipality's or the joint agency's debt will be managed in strict compliance with law;

(2)   The requirements of this Chapter with respect to the issuance of its bonds and the details thereof and security therefor have been and will be satisfied;

(3)   The estimated revenues of the project or the revenues of the municipality's electric system, as the case may be, will be sufficient to service all bonds to be outstanding after the issuance of the refunding bonds;

(4)   The application of the proceeds of the refunding bonds will result in the deferral of recovery in rates of a portion of the capital costs of the project for a reasonable period of time;

(5) All capital costs of the project will be recovered over a period ending, and all bonds issued for the project will mature, no later than the end of the then estimated useful economic life of the project;

(6) The issuance of the bonds is in the best interest of the municipality's or joint agency's electricity customers; and

(7) The bond rating of the State and its several political subdivisions and agencies allowed to issue bonds should not be adversely affected.

(c) The issuance of such bonds, the maturities and other details thereof, the rights of the holders thereof, and the rights, duties and obligations of the municipality or joint agency in respect to the same shall be governed by the provisions of this Chapter which relate to the issuance of bonds, insofar as such provisions may be appropriate thereto. (1975, c. 186, s. 1; 1989, c. 735, s. 2; 1995, c. 412, s. 16.)

§ 159B-26. Tax exemption.

Bonds shall at all times be free from taxation by the State or any political subdivision or any of their agencies, excepting inheritance or gift taxes, income taxes on the gain from the transfer of the bonds, and franchise taxes. The interest on the bonds is not subject to taxation as income. (1975, c. 186, s. 1; 1995, c. 46, s. 18.)

§ 159B-27. Taxes; payments in lieu of taxes.

(a) A project jointly owned by municipalities or owned by a joint agency shall be exempt from property taxes; provided, however, that each municipality possessing an ownership share of a project, and a joint agency owning a project, shall, in lieu of property taxes, pay to any governmental body authorized to levy property taxes the amount which would be assessed as taxes on real and personal property of a project if such project were otherwise subject to valuation and assessment by the Department of Revenue. Such payments in lieu of taxes shall be due and shall bear interest if unpaid, as in the cases of taxes on other property. Payments in lieu of taxes made hereunder shall be treated in the same manner as taxes for purposes of all procedural and substantive provisions of law. Any administrative building and associated land shall be deemed a project for purposes of this paragraph.

(b) (Repealed effective July 1, 2014) Each municipality having an ownership share in a project shall pay to the State in lieu of an annual franchise or privilege tax an amount equal to three and twenty-two hundredths percent (3.22%) of that percentage of all moneys expended by said municipality on account of its ownership share, including payment of principal and interest on bonds issued to finance such ownership share, which is equal to the percentage of such city or town's total entitlement that is used or sold by it to any person, firm or corporation exempted by law from the payment of the tax on gross receipts pursuant to G.S. 105-116.

(c) (Repealed effective July 1, 2014) In lieu of an annual franchise or privilege tax, each joint agency shall pay to the State an amount equal to three and twenty-two hundredths percent (3.22%) of the gross receipts from sales of electric power or energy, less receipts from sales of electric power or energy to a vendee subject to tax under G.S. 105-116.

(d) (Repealed effective July 1, 2014) The State shall distribute to cities and towns which receive electric power and energy from their ownership share of a project or to which electric power and energy is sold by a joint agency an amount equal to a tax of three and nine hundredths percent (3.09%) of all moneys expended by a municipality on account of its ownership share of a project, including payment of principal and interest on bonds issued to finance such ownership share, or an amount equal to a tax of three and nine hundredths percent (3.09%) of the gross receipts from all sales of electric power and energy to such city or town by a joint agency, as the case may be. The General Assembly finds that the revenue distributed under this section is local revenue, not a State expenditure, for the purpose of Section 5(3) of Article III of the North Carolina Constitution. Therefore, the Governor may not reduce or withhold the distribution.

(e) (Repealed effective July 1, 2014) The reporting, payment and collection procedures contained in G.S. 105-116 shall apply to the levy herein made.

(f) Except as herein expressly provided with respect to jointly owned projects or projects owned by a joint agency, no other property of a municipality used or useful in the generation, transmission and distribution of electric power and energy shall be subject to payments in lieu of taxes. (1973, c. 476, s. 193; 1975, c. 186, s. 1; 1977, c. 385, s. 12; 1981, c. 487; 1983, c. 574, s. 10; 1983

(Reg. Sess., 1984), c. 1097, s. 11; 1995, c. 412, s. 17; 2002-120, s. 6; 2013-316, s. 4.1(a).)

§ 159B-28. Personnel.

Personnel employed or appointed by a municipality to work on a joint project or for a joint agency shall have the same authority, rights, privileges and immunities (including coverage under the workers' compensation laws) which the officers, agents and employees of the appointing municipality enjoy within the territory of that municipality, whether within or without the territory of the appointing municipality, when they are acting within the scope of their authority or in the course of their employment.

Personnel employed or appointed directly by a joint agency or by a nonprofit operating agency of the participating municipalities or of the joint agency, shall be qualified for participation in the North Carolina Local Government Employees Retirement System with the same rights, privileges, obligations and responsibilities as they would have if they were employees of a municipality. (1975, c. 186, s. 1; 1991, c. 636, s. 3.)

§ 159B-29. Dissolution of joint agencies.

Whenever the governing board of a joint agency and the governing boards of its member municipalities shall by resolution or ordinance determine that the purposes for which the joint agency was formed have been substantially fulfilled and that all bonds theretofore issued and all other obligations theretofore incurred by the joint agency have been fully paid or satisfied, the governing board of the joint agency may by resolution declare the joint agency to be dissolved. On the effective date of such resolution declaring the joint agency to be dissolved, the title to all funds and other property owned by the joint agency at the time of such dissolution shall vest in the member municipalities of the joint agency as provided in this Chapter and the bylaws of the joint agency. Notice of such dissolution shall be filed with the Secretary of State. (1975, c. 186, s. 1; 1995, c. 412, s. 18.)

§ 159B-30. Annual reports.

Each joint agency shall, following the closing of each fiscal year, submit an annual report of its activities for the preceding year to the governing boards of its member municipalities and to the North Carolina Utilities Commission. Each such report shall set forth in a form prescribed by the North Carolina Utilities Commission a complete operating and financial statement covering the operations of the joint agency during such year. The joint agency shall cause an audit of its books of record and accounts to be made at least once in each year by certified public accountant(s) and the cost thereof may be treated as a part of the cost of construction of a project or projects, or otherwise as part of the expense of administration of a project covered by such audit.

The municipalities possessing ownership interests in a project shall, following the closing of each fiscal year, submit a consolidated or combined annual report of their activities with respect to such project for the preceding year to the respective governing board of such municipalities and to the North Carolina Utilities Commission. Each such report shall set forth in a form prescribed by the North Carolina Utilities Commission a complete operating and financial statement covering the operations of the jointly owned project during such year. The municipalities possessing ownership interests in a project shall cause an audit of the books of record and accounts relating to such project to be made at least once in each year by certified public accountant(s) and the cost thereof may be treated as a cost of construction of the project, or otherwise as part of the expenses of the administration of the project covered by such audit. (1975, c. 186, s. 1.)

§ 159B-30.1. Additional reports.

Beginning March 1, 1996, and annually thereafter, each joint agency operating under the authority of Chapter 159B of the General Statutes shall file a report with the Joint Legislative Commission on Governmental Operations describing the activities of the joint agency carried out pursuant to the authority granted by G.S. 159B-2, 159B-11(19b), 159B-12 and 159B-17(c). The report shall cover the preceding calendar year. Each joint agency shall file such additional reports as the Joint Legislative Commission on Governmental Operations shall request. (1991 (Reg. Sess., 1992), c. 888, s. 7; 1995, c. 412, s. 19; 2011-291, s. 2.62.)

§ 159B-31. Legislative consent to the application of laws of other states.

Legislative consent is hereby given

(1)   To the application of the laws of other states with respect to taxation, payments in lieu of taxes, and the assessment thereof, to any municipality or joint agency created pursuant to this Chapter, which has acquired or has an interest in a project, real or personal, situated without the State, or which owns or operates a project without the State pursuant to this Chapter, and

(2)   To the application of regulatory and other laws of other states and of the United States to any municipality or joint agency which owns or operates a project without the State. (1975, c. 186, s. 1.)

§ 159B-32. Government grants and loans.

The governing board of any municipality or joint agency is hereby authorized to make application and to enter into contracts for and to accept grants-in-aid and loans from the federal and State governments and their agencies for planning, acquiring, constructing, expanding, maintaining and operating any project or facility, or participating in any research or development program, or performing any function which such municipality or joint agency may be authorized by general or local law to provide or perform.

In order to exercise the authority granted by this section, the governing board of any municipality or joint agency may:

(1)   Enter into and carry out contracts with the State or federal government or any agency or institution thereof under which such government, agency or institution grants financial or other assistance to the municipality or joint agency;

(2)   Accept such assistance or funds as may be granted or loaned by the State or federal government with or without such a contract;

(3)   Agree to and comply with any reasonable conditions which are imposed upon such grants or loans;

(4)   Make expenditures from any funds so granted. (1975, c. 186, s. 1.)

§ 159B-33. Eminent domain.

Municipalities participating in a joint project and joint agencies shall possess the power of eminent domain to the extent and in the same manner and under the same laws as municipalities pursuant to Chapter 40A of the General Statutes of North Carolina; provided, however, that a municipality or joint agency exercising the power of eminent domain for a purpose authorized by this Chapter shall have no power to condemn an existing facility used for the generation, transmission or distribution of electric power and energy; provided, further, that the North Carolina Utilities Commission shall have the power and authority to order that the lines and rights-of-way of any public utility or electric membership corporation, municipalities participating in a joint project or any joint agency may be crossed by any municipalities participating in a joint project or any joint agency or that the lines of any municipalities participating in a joint project or any joint agency may be crossed by any public utility or electric membership corporation pursuant to the provisions of G.S. 62-39; provided, further, when any municipalities participating in a joint project, or any joint agency, proposes to condemn the lands or rights-of-way of any public utility, electric membership corporation, municipalities participating in a joint project or any joint agency, or any public utility or electric membership corporation proposes to condemn the lands or rights-of-way of any municipalities participating in a joint project or any joint agency, not then used for the generation, transmission or distribution of electric power and energy but held for future use or development, the party desiring to condemn shall file a petition with the North Carolina Utilities Commission requesting authority to condemn such lands or rights-of-way. Upon such petition, the North Carolina Utilities Commission shall have the power and authority, after notice and hearing, to order that such lands or rights-of-way, or parts thereof, may be condemned, and its order shall be final, subject to appeal as provided in this section. In all such cases in which the Commission permits condemnation and when the parties affected cannot agree upon the damages to be paid for the lands or rights-of-way to be condemned, it shall be the duty of the Commission to fix the damages, if any, to be paid in such amounts as may be just and equitable. Any party shall have the right of appeal from any final order or decision or determination of the North Carolina Utilities Commission as to matters of crossings and condemnation of property held for future use or development pursuant to the provisions of Article 5 of Chapter 62 of the General Statutes of North Carolina. (1975, c. 186, s. 1; 1981, c. 919, s. 27.)

§ 159B-34. Liability and defense.

(a) No commissioner or officer of any joint agency or municipality, or member of an executive committee created pursuant to G.S. 159B-10, or person or persons acting in their behalf, while acting within the scope of their authority, shall be subject to any personal liability or accountability by reason of his carrying out any of the powers expressly or impliedly given in this Chapter.

(b) The governing board of a joint agency may provide for the defense of a criminal or civil proceeding brought against any current or former commissioner, member of an executive committee, officer, agent or employee either in his official or individual capacity, or both, on account of any act done or omission made in the scope and course of his employment or duty as a commissioner, member of an executive committee, officer, agent, or employee of the joint agency. The defense may be provided by the agency by its own counsel, by employing other counsel or by purchasing insurance which requires that the insurer provide the defense.

(c) The governing board may appropriate funds for the purpose of paying all or part of a claim made or any civil judgment entered against any of its current or former commissioners, members of executive committees, officers, agents or employees, when such claim is made or such judgment is rendered as damages on account of any act done or omission made in the scope and course of his current or former employment or duty as a commissioner, member of an executive committee, officer, agent or employee; provided, however, that nothing in this section shall authorize any joint agency to appropriate funds for the purpose of paying any claim made or civil judgment entered against any current or former commissioners, members of executive committees, officers, agents or employees if the board of commissioners finds that commissioner, member of an executive committee, officer, agent or employee acted or failed to act because of actual fraud, corruption or actual malice on his part. Any joint agency may purchase insurance coverage for payment of claims or judgments pursuant to this section. (1975, c. 186, s. 1; 1985, c. 225, s. 1; 1995, c. 412, s. 20.)

§ 159B-35. Additional method.

The foregoing sections of this Chapter shall be deemed to provide an additional, alternative and complete method for the doing of the things authorized thereby and shall be deemed and construed to be supplemental and additional to powers conferred by other laws, and shall not be regarded as in derogation of any powers now existing; provided, however, that insofar as the provisions of this Chapter are inconsistent with the provisions of any other general, special or local law, the provisions of this Chapter shall be controlling. Nothing in this Chapter shall be construed to authorize the issuance of bonds for the purpose of financing facilities to be owned exclusively by any private corporation. (1975, c. 186, s. 1; 1977, c. 385, s. 13.)

§ 159B-36: Recodified as § 159B-52 by Session Laws 1983, c. 609, s. 8.

§ 159B-37. Actions relating to bonds or to security for bonds.

Notwithstanding the general provisions concerning venue contained in Chapter 1, Subchapter IV, Article 7, or elsewhere in the General Statutes, any action or proceeding by or against a municipality or a joint agency that concerns or relates to (a) any bonds issued pursuant to this Chapter, (b) any contract or document the revenues from which secure in whole or in part the payment of said bonds or (c) any other security or source for payment of said bonds must be tried in the Superior Court of Wake County. (1985, c. 414, s. 1.)

§ 159B-38. Confidentiality of contract discussions.

Discussions of a proposed or existing contract to which a joint agency may be or is a party for the construction, ownership, or operation of works, plants, and facilities for or incident to the generation, transmission, or use of electric power and energy or the purchase, sale, exchange, interchange, wheeling, pooling, transmission, or use of electric power and energy shall be confidential and information relating to such discussions shall not be a public record under Chapter 132 of the General Statutes; provided that any contract entered into by or on behalf of a joint agency as defined by G.S. 159B-3 shall be a public record unless otherwise exempted by law. (1993 (Reg. Sess., 1994), c. 570, s. 11.)

§ 159B-39. (Effective July 1, 2014) Permitted uses of revenue from electric power rates.

(a) A municipality as authorized in this Chapter shall use revenue derived from rates for electric service to (i) pay the direct and indirect costs of operating the electric system and (ii) transfer to other funds of the municipality a sum that reflects a rate of return on the investment in the electric system to the extent allowed in subsection (c) of this section. Any remaining revenue shall be used to produce lower rates on electric service within the area served by the municipal electric system and to make additional debt service payments on bonds or other indebtedness incurred by the municipality to finance improvements to the electric system. A municipality shall not otherwise transfer revenue from an electric utility fund to any other fund of the municipality for any other purpose not explicitly authorized by law.

(b)   The direct and indirect costs of operating the electric system include all of the following:

(1)   Debt service payments on indebtedness incurred for the electric system or secured by revenues of the electric system.

(2)   Capital improvements or equipment for the electric system.

(3)   Payments for the cost of power purchased under contractual arrangements.

(4)   Debt service, maintenance, renewal, and replacement or other reserves required by legal documents entered into by the municipality in connection with the issuance of bonds or other indebtedness for the electric system.

(5)   Reserves deemed necessary by the governing body of the municipality to assure that funds are available to maintain the financial and operational integrity of the electric system.

(6)   Maintaining a rate stabilization fund to minimize the impact of periodic rate changes that would otherwise be required to reflect changes in costs of operations and demand for electric service.

(7)   Making payments in lieu of taxes to other governmental units to reflect property taxes that would have been collected by the other governmental unit if the municipality were not the owner of the electric system.

(8)   Making transfers to the general fund or other funds of the municipality to reimburse the general fund or other funds for costs paid from the fund that are reasonably allocable to the electric system.

(c) The total amount transferred to other funds of the municipality authorized as a rate of return on the investment of the municipality in the electric system shall be calculated using amounts reported in the municipality's audited financial statements for the preceding fiscal year. The amount transferred may be less than the following, but in no event may the amount transferred exceed the greater of the following:

(1) Three percent (3%) of the gross capital assets of the electric system at the end of the preceding fiscal year.

(2) Five percent (5%) of the gross annual revenues of the electric system for the preceding fiscal year.

(d) The restrictions in this section shall not apply to any action required to be taken for a municipality by the Local Government Commission in accordance with G.S. 159-181(c).

(e) This section applies only to the following cities and towns that are members of the North Carolina Eastern Municipal Power Agency: Apex, Ayden, Belhaven, Benson, Clayton, Edenton, Elizabeth City, Farmville, Fremont, Greenville, Hamilton, Hertford, Hobgood, Hookerton, Kinston, LaGrange, Laurinburg, Louisburg, Lumberton, New Bern, Pikeville, Red Springs, Robersonville, Rocky Mount, Scotland Neck, Selma, Smithfield, Southport, Tarboro, Wake Forest, Washington, and Wilson. (2011-129, ss. 1, 2; 2012-181, ss. 1, 2.)

§ 159B-40. Reserved for future codification purposes.

§ 159B-41. Reserved for future codification purposes.

Article 3.

Joint Municipal Assistance Agencies.

§ 159B-42. Joint municipal assistance agencies.

The purpose of this Article is to authorize joint agencies or municipalities to form one or more joint municipal assistance agencies which shall be empowered to provide aid and assistance to municipalities in the construction, ownership, maintenance, expansion and operation of their electric systems, to do such other acts and things as hereinafter provided and to carry out the powers and responsibilities hereinafter granted in this Chapter. It shall also be the purpose of a joint municipal assistance agency to provide aid and assistance to any joint agency in the exercise of its respective powers and functions. The term "provide aid and assistance" shall be liberally construed. (1983, c. 609, s. 7; 1995, c. 412, s. 21.)

§ 159B-43. Joint municipal assistance agencies authorized.

(a) Any two or more joint agencies, or any two or more municipalities, may organize a joint municipal assistance agency, which shall be a public body and body corporate and politic. Any joint agency or municipality is hereby authorized to become a member of any such joint municipal assistance agency upon a determination, by resolution or ordinance of its governing board, that economies, efficiencies and other benefits might be achieved from participation in such an agency.

The resolution or ordinance determining it desirable for a joint agency or municipality to become a member of a joint municipal assistance agency (which need not prescribe in detail the basis for the determination) shall set forth the names of the joint agencies or municipalities which are proposed to be initial members of the joint municipal assistance agency. The governing board of the joint agency or municipality shall thereupon by ordinance or resolution appoint one commissioner and up to two alternate commissioners of the joint municipal assistance agency who may, at the discretion of the governing board, be an officer or employee of the joint agency or municipality. If two alternate commissioners are appointed, the governing board shall designate them as first or second alternate commissioner.

Any two or more commissioners so named may file with the Secretary of State an application signed by them setting forth (i) the names of all the proposed member joint agencies or municipalities; (ii) the name and official residence of each of the commissioners so far as known to them; (iii) a certified copy of the appointment evidencing their right to office; (iv) a statement that each governing board of each respective joint agency or municipality appointing a commissioner has made the aforesaid determination; (v) the desire that a joint municipal assistance agency be organized as a public body and a body corporate and politic under this Chapter; and (vi) the name which is proposed for the joint municipal assistance agency.

The application shall be subscribed and sworn to by such commissioners before an officer or officers authorized by the laws of the State to administer and certify oaths.

The Secretary of State shall examine the application and, if he finds that the name proposed for the joint municipal assistance agency is not identical with that of any other corporation of this State or of any agency or instrumentality thereof, or so nearly similar as to lead to confusion and uncertainty, he shall receive and file it and shall record it in an appropriate book of record in his office.

When the application has been made, filed and recorded as herein provided, the joint municipal assistance agency shall constitute a public body and a body corporate and politic under the name proposed in the application. The Secretary of State shall make and issue to the commissioners executing the application a certificate of incorporation pursuant to this Chapter under the seal of the State, and shall record the same with the application. The certificate shall set forth the names of the member municipalities.

In any suit, action or proceeding involving the validity or enforcement of, or relating to, any contract of the joint municipal assistance agency, the joint municipal assistance agency, in the absence of establishing fraud in the premises, shall be conclusively deemed to have been established in accordance with the provisions of this Chapter upon proof of the issuance of the aforesaid certificate by the Secretary of State. A copy of such certificate or of any new or supplemental certificate hereinafter provided for, duly certified by the Secretary of State, shall be admissible in evidence in any suit, action or proceeding, and shall be conclusive proof of the filing and contents thereof.

Notice of the issuance of such certificate shall be given to all of the proposed member joint agencies or municipalities by the Secretary of State. If a commissioner of any such joint agency or municipality has not signed the application to the Secretary of State and such joint agency or municipality does not notify the Secretary of State of the appointment of a commissioner within 60 days after receipt of such notice, such joint agency or municipality shall be deemed to have elected not to be a member of the joint municipal assistance agency. As soon as practicable after the expiration of such 60-day period, the Secretary of State shall issue a new certificate of incorporation, if necessary, setting forth the names of those joint agencies or municipalities which have elected to become members of the joint municipal assistance agency. The failure of any proposed member to become a member shall not affect the validity of the corporate existence of the joint municipal assistance agency.

(b)   After the creation of a joint municipal assistance agency, any other joint agency (if organized by joint agencies) or municipality (if organized by municipalities) may become a member thereof upon application to such joint municipal assistance agency after the adoption of a resolution or ordinance by the governing board of the joint agency or municipality setting forth the determination and finding prescribed above for the original members and authorizing said municipality to become a member and appointing one commissioner, and with the consent of a majority of the board of commissioners of the joint municipal assistance agency. Any joint agency or municipality may withdraw from a joint municipal assistance agency, provided, however, that all obligations incurred by a joint agency or municipality while it was a member shall remain in full force and effect. Notice that a joint agency or municipality has been added to or withdrawn from membership in the joint municipal assistance agency shall be filed with the Secretary of State, and the Secretary of State shall thereupon issue a new or supplemental certificate of incorporation setting forth the names of all members of the joint municipal assistance agency. Additions of new members or withdrawal of members shall not affect the validity of the corporate existence of the joint municipal assistance agency.

(c)   The joint municipal assistance agency may be governed by a board of commissioners appointed as provided in subsections (a) and (b) of this section. It shall not be necessary to notify the Secretary of State of the appointment of any commissioners following the notifications referred to in subsections (a) and (b) of this section. Each commissioner shall have one vote and shall serve at the pleasure of the governing board by which he was appointed. Each appointed commissioner before entering upon his duties shall take and subscribe to an oath before some person authorized by law to administer oaths to execute the duties of his office faithfully and impartially, and a record of each such oath shall be filed with the governing board of the appointing joint agency or municipality and spread upon its minutes. The governing board of each of the joint agencies or municipalities may appoint up to two alternate commissioners to act in lieu of its appointed commissioner when the appointed commissioner is unable for any reason to attend meetings of the board of commissioners or any committee thereof, and the governing board shall designate them as first or second alternate commissioner. Each alternate commissioner shall serve at the pleasure of the governing board by which he is appointed and shall take, subscribe to and file an oath in the same manner as prescribed for regularly appointed commissioners. Such alternate commissioner when acting in lieu of the regularly appointed commissioner shall be deemed to be the commissioner representing such joint agency or municipality, and shall have the rights, powers and authority of the regularly appointed commissioner, other than such commissioner's position as an officer, director or member of the executive committee. A certificate entered into the minutes of the board of commissioners of a joint agency by the clerk or other custodian of the minutes and records of the governing body of a municipality, appointing commissioners and alternate commissioners and reciting their appointments, shall constitute conclusive evidence of their appointment. All powers, functions, rights and privileges of the joint municipal assistance agency shall be exercised or delegated by the board of commissioners.

(d)   The board of commissioners of the joint municipal assistance agency shall annually elect one of the commissioners as president, another as vice president, and another person or persons, who may but need not be commissioners, as treasurer, secretary, and, if desired, assistant secretary or secretaries and assistant treasurer. The office of treasurer or assistant treasurer may be held by the secretary or any assistant secretary. The board of commissioners may also appoint and prescribe the duties of such additional officers as it deems necessary. The secretary or any assistant secretary of the joint municipal assistance agency shall keep a record of the proceedings of the joint municipal assistance agency, and the secretary shall be the custodian of all records, books, documents and papers filed with the joint municipal assistance agency, the minute book or journal of the joint municipal assistance agency and its official seal. Either the secretary or any assistant secretary of the joint municipal assistance agency may cause copies to be made of all minutes and other records and documents of the joint municipal assistance agency and may give certificates under the official seal of the joint municipal assistance agency to the effect that such copies are true copies, and all persons dealing with the joint municipal assistance agency may rely upon such certificates.

(e)   Fifty-one percent (51%) of the commissioners of a joint municipal assistance agency then in office shall constitute a quorum, and the commissioners may by written consent executed before or after any meeting waive notice and all other formalities incident to the calling or conduct of the same. Meetings of the commissioners may be held at any place within the State or any state contiguous to the State. A vacancy in the board of commissioners of the joint municipal assistance agency shall not impair the right of a quorum to exercise all the rights and perform all the duties of the joint municipal assistance agency. Any action taken by the joint municipal assistance agency under the provisions of this Chapter may be authorized by resolution at any regular or special meeting, and each such resolution may take effect immediately and need not be published or posted. Except as specifically provided by the bylaws, a majority of the votes of the commissioners present shall be necessary and sufficient to take any action or to pass any resolution.

(f) The board of commissioners of the joint municipal assistance agency may, in its bylaws, provide for a board of directors of the joint municipal assistance agency to be selected from the commissioners and alternate commissioners. The board of directors shall have and exercise such of the powers and authority of the board of commissioners during the intervals between the board of commissioners' meetings as shall be prescribed in the bylaws, rules, motions and resolutions of the board of commissioners. The terms of office of the members of the board of directors and the method of filling vacancies therein shall be fixed by the bylaws of the board of commissioners of the joint municipal assistance agency. The bylaws of the joint municipal assistance agency shall provide that the officers of the board of commissioners elected pursuant to subsection (d) of this section must also serve on the board of directors and hold the same offices thereon.

(g) The board of commissioners may also provide, in its bylaws or otherwise, that the board of directors shall create an executive committee of the board of directors composed of the officers of the board of directors, together with such other members of the board of directors as may be prescribed and that such executive committee shall have and shall exercise such of the powers and authority of the board of directors during the intervals between that board's meetings as shall be prescribed in the bylaws of the joint municipal assistance agency or in the rules or resolutions of the board of directors.

(h) The board of commissioners, board of directors and executive committee may provide or adopt methods and procedures consistent with other applicable laws for the calling or conducting of meetings or the taking of any action.

(i) No commissioner or director of a joint municipal assistance agency shall receive any compensation for the performance of his or her duties hereunder, provided, however, that each commissioner and director may be paid his or her necessary expenses incurred while engaged in the performance of such duties. (1983, c. 609, s. 7; 1985, c. 243, ss. 2, 3; 1995, c. 412, s. 22.)

§ 159B-43.1. Alternative to board of commissioners.

(a) In lieu of the provisions of G.S. 159B-43(c) through (i), a joint municipal assistance agency organized by two or more joint agencies, by resolutions adopted by each of those joint agencies, may be governed by an executive committee created pursuant to the provisions of G.S. 159B-10. In that case, the commissioners of the joint municipal assistance agency appointed pursuant to the provisions of G.S. 159B-43(a) and (b) shall adopt a resolution substantially identical to the resolutions adopted by the joint agencies creating the executive committee. The terms of office, methods of filling vacancies, and such other matters involving the executive committee shall be as set forth in those resolutions.

(b) In connection with a joint municipal assistance agency governed pursuant to the provisions of subsection (a) of this section, member municipalities of that joint municipal assistance agency which are not members of the joint agencies organizing that joint municipal assistance agency and nonmunicipal members, as defined in G.S. 159B-50, may elect members to the executive committee pursuant to those procedures as they agree upon among themselves, but subject to the following: if the number of the member municipalities and nonmunicipal members is seven or less, those municipalities and nonmunicipal members, acting jointly, may appoint one member to the executive committee, and if the number of the member municipalities and nonmunicipal members is more than seven, those member municipalities and nonmunicipal members, acting jointly, may appoint two members to the executive committee.

(c) Members of the executive committee appointed by the member municipalities and nonmunicipal members, and members of any subcommittee created by those member municipalities and nonmunicipal members, may receive compensation, and be paid expenses, for the performance of their duties as determined by the member municipalities and nonmunicipal members appointing those members. However, for any member of an executive committee who is an employee of a member municipality or nonmunicipal member, a payment in lieu of any compensation shall be made to the member municipality or nonmunicipal member for distribution to the executive committee member in the manner and amount, if any, it deems appropriate. (1995, c. 412, s. 23.)

§ 159B-44. General powers of joint municipal assistance agencies and municipalities.

Each joint municipal assistance agency shall have all of the rights and powers necessary or convenient to carry out and effectuate the purposes and provisions of this Article, including, but without limiting the generality of the foregoing, the rights and powers:

(1) To establish and from time to time modify a schedule of dues and assessments and to provide that the payment thereof when due shall be prerequisite to voting at any meeting and participation in and enjoyment of rights or benefits of the joint municipal assistance agency;

(2) To appropriate for the purposes of the joint municipal assistance agency the funds derived from dues and assessments, and from any other source;

(3) To provide aid and assistance to any one or more municipalities, and to act for or on behalf of any one or more municipalities, in any activity related to the construction, ownership, maintenance, expansion or operation of an electric system, upon such terms, conditions and considerations as may be agreed to between the municipalities and the joint municipal assistance agency;

(4) To provide aid and assistance to any one or more joint agencies, and to act for or on behalf of any one or more joint agencies in the exercise of any power, function, right, privilege or immunity granted by Article 2 of this Chapter, upon such terms, conditions and considerations as may be agreed to between the joint agency and the joint municipal assistance agency;

(5) To provide property and services to any one or more municipalities or joint agencies upon such terms, conditions and considerations as may be agreed to between the municipalities or joint agency and the joint municipal assistance agency;

(6) To adopt bylaws for the regulation of the affairs and the conduct of its business, and to prescribe rules, regulations and policies in connection with the performance of its functions and duties;

(7) To adopt an official seal and alter the same at pleasure;

(8) To acquire and maintain an administrative office building or office at such place or places as it may determine, which building or office may be used

or owned together with any joint agency or agencies, municipalities, corporations, associations or persons under such terms and provisions for sharing costs and otherwise as may be determined;

(9)   To sue and be sued in its own name, and to plead and be impleaded;

(10)   To receive, administer and comply with the conditions and requirements respecting any gift, grant or donation of any property or money;

(11)   To acquire by purchase, lease, gift, or otherwise, or to obtain options for the acquisition of, any property, real or personal, improved or unimproved, including an interest in land less than the fee thereof;

(12)   To sell, lease, exchange, transfer or otherwise dispose of, or to grant options for any such purposes with respect to, any real or personal property or interest therein; provided, however, that property acquired by a joint municipal assistance agency from a municipality without consideration or for a consideration other than the fair market value thereof as determined by the governing board of the municipality may only be disposed of in accordance with the procedures set forth in Article 12 of Chapter 160A of the General Statutes;

(13)   To make and execute contracts and other instruments necessary or convenient in the exercise of the powers and functions of the joint municipal assistance agency, including contracts with municipalities, joint agencies, persons, firms, corporations and others, provided, however, that such contracts shall not unreasonably preclude the municipality or joint agency from contracting with other parties in order to achieve economy, adequacy and reliability in the operation of their electric systems;

(14)   To employ engineers, architects, attorneys, real estate counselors, appraisers, financial advisors and such other consultants and employees as may be required in the judgment of the joint municipal assistance agency and to fix and pay their compensation from funds available to the joint municipal assistance agency therefor; and

(15)   To do all acts and things necessary, convenient or desirable to carry out the purposes, and to exercise the powers granted to the joint municipal assistance agency herein.

Any municipality or joint agency is authorized to appropriate and pay funds to a joint municipal assistance agency and to enter into contracts or arrangements with a joint municipal assistance agency for the purposes and in the execution of the functions and powers of the municipality or joint agency.

Joint municipal assistance agencies shall comply with Article 8 of Chapter 143 of the General Statutes respecting acquisition or construction of property to the same extent required of municipalities; provided, however, that Article 8 of Chapter 143 of the General Statutes shall not apply to a municipality, joint municipal assistance agency or joint agency in transactions between a joint municipal assistance agency and a municipality or joint agency involving the transfer or construction of property.

Property owned by a joint municipal assistance agency or jointly owned by municipalities or joint agencies and joint municipal assistance agencies shall be exempt from property taxes; provided, however, that each joint municipal assistance agency shall, in lieu of property taxes, pay to any governmental agency authorized to levy property taxes the amount which would be assessed as taxes on real and personal property of such agency if such property were otherwise subject to valuation and assessment by the Department of Revenue. Such payments in lieu of taxes shall be due and shall bear interest if unpaid, as in the cases of taxes on other property. Payments in lieu of taxes made hereunder shall be treated in the same manner as taxes for purposes of all procedural and substantive provisions of law. (1983, c. 609, s. 7; 1995, c. 412, s. 24; 2008-38, s. 1.)

§ 159B-45. Dissolution.

Whenever the governing board of a joint municipal assistance agency and the governing boards of its member joint agencies or municipalities shall by resolution or ordinance determine that the purposes for which the joint municipal assistance agency was formed have been substantially fulfilled and that all obligations incurred by the joint municipal assistance agency have been fully paid or satisfied, the governing board of the joint municipal assistance agency may by resolution declare the joint municipal assistance agency to be dissolved. On the effective date of such resolution declaring the joint agency to be dissolved, the title to all funds and other property owned by the joint municipal assistance agency at the time of such dissolution shall vest in the members of the joint municipal assistance agency as provided in this Chapter and the bylaws of the joint municipal assistance agency. Notice of such dissolution shall be filed with the Secretary of State. (1983, c. 609, s. 7; 1995, c. 412, s. 25.)

§ 159B-46. Reports, liability, and personnel.

(a) Each joint municipal assistance agency shall, following the closing of each fiscal year, submit an annual report of its activities for the preceding year to the governing boards of its members. Each such report shall set forth an operating and financial statement covering the operations of the joint municipal assistance agency during such year. The joint municipal assistance agency shall cause an audit of its books of record and accounts to be made at least once in each year by independent certified public accountants.

(b) No commissioner, alternate commissioner or director or officer of any joint municipal assistance agency, member of an executive committee created pursuant to G.S. 159B-10, officer of any joint agency or municipality, or person or persons acting in their behalf, while acting within the scope of his authority, shall be subject to any personal liability or accountability by reason of his carrying out any of the powers expressly or impliedly given in this Article.

(c) Each municipality, joint agency and joint municipal assistance agency shall be severally liable for its own acts or omissions and not jointly or severally liable for the acts, omissions, or obligations of others, including other municipalities.

(d) In no event shall any municipality or joint agency be liable or responsible for any acts, omissions or obligations of any joint municipal assistance agency or any of its officers, members of an executive committee, employees or agents; provided, however, that contracts between the joint municipal assistance agency and one or more municipalities or one or more joint agencies may expressly provide for the imputation of or indemnification for any liability of one party thereto by the other, or for the assumption of any obligation of one party thereto by the other.

(e) Personnel employed or appointed by a municipality and performing services for or on behalf of a joint municipal assistance agency shall have the same authority, rights, privileges and immunities (including coverage under the workers' compensation laws) which the officers, agents and employees of the appointing municipality enjoy within the territory of that municipality, whether within or without the territory of the appointing municipality, when they are acting within the scope of their authority or in the course of their employment.

(f) Personnel employed or appointed by a joint municipal assistance agency shall be qualified for participation in the North Carolina Local Government

Employees' Retirement System with the same rights, privileges, obligations and responsibilities as they would have if they were employees of a municipality.

(g) The offices of commissioner, alternate commissioner, officer, director and member of the executive committee of a joint municipal assistance agency are hereby declared to be offices which may be held by the holder of any office, place of trust or profit in addition to and concurrently with those offices permitted by G.S. 128-1.1 and other offices permitted by other General Statute. (1983, c. 609, s. 7; 1991, c. 636, s. 3; 1995, c. 412, s. 26.)

§ 159B-47. Defense.

(a) The board of commissioners of a joint municipal assistance agency may provide for the defense of a criminal or civil proceeding brought against any current or former commissioner, member of an executive committee, director, officer, agent or employee either in his official or individual capacity, or both, on account of any act done or omission made in the scope and course of his employment or duty as a commissioner, member of an executive committee, director, officer, agent or employee of the joint municipal assistance agency. The defense may be provided by the agency by its own counsel, by employing other counsel or by purchasing insurance which requires that the insurer provide the defense.

(b) The board of commissioners may appropriate funds for the purpose of paying all or part of a claim made or any civil judgment entered against any of its current or former commissioners, members of executive committees, directors, officers, agents or employees, when such claim is made or such judgment is rendered as damages on account of any act done or omission made or any act allegedly done or omission allegedly made in the scope and course of his current or former employment or duty as a commissioner, member of an executive committee, director, officer, agent or employee; provided, however, that nothing in this section shall authorize any joint municipal assistance agency to appropriate funds for the purpose of paying any claim made or civil judgment entered against any current or former commissioners, members of executive committees, directors, officers, agents or employees if the board of commissioners finds that commissioner, member of an executive committee, director, officer, agent or employee acted or failed to act because of actual fraud, corruption or actual malice on his part. Any joint municipal assistance agency may purchase insurance coverage for payment of claims or judgments pursuant to this section. (1985, c. 225, s. 2; 1995, c. 412, s. 27.)

§ 159B-48. Nonmunicipal members; constituent institutions of The University of North Carolina.

Notwithstanding the provisions of Article 1 of Chapter 159B of the General Statutes or any other provision of law, any constituent institution of The University of North Carolina, as defined in Article 1 of Chapter 116 of the General Statutes, that owns a system or facility for the generation, transmission, or distribution of electric power and energy for public and private use, may become a member of a joint municipal assistance agency. The commissioner and one or more alternate commissioners designated by any such members shall be appointed by its local governing board. As a member, the constituent institution has all the rights, privileges, immunities, powers, authority, and responsibilities of a municipal member of a joint municipal assistance agency under Article 3 of this Chapter, including, the protection and immunities granted under Article 3 to those employed, appointed or otherwise acting on behalf of the constituent institutions, and the power and authority to enter into contracts and arrangements with a joint municipal assistance agency. (1991, c. 291, s. 1; 1995, c. 412, s. 28.)

§ 159B-49. Associate members.

Notwithstanding the provisions of Article 1 of Chapter 159B of the General Statutes or any other provision of law, a joint municipal assistance agency may, in its bylaws, create associate memberships. An associate member of a joint municipal assistance agency shall have only those rights, privileges, immunities, powers, authority, and responsibilities as set forth in the bylaws of the joint municipal assistance agency; provided, that:

(1) An associate member shall not have the right to appoint a commissioner or alternate commissioner, have the right to vote or otherwise participate in decisions of the joint municipal assistance agency;

(2) An associate member shall not have the right to a distribution of assets upon dissolution of the joint municipal assistance agency; and

(3) Income from the joint municipal assistance agency shall not accrue to, or otherwise inure to the benefit of, an associate member. (1991, c. 291, s. 2.)

§ 159B-50. Reserved for future codification purposes.

§ 159B-51. Reserved for future codification purposes.

Article 4.

Construction.

§ 159B-52. Chapter liberally construed.

In order to effectuate the purposes and policies prescribed in this Chapter the provisions hereof shall be liberally construed. (1975, c. 186, s. 3; 1983, c. 609, s. 8.)

Chapter 159C.

Industrial and Pollution Control Facilities Financing Act.

§ 159C-1. Short title.

This Chapter may be referred to as the "Industrial and Pollution Control Facilities Financing Act." (1975, c. 800, s. 1.)

§ 159C-2. Legislative findings and purposes.

(a) The General Assembly finds and determines that there exists in the State a critical condition of unemployment and a scarcity of employment opportunities; that the economic insecurity which results from such unemployment and scarcity of employment opportunities constitutes a serious menace to the safety, morals and general welfare of the entire State; that such unemployment and scarcity of employment opportunities have caused many workers and their families, including young adults upon whom future economic prosperity is dependent, to migrate elsewhere to find employment and establish homes; that such emigration has resulted in a reduced rate of growth in the tax base of the counties and other local governmental units of the State which impairs the financial ability of such counties and other local governmental units to support education and other local governmental services; that such unemployment results in obligations to grant public assistance and to pay unemployment compensation; that the aforesaid conditions can best be remedied by the attraction, stimulation, expansion and rehabilitation and revitalization of industrial and manufacturing facilities for industry in the State; and that there is a need to stimulate a larger flow of private investment funds into industrial building programs into the State.

(b)   The General Assembly further finds and determines that the development and expansion of industry within the State, and the generation of electric power and the supply of other services by public utilities, which are essential to the economic growth of the State and to the full employment and prosperity of its people, are accompanied by the increased production and discharge of gaseous, liquid, and solid pollution and wastes which threaten and endanger the health, welfare and safety of the inhabitants of the State by polluting the air, land and waters of the State; that in order to reduce, control, and prevent such environmental pollution, it is imperative that action be taken at various levels of government to require the provision of devices, equipment and facilities for the collection, reduction, treatment, and disposal of such pollution and wastes; that the assistance provided in this Chapter, especially with respect to financing, is therefore in the public interest and serves a public purpose of the State in promoting the health, welfare and safety of the inhabitants of the State not only physically by collecting, reducing, treating and preventing environmental pollution but also economically by securing and retaining private industry thereby maintaining a higher level of employment and economic activity and stability.

(c)   It is therefore declared to be the policy of the State to promote the right to gainful employment opportunity, private industry, the prevention and control of the pollution of the air, land and waters of the State, and the safety, morals and health of the people of the State, and thereby promote general welfare of the people of the State, by authorizing counties to create county authorities which shall be political subdivisions and bodies corporate and politic of the State. These bodies are to be formed (i) to aid in the financing of industrial and manufacturing facilities for the purpose of alleviating unemployment or raising below average manufacturing wages by financing industrial and manufacturing facilities which provide job opportunities or pay better wages than those prevalent in the area and (ii) to aid in financing pollution control facilities for industry in connection with manufacturing and industrial facilities and for public utilities; provided, however, that it is the policy of the State to finance only those facilities where there is a direct or indirect favorable impact on employment or an improvement in the degree of prevention or control of pollution commensurate with the size and cost of the facilities. (1975, c. 800, s. 1.)

§ 159C-3. Definitions.

The following definitions apply in this Chapter:

(1) Agency. - Any agency, bureau, commission, department, or instrumentality.

(2) Air pollution control facility. - Any structure, equipment, or other facility for, including any increment in the cost of any structure, equipment, or facility attributable to, the purpose of treating, neutralizing, or reducing gaseous industrial waste and other air pollutants, including recovery, treatment, neutralizing, or stabilizing plants and equipment and their appurtenances, which have been certified by the government entity having jurisdiction to be in furtherance of the purpose of abating or controlling atmospheric pollutants or contaminants.

(3) Bonds. - Revenue bonds of an authority issued under the provisions of this Chapter.

(3a) Code. - The Internal Revenue Code of 1986, as amended.

(4) Cost. - This term as applied to any project embraces all capital costs of the project, including all of the following:

a. The cost of construction.

b. The cost of acquisition of all property, including rights in land and other property, real and personal and improved and unimproved.

c. The cost of demolishing, removing or relocating any buildings or structures on lands so acquired, including the cost of acquiring any lands to which those buildings or structures may be moved or relocated.

d. The cost of all machinery and equipment, installation, start-up expenses, financing charges, and interest prior to, during and for a period not exceeding one year after completion of construction.

e. The cost of engineering and architectural surveys, plans and specifications.

f. The cost of consultants' and legal services, other expenses necessary or incident to determining the feasibility or practicability of the project, administrative and other expenses necessary or incident to the acquisition or construction of the project and the financing of the acquisition and construction of the project.

(5) Repealed by Session Laws 2000, c. 179, s. 3, effective August 1, 2000.

(6) Financing agreement. - A written instrument establishing the rights and responsibilities of the authority, operator, and obligor with respect to a project financed by the issuance of bonds. A financing agreement may be in the nature of a lease, a lease and leaseback, a sale and leaseback, a lease purchase, an installment sale and purchase agreement, a conditional sales agreement, a secured or unsecured loan agreement or other similar contract and may involve property in addition to the property financed with the bonds.

(6a) Governing body. - The board, commission, council, or other body in which the general legislative powers of any county or other political subdivision are vested.

(6b) Industrial project. - Any industrial or manufacturing factory, mill, assembly plant, or fabricating plant; freight terminal; industrial research, development, or laboratory facility; industrial processing facility; facility used in the manufacturing or production of tangible personal property; facility used in the creation or production of intangible property as described in section 197(d)(1)(C)(iii) of the Code; or distribution facility for industrial or manufactured products.

(7) Obligor. - Any person, which may include the operator, who is obligated under a financing agreement or guaranty agreement or other contract or agreement to make payments to, or for the benefit of, the holders of bonds of the authority. Any requirement of an obligor may be satisfied by any one or more persons who are defined collectively by this Chapter as the obligor.

(8) Operator. - The person entitled to the use or occupancy of a project.

(9) Political subdivision. - Any county, city, town, other unit of local government or any other governmental corporation, authority, or instrumentality of the State now or hereafter existing.

(10) Pollution or pollutants. - Any noxious or deleterious substances in any air or waters of or adjacent to the State of North Carolina or affecting the physical, chemical or biological properties of any air or waters of or adjacent to the State of North Carolina in a manner and to an extent which renders or is likely to render the air or waters harmful or inimical to the public health, safety or welfare, or to animal, bird or aquatic life, or to the use of such air or waters for domestic, industrial or agricultural purposes or recreation.

(10a) Pollution control project. - Any air pollution control facility, water pollution control facility, or solid waste disposal facility if the facility is in connection with either an industrial project or a public utility plant.

(11) Project. - Any land or equipment or one or more buildings or other structures, whether or not on the same site or sites, and any rehabilitation, improvement, renovation or enlargement of, or any addition to, any building or structure for use as or in connection with (i) any industrial project, (ii) any pollution control project for industry or for public utilities, (iii) any special purpose project, or (iv) any combination of projects mentioned in clauses (i) through (iii) of this subdivision. Any project may include all appurtenances and incidental facilities such as land, headquarters or office facilities, warehouses, distribution centers, access roads, sidewalks, utilities, railway sidings, trucking and similar facilities, parking facilities, landing strips and other facilities for aircraft, waterways, docks, wharves and other improvements necessary or convenient for the construction, maintenance and operation of any building or structure, or addition to it.

(12) Revenues. - With respect to any project, the rents, fees, charges, payments, proceeds and other income or profit derived from the project or from the financing agreement or security document in connection with the project.

(13) Security document. - A written instrument establishing the rights and responsibilities of the authority and the holders of bonds issued to finance a project, which may provide for, or be in the form of an agreement with, a trustee for the benefit of the bondholders. A security document may contain an assignment, pledge, mortgage or other encumbrance of all or part of the

authority's interest in, or right to receive revenues with respect to, a project and any other property provided by the operator or other obligor under a financing agreement and may bear any appropriate title. A financing agreement and a security document may be combined as one instrument.

(14)   Solid waste. - Solid waste materials resulting from any industrial or manufacturing activities or from any pollution control facility.

(15)   Solid waste disposal facility. - A facility for the purpose of treating, burning, compacting, composting, storing or disposing of solid waste.

(15a)   Special purpose project. - Any structure, equipment, or other facility for any one or more of the following purposes:

a.   Water systems or facilities, including all plants, works, instrumentalities, and properties used or useful in obtaining, conserving, treating, and distributing water for domestic or industrial use, irrigation, sanitation, fire protection, or any other public or private use.

b.   Sewage disposal systems or facilities, including all plants, works, instrumentalities, and properties used or useful in the collection, treatment, purification, or disposal of sewage, other than facilities constituting a water pollution control facility.

c.   Public transportation systems, facilities, or equipment, including bus, truck, ferry, and railroad terminals, depots, trackages, vehicles, and ferries, and mass transit systems.

d.   Public parking lots, areas, garages, and other public vehicular parking structures and facilities.

e.   Public auditoriums, gymnasiums, stadiums, and convention centers.

f.   Recreational facilities, including museums.

g.   Land, equipment, and facilities for the disposal, treatment, or recycling of (i) solid or other waste that are described in G.S. 159I-8 or (ii) solid, forestry, agricultural, or other waste, including any residual material which is the by-product or excess raw material remaining after the completion of any commercial, consumer, governmental, agricultural, or industrial production process. Facilities for the handling and transport of products resulting from treatment and recycling are included within this purpose.

h. Facilities for the provision of rehabilitation services, education, training, and employment opportunities for persons with disabilities and the disadvantaged. The term does not include a retail facility, however, unless the proposed operator of the facility certifies that at least seventy-five percent (75%) of its employees will be disadvantaged or disabled persons and at least seventy-five percent (75%) of its inventory will be composed of used, donated items and items manufactured by disadvantaged or disabled persons.

i. Orphanages and similar housing facilities for children or disadvantaged or disabled persons.

j. Facilities for the provision of material salvage and recycling services, the proceeds of which are used to provide for low, moderate, or affordable housing.

k. Research facilities owned or operated by a nonprofit corporation incorporated by two or more accredited universities whose main campuses are located in North Carolina or by the Chancellor, President, or similar official of such universities.

l. Facilities for housing the international headquarters of a nonprofit scholarly society that is a member of the Scholarly Societies Project.

m. Facilities that qualify as recovery zone property in connection with the issuance of recovery zone facility bonds pursuant to the American Recovery and Reinvestment Tax Act of 2009.

(16) Water pollution control facility. - Any structure, equipment or other facility for, including any increment in the cost of any structure, equipment or facility attributable to, the purpose of treating, neutralizing or reducing liquid industrial waste and other water pollution, including collecting, treating, neutralizing, stabilizing, cooling, segregating, holding, recycling, or disposing of liquid industrial waste and other water pollution, including necessary collector, interceptor, and outfall lines and pumping stations, which have been certified by the agency exercising jurisdiction to be in furtherance of the purpose of abating or controlling water pollution. (1975, c. 800, s. 1; 1977, 2nd Sess., c. 1197; 1979, c. 109, s. 1; 1995 (Reg. Sess., 1996), c. 575, ss. 4, 5; 2000-179, s. 3; 2005-238, s. 10; 2007-128, s. 1; 2009-140, s. 6; 2013-135, s. 1.)

§ 159C-4. Creation of authorities.

(a) The governing body of any county is hereby authorized to create by resolution a political subdivision and body corporate and politic of the State known as "The _____ (the blank space to be filled in with the name of the county) County Industrial Facilities and Pollution Control Financing Authority," which shall consist of a board of seven commissioners, to be appointed by the governing body of such county in the resolution creating such authority, or by subsequent resolution. At least 30 days prior to the adoption of such resolution, the governing body of such county shall file with the Department of Commerce and the Local Government Commission of the State notice of its intention to adopt a resolution creating an authority. At the time of the appointment of the first board of commissioners the governing body of the county shall appoint two commissioners for initial terms of two years each, two commissioners for initial terms of four years each and three commissioners for initial terms of six years each and thereafter the terms of all commissioners shall be six years, except appointments to fill vacancies which shall be for the unexpired terms. Each appointed commissioner before entering upon his duties shall take and subscribe to an oath before some person authorized by law to administer oaths to execute the duties of his office faithfully and impartially, and a record of each such oath shall be filed with the governing body of the county and entered in its minutes. All authority commissioners will serve at the pleasure of the governing body of the county. If at the end of any term of office of any commissioner a successor thereto shall not have been appointed, then the commissioner whose term of office shall have expired shall continue to hold office until his successor shall be so appointed and qualified.

(b) Each commissioner of an authority shall be a qualified elector and resident of the county for which the authority is created, and no commissioner shall be an elected official of the county for which the authority is created. Any commissioner of an authority may be removed, with or without cause, by the governing body of the county.

(c) The board of commissioners of the authority shall annually elect from its membership a chairman and a vice-chairman and another person or persons, who may but need not be commissioners, as treasurer, secretary and, if desired, assistant secretary. The position of secretary and treasurer or assistant secretary and treasurer may be held by the same person. The secretary of the authority shall keep a record of the proceedings of the authority and shall be the custodian of all books, documents and papers filed with the authority, the minute book or journal of the authority and its official seal. Either the secretary or the assistant secretary of the authority may cause copies to be made of all minutes and other records and documents of the authority and may give certificates under the official seal of the authority to the effect that such copies are true copies, and all persons dealing with the authority may rely upon such certificates.

(d)   A majority of the commissioners of an authority then in office shall constitute a quorum. The affirmative vote of a majority of the commissioners of an authority then in office shall be necessary for any action taken by the authority. A vacancy in the board of commissioners of the authority shall not impair the right of a quorum to exercise all the rights and perform all the duties of the authority. Any action taken by the authority under the provisions of this Chapter may be authorized by resolution at any regular or special meeting, and each resolution shall take effect immediately and need not be published or posted. No bonds shall be issued under the provisions of this Chapter unless the issuance thereof shall have been approved by the governing body of the county.

(e)   No commissioner of an authority shall receive any compensation for the performance of his duties under this Chapter; provided, however, that each commissioner shall be reimbursed for his necessary expenses incurred while engaged in the performance of duties but only from moneys provided by obligors.

(f)   Within 30 days of the date of creation of the authority, the authority shall advise the Department of Commerce and the Local Government Commission that an authority has been formed. The authority shall also furnish such Department and such Commission with (i) a list of its commissioners and its officers and (ii) a description of any projects that are under consideration by the authority. The authority shall, from time to time, notify the Department of Commerce and the Local Government Commission of changes in commissioners and officers and of new projects under consideration by the authority. (1975, c. 800, s. 1; 1977, c. 198, s. 23; c. 719, s. 1; 1989, c. 751, s. 7(47); 1991 (Reg. Sess., 1992), c. 959, s. 78.)

§ 159C-5. General powers.

Each authority shall have all of the powers necessary or convenient to carry out and effectuate the purposes and provisions of this Chapter, including, but without limiting the generality of the foregoing, the powers:

(1) To adopt bylaws for the regulation of its affairs and the conduct of its business and to prescribe rules, regulations and policies in connection with the performance of its functions and duties;

(2) To adopt an official seal and alter the same at pleasure;

(3) To maintain an office at such place or places within the boundaries of the county for which it was created as it may determine;

(4) To sue and be sued in its own name, plead and be impleaded;

(5) To receive, administer and comply with the conditions and requirements respecting any gift, grant or donation of any property or money;

(6) To make and execute financing agreements, security documents and other contracts and instruments necessary or convenient in the exercise of the powers and functions of the authority under this Chapter;

(7) To acquire by purchase, lease, gift or otherwise, but not by eminent domain, or to obtain options for the acquisition of, any property, real or personal, improved or unimproved, and interests in land less than the fee interest, for the construction, operation or maintenance of any project;

(7a) Repealed by Session Laws 2001-487, s. 94.

(8) To sell, lease, exchange, transfer or otherwise dispose of, or to grant options for any such purposes with respect to, any real or personal property or interest therein;

(9) To pledge or assign revenues of the authority;

(10) To construct, acquire, own, repair, maintain, extend, improve, rehabilitate, renovate, furnish and equip one or more projects and to pay all or any part of the costs thereof from the proceeds of bonds of the authority or from any contribution, gift or donation or other funds made available to the authority for such purpose;

(11) To fix, charge and collect revenues with respect to any project;

(12) To employ consulting engineers, architects, attorneys, real estate counselors, appraisers and such other consultants and employees as may be required in the judgment of the authority and to fix and pay their compensation from funds available to the authority therefor and to select and retain subject to approval of the Local Government Commission the financial consultants, underwriters and bond attorneys to be associated with the issuance of any bonds and to pay for services rendered by underwriters, financial consultants or bond attorneys out of the proceeds of any such issue with regard to which the services were performed; and

(13) To do all acts and things necessary, convenient or desirable to carry out the purposes, and to exercise the powers herein granted. (1975, c. 800, s. 1; 1979, c. 109, s. 1; 1985, c. 723, s. 3; 2000-179, s. 4; 2001-487, s. 94.)

§ 159C-6. Bonds.

(a) Each authority is authorized to provide for the issuance, at one time or from time to time, of bonds of the authority for the purpose of paying all or any part of the cost of any project. The principal of, the interest on and any premium payable upon the redemption of the bonds shall be payable solely from the funds authorized in this Article for their payment. The bonds of each issue shall bear interest as may be determined by the Local Government Commission with the approval of the authority and the obligor irrespective of the limitations of G.S. 24-1.1, as amended, and successor provisions. The bonds of each issue shall be dated, shall mature at any time or times not exceeding 35 years after the date of their issuance, and may be made redeemable before maturity at any price or prices and under any terms and conditions, as may be fixed by the authority before the issuance of the bonds. The authority shall determine the form and the manner of execution of the bonds, including any interest coupons to be attached to them, and shall fix the denomination or denominations of the bonds and the place or places of payment of principal and interest. In case any officer whose signature or a facsimile of whose signature appears on any bonds or coupons ceases to be that officer before the delivery of the bonds, the signature or the facsimile shall nevertheless be valid and sufficient for all purposes the same as if the officer had remained in office until the delivery. The authority may also provide for the authentication of the bonds by a trustee or fiscal agent. The bonds may be issued in coupon or in fully registered form, or both, as the authority may determine, and provision may be made for the registration of any coupon bonds as to principal alone and also as to both principal and interest, and for the reconversion into coupon bonds of any bonds registered as to both principal and interest, and for the interchange of registered and coupon bonds.

(a1) A county or city that receives an allocation to issue recovery zone facility bonds within the meaning of the American Recovery and Reinvestment Tax Act of 2009 to finance recovery zone property may designate any authority as the governmental entity authorized to issue recovery zone facility bonds.

(b) The proceeds of the bonds of each issue shall be used solely for the payment of the cost of all or part of the project for which the bonds were issued, and shall be disbursed in any manner and under any restrictions, as the authority may provide in the financing agreement and the security document. If the proceeds of the bonds of any issue, by reason of increased construction costs or error in estimates or otherwise, are less than this cost, additional bonds may in like manner be issued to provide the amount of the deficiency.

(c) The proceeds of bonds shall not be used to refinance the cost of an industrial project or a pollution control project. For the purposes of this section, a cost of an industrial project or a pollution control project is considered refinanced if both of the following conditions are met:

(1) The cost is initially paid from sources other than bond proceeds, and the original expenditure is to be reimbursed from bond proceeds.

(2) The original expenditure was paid more than 60 days before the authority took some action indicating its intent that the expenditure would be financed or reimbursed from bond proceeds.

(d) Notwithstanding subsection (c) of this section, preliminary expenditures that are incurred prior to the commencement of the acquisition, construction, or rehabilitation of an industrial project or a pollution control project, such as architectural costs, engineering costs, surveying costs, soil testing costs, bond issuance costs, and other similar costs, may be reimbursed from bond proceeds even if these costs are incurred or paid more than 60 days prior to the authority's action. This exception that allows preliminary expenditures to be reimbursed from bond proceeds, regardless of whether or not they are incurred or paid within 60 days of the authority's action, does not include costs that are incurred incident to the commencement of the construction of an industrial project or a pollution control project, such as expenditures for land acquisition and site preparation. In any event, an expenditure in connection with an industrial project or a pollution control project originally paid before the authority took some action indicating its intent that the expenditures would be financed or reimbursed from bond proceeds may be reimbursed from bond proceeds only if the authority finds that reimbursing those costs from bond proceeds will promote the purposes of this Chapter.

(e) An authority may make loans to an obligor to refund outstanding loans, obligations, deeds of trust, or advances issued, made, or given by the obligor for the cost of a special purpose project.

(f) The authority may issue interim receipts or temporary bonds, with or without coupons, exchangeable for definitive bonds when the bonds have been executed and are available for delivery. The authority may also provide for the replacement of any bonds that become mutilated or are destroyed or lost.

(g) Bonds may be issued under the provisions of this Chapter without obtaining, except as otherwise expressly provided in this Chapter, the consent of the State or of any political subdivision or of any agency of either, and without any other proceedings or the happening of any conditions or things other than those proceedings, conditions, or things that are specifically required by this Chapter and the provisions of the financing agreement and security document authorizing the issuance of the bonds and securing the bonds. (1975, c. 800, s. 1; 1979, c. 109, s. 1; 1997-111, s. 1; 1997-463, s. 1; 2000-179, s. 5; 2009-140, s. 7.)

§ 159C-7. Approval of industrial projects and pollution control projects by Secretary of Commerce.

(a) Approval Required. - No bonds may be issued by an authority to finance an industrial project or a pollution control project unless the project for which their issuance is proposed is first approved by the Secretary of Commerce. The authority shall file an application for approval of its proposed industrial project or pollution control project with the Secretary of Commerce, and shall notify the Local Government Commission of the filing.

(b) Findings. - The Secretary shall not approve any proposed industrial project or pollution control project unless the Secretary makes all of the following, applicable findings:

(1) In the case of a proposed industrial project, that the proposed project will not have a materially adverse effect on the environment.

(2) In the case of a proposed pollution control project, that the project will have a materially favorable impact on the environment or will prevent or diminish materially the impact of pollution which would otherwise occur.

(2a) In the case of a hazardous waste facility or low-level radioactive waste facility that is used as a reduction, recovery or recycling facility, that such project will further the waste management goals of North Carolina and will not have an adverse effect upon public health or a significant adverse effect on the environment.

(3) In the case of an industrial project or a pollution control project, except a pollution control project for a public utility,

a. That the jobs to be generated or saved, directly or indirectly, by the proposed project will be large enough in number to have a measurable impact on the area immediately surrounding the proposed project and will be commensurate with the size and cost of the proposed project,

b. That the proposed operator of the proposed project has demonstrated or can demonstrate the capability to operate the project, and

c. That the financing of the project by the authority will not cause or result in the abandonment of an existing industrial or manufacturing facility of the proposed operator or an affiliate elsewhere within the State unless the facility is to be abandoned because of obsolescence, lack of available labor in the area, or site limitations.

(b1) Initial Operator. - If the initial proposed operator of an industrial project or a pollution control project is not expected to be the operator for the term of the bonds proposed to be issued, the Secretary may make the findings required pursuant to subdivisions (b)(1)a. and (3)b. of this section only with respect to the initial operator. The initial operator shall be identified in the application for approval of the proposed project.

(c) Public Hearing. - The Secretary of Commerce shall not approve any proposed industrial project or pollution control project pursuant to this section unless the governing body of the county in which the project is located has first conducted a public hearing and, at or after the public hearing, approved in principle the issuance of bonds under this Chapter for the purpose of paying all or part of the cost of the proposed project. Notice of the public hearing shall be published at least once in at least one newspaper of general circulation in the county not less than 14 days before the public hearing. The notice shall describe generally the bonds proposed to be issued and the proposed project, including its general location, and any other information the governing body considers appropriate or the Secretary of Commerce prescribes for the purpose of providing the Secretary with the views of the community. The notice shall also state that following the public hearing the authority intends to file an application for approval of the proposed project with the Secretary of Commerce.

(d) Certificate of Department of Environment and Natural Resources. - The Secretary of Commerce shall not make the findings required by subdivisions (b)(1)b and (2) of this section unless the Secretary has first received a certification from the Department of Environment and Natural Resources that, in the case of a proposed industrial project, the proposed project will not have a materially adverse effect on the environment and that, in the case of a proposed pollution control project, the proposed project will have a materially favorable impact on the environment or will prevent or diminish materially the impact of pollution which would otherwise occur. The Secretary of Commerce shall not make the findings required by subdivision (2a) unless the Secretary has first received a certification from the Department of Environment and Natural Resources that the proposed project is environmentally sound, will not have an adverse effect on public health and will further the waste management goals of North Carolina. The Secretary of Commerce shall deliver a copy of the application to the Department of Environment and Natural Resources. The Department of Environment and Natural Resources shall provide each certification to the Secretary of Commerce within seven days after the applicant satisfactorily demonstrates to it that all permits, including environmental permits, necessary for the construction of the proposed project have been obtained, unless the authority consents to a longer period of time.

(e) Waiver of Wage Requirement. - If the Secretary of Commerce has made all of the required findings respecting a proposed industrial project except that prescribed in subdivision (b)(1)a of this section, the Secretary may, in the Secretary's discretion, approve the proposed industrial project if the Secretary has received (i) a resolution of the governing body of the county requesting that the proposed industrial project be approved notwithstanding that the operator will not pay an average weekly manufacturing wage above the average weekly manufacturing wage in the county and (ii) a letter from an appropriate State official, selected by the Secretary, to the effect that unemployment in the county is especially severe.

(f) Rules. - To facilitate review of each proposed industrial project or pollution control project, the Secretary may require the authority to obtain and submit any data and information about the project the Secretary may prescribe. The Secretary may also prescribe forms and rules the Secretary considers reasonably necessary to implement the provisions of this section.

(g) Certificate of Approval. - If the Secretary approves the proposed industrial project or pollution control project, the Secretary shall prepare a certificate of approval evidencing the approval and setting forth the findings and shall cause the certificate of approval to be published in a newspaper of general circulation within the county. This approval shall be reviewable as provided in Article 4 of Chapter 150B of the General Statutes only by an action filed, within 30 days after notice of the findings and approval have been so published, in the Superior Court of Wake County. The superior court is vested with jurisdiction to hear the action, but if no action is filed within the 30 days prescribed, the validity of the approval is conclusively presumed, and no court has authority to inquire into the approval. Copies of the certificate of approval of the proposed industrial project or pollution control project will be given to the authority, the board of county commissioners, and the Secretary of the Local Government Commission.

The certificate of approval becomes effective immediately following the expiration of the 30-day period or the expiration of any appeal period after a final determination by any court of any action timely filed pursuant to this section. The certificate expires one year after its date unless extended by the Secretary who shall not extend the certificate unless the Secretary again approves the proposed industrial project or pollution control project as provided in this section. If bonds are issued within that year pursuant to the authorization of this Chapter to pay all or part of the costs of the industrial project or pollution control project, however, the certificate expires three years after the date of the first issuance of the bonds. (1975, c. 800, s. 1; 1977, c. 198, s. 23; c. 719, ss. 2, 3; c. 771, s. 4; 1979, c. 109, s. 1; 1981, c. 704, s. 22; 1987, c. 827, s. 1; 1989, c. 727, ss. 218(161), 219(38); c. 751, s. 8(29); 1991 (Reg. Sess., 1992), c. 959, s. 79; 1995 (Reg. Sess., 1996), c. 575, s. 6; 1997-443, s. 11A.123; 1997-463, s. 2; 2000-179, s. 6; 2004-132, s. 1.)

§ 159C-8. Approval of bonds.

(a) No bonds may be issued by an authority unless the issuance of the bonds is first approved by the Local Government Commission.

The authority shall file an application for approval of its proposed bond issue with the Secretary of the Local Government Commission, and shall notify the Secretary of Commerce of the filing if the project is an industrial project or pollution control project.

(b) In determining whether a proposed bond issue should be approved, the Local Government Commission may consider any of the following:

(1) Whether the proposed operator and obligor have demonstrated or can demonstrate the financial responsibility and capability to fulfill their obligations with respect to the financing agreement. In making such determination, the Commission may consider the operator's experience and the obligor's ratio of current assets to current liabilities, net worth, earnings trends and coverage of fixed charges, the nature of the industry or business involved and its stability and any additional security such as credit enhancement, insurance, guaranties or property to be pledged to secure such bonds.

(2) Whether the political subdivisions in or near which the proposed project is to be located have the ability to cope satisfactorily with the impact of the project and to provide, or cause to be provided, the public facilities and services, including utilities, that will be necessary for the project and on account of any increase in population which are expected to result from the project.

(3) Whether the proposed date and manner of sale will have an adverse effect upon any scheduled or anticipated sale of obligations by the State or any political subdivision or any agency of either of them.

(4) Any other factors the Commission considers relevant.

(c) The Local Government Commission shall not approve the issuance of bonds for a special purpose project unless the governing body of the county in which the special purpose project is located has conducted a public hearing and, at or after the public hearing, approved in principle the issuance of bonds under this Chapter for the purposes of paying all or a part of the proposed special purpose project. Notice of the public hearing must be published at least once in at least one newspaper of general circulation in the county not less than

14 days before the public hearing. The notice must describe generally the bonds proposed to be issued and the proposed special purpose project, including its general location, and any other information the governing body considers appropriate.

(d)   If the initial proposed operator of the project is not expected to be the operator for the term of the bonds proposed to be issued, the Local Government Commission may consider the matters required under subdivision (b)(1) of this section only with respect to the initial operator. The obligor shall be obligated to perform all of the duties of the obligor required hereunder during the term the bonds are outstanding. The Local Government Commission shall evaluate the obligor's ability to perform these duties without regard to whether the initial proposed operator of the project is expected to be the operator for the term of the bonds proposed to be issued. To facilitate the review of the proposed bond issue by the Commission, the Secretary may require the authority to obtain and submit any financial data and information about the proposed bond issue and the security for it, including the proposed prospectus or offering circular, the proposed financing agreement and security document and annual and other financial reports and statements of the obligor, as the Secretary may prescribe. The Secretary may also prescribe any forms and rules the Secretary considers reasonably necessary to implement the provisions of this section. (1975, c. 800, s. 1; 1977, c. 198, s. 23; 1979, c. 109, s. 1; 1989, c. 751, s. 7(49); 1991 (Reg. Sess., 1992), c. 959, s. 80; 1995 (Reg. Sess., 1996), c. 575, s. 7; 2000-179, s. 7.)

§ 159C-9. Sale of bonds.

Bonds may be sold in such manner, either at public or private sale, and for such price as the Local Government Commission shall determine to be for the best interests of the authority and effectuate best the purposes of this Chapter irrespective of the interest limitations set forth in G.S. 24-1.1, as amended, and successor provisions, provided that such sale shall be approved by the authority and the obligor. (1975, c. 800, s. 1.)

§ 159C-10. Location of projects.

Except as provided in this section, any project or projects of an authority shall be located within the boundaries of the county for which the authority was created. A portion or portions of any project including, but not limited to, any real or personal property or improvements necessary or convenient for the construction, maintenance, and operation of the project, may be located in a county or counties other than the county in which the principal part of the project is located so long as the additional portion or portions constitute functionally appurtenant or incidental facilities and the governing body of each other county in which the additional portion or portions of the project is or are located approves the project. In addition, if a project or a group of related projects is located in two or more adjacent counties, the authority created for any one of the counties may issue bonds as provided in G.S. 159C-6 for the purpose of paying all or any part of the cost of the project or group of related projects if the following conditions are met:

(1) The board of commissioners of each county in which the project or group of related projects is located has consented.

(2) The governing body of the authority created for each county in which the project or group of related projects is located has consented.

(3) The bonds are issued in compliance with all other provisions of this Chapter. (1975, c. 800, s. 1; 1993, c. 130, s. 1; 1997-463, s. 3.)

§ 159C-11. Financing agreements.

(a) Every financing agreement shall provide that:

(1) The amounts payable under the financing agreement shall be sufficient to pay all of the principal of and redemption premium, if any, and interest on the bonds issued by the authority to pay the cost of the project as they respectively become due.

(2) The obligor shall pay all costs incurred by the authority in connection with the financing and administration of the project, except as may be paid out of the proceeds of bonds or otherwise, including insurance costs, the cost of administering the financing agreement and the security document and the fees and expenses of the fiscal agent or trustee, paying agents, attorneys, consultants and others.

(3) The obligor shall pay all the costs and expenses of operation, maintenance and upkeep of the project.

(4) The obligor's obligation to provide for the payment of the bonds in full is not subject to cancellation, termination or abatement until payment of the bonds or provision for their payment has been made.

(5) If the proposed initial operator of the project is not expected to be the operator for the term of the bonds proposed to be issued, the financing agreement shall require that the obligor attempt to arrange for a new operator when the current operator discontinues serving as operator. The new operator is subject to the approval of the Secretary under subdivisions (b)(1)a. and (3)b. of G.S. 159C-7 if the project is an industrial project or a pollution control project, and is subject in any event to the approval of the Local Government Commission under G.S. 159C-8.

(b) The financing agreement, if in the nature of a lease agreement, shall either provide that the obligor has an option to purchase, or require that the obligor purchase, the project upon the expiration or termination of the financing agreement subject to the condition that payment in full of the principal of, and the interest and any redemption premium on, the bonds, or provision for payment, has been made.

The financing agreement may provide the authority with rights and remedies in the event of a default by the obligor under the agreement, including any one or more of the following:

(1) Acceleration of all amounts payable under the financing agreement;

(2) Reentry and repossession of the project;

(3) Termination of the financing agreement;

(4) Leasing or sale or foreclosure of the project to others; and

(5) Taking whatever actions at law or in equity may appear necessary or desirable to collect the amounts payable under, and to enforce covenants made in, the financing agreement.

(c) The authority's interest in a project under a financing agreement may be that of owner, lessor, lessee, conditional or installment vendor, mortgagor, mortgagee, secured party or otherwise, but the authority need not have any ownership or possessory interest in the project.

The authority may assign all or any of its rights and remedies under the financing agreement to the trustee or the bondholders under a security document.

The financing agreement may contain any additional provisions the authority considers necessary or convenient to effectuate the purposes of this Chapter. (1975, c. 800, s. 1; 1979, c. 109, s. 1; 1995 (Reg. Sess., 1996), c. 575, s. 8; 2000-179, s. 8.)

§ 159C-12. Security documents.

Bonds issued under the provisions of this Chapter may be secured by a security document which may be a trust instrument between the authority and a bank or trust company or individual within the State, or a bank or a trust company without the State, as trustee. Such security document may pledge and assign the revenues provided for the security of the bonds, including proceeds from the sale of any project, or part thereof, insurance proceeds and condemnation awards, and may convey or mortgage the project and other property to secure a bond issue.

The revenues and other funds derived from the project, except such part thereof as may be necessary to provide reserves therefor, if any, shall be set aside at such regular intervals as may be provided in such security document in a sinking fund which may be thereby pledged to, and charged with, the payment of the principal of and the interest on such bonds as the same shall become due and the redemption price or the purchase price of bonds retired by call or purchase as therein provided. Such pledge shall be valid and binding from the time when the pledge is made. The revenues so pledged and thereafter received by the authority shall immediately be subject to the lien of such pledge without any physical delivery thereof or further act, and the lien of any such pledge shall be valid and binding as against all parties having claims of any kind in tort, contract or otherwise against the authority, irrespective of whether such parties have notice thereof. The use and disposition of money to the credit of such sinking fund shall be subject to the provisions of the security document. Such security document may contain such provisions for protecting and enforcing the rights and remedies of the bondholders as may be reasonable and proper and not in violation of law, including, without limitation, any one or more of the following:

(1)   Acceleration of all amounts payable under the security document;

(2) Appointment of a receiver to manage the project and any other property mortgaged or assigned as security for the bonds;

(3) Foreclosure and sale of the project and any other property mortgaged or assigned as security for the bonds; and

(4) Rights to bring and maintain such other actions at law or in equity as may appear necessary or desirable to collect the amounts payable under, or to enforce the covenants made in, the security document.

It shall be lawful for any bank or trust company incorporated under the laws of this State which may act as depositary of the proceeds of bonds, revenues or other funds provided under this Chapter to furnish such indemnifying bonds or to pledge such securities as may be required by the authority. All expenses incurred in carrying out the provisions of such security document may be treated as a part of the cost of the project in connection with which bonds are issued or as an expense of administration of such project.

The authority may subordinate the bonds or its rights under the financing agreement or otherwise to any prior, contemporaneous or future securities or obligations or lien, mortgage or other security interest. (1975, c. 800, s. 1; 1977, c. 719, s. 4; 1979, c. 109, s. 1.)

§ 159C-13. Trust funds.

Notwithstanding any other provisions of law to the contrary, all money received pursuant to the authority of this Chapter, whether as proceeds from the sale of bonds or as revenues, shall be deemed to be trust funds to be held and applied solely as provided in this Chapter. The security document may provide that any of such moneys may be temporarily invested and reinvested pending the disbursement thereof in such securities and other investments as shall be provided in such security document, and shall provide that any officer with whom, or any bank or trust company with which, such moneys shall be deposited shall act as trustee of such moneys and shall hold and apply the same for the purpose hereof, subject to such regulations as this Chapter and such security document may provide. (1975, c. 800, s. 1.)

§ 159C-14. Tax exemption.

The authority shall not be required to pay any taxes on any project or on any other property owned by the authority under the provisions of this Chapter or upon the income therefrom.

The interest on bonds issued by the authority shall be exempt from all income taxes within the State.

All projects and all transactions therefor shall be subject to taxation to the extent such projects and transactions would be subject to taxation if no public body were involved therewith. (1975, c. 800, s. 1; 1977, c. 719, s. 5.)

§ 159C-15. Construction contracts.

The authority may agree with the prospective operator that all contracts relating to the acquisition, construction, installation and equipping of a project shall be solicited, negotiated, awarded and executed by the prospective operator and its agents subject only to such approvals by the authority as the authority may require in such agreement. Such agreement may provide that the authority may, out of the proceeds of bonds, make advances to or reimburse the operator for all or a portion of its costs incurred in connection with such contracts. (1975, c. 800, s. 1; 1977, c. 719, s. 6.)

§ 159C-16. Conflict of interest.

If any officer, commissioner or employee of the authority, or any member of the governing body of the county for which the authority is created, shall be interested either directly or indirectly in any contract with the authority, such interest shall be disclosed to the authority and the county board of commissioners and shall be set forth in the minutes of the authority and the county board of commissioners, and the officer, commissioner, employee or member having such interest therein shall not participate on behalf of the authority in the authorization of any such contract or on behalf of the governing body of the county in the approval of the bonds to be issued by the authority to finance the project, respectively; provided, however, that this section shall not apply to the ownership of less than one per centum (1%) of the stock of any operator or obligor. Failure to take any or all actions necessary to carry out the purposes of this section shall not affect the validity of bonds issued pursuant to the provisions of this Chapter. (1975, c. 800, s. 1; 1977, c. 719, s. 7.)

§ 159C-17. Credit of State not pledged.

Bonds issued under the provisions of this Chapter shall not be deemed to constitute a debt of the State or any political subdivision or any agency thereof or a pledge of the faith and credit of the State or any political subdivision or any such agency, but shall be payable solely from the revenues and other funds provided therefor. Each bond issued under this Chapter shall contain on the face thereof a statement to the effect that the authority shall not be obligated to pay the same or the interest thereon except from the revenues and other funds pledged therefor and that neither the faith and credit nor the taxing power of the State or any political subdivision or any agency thereof is pledged to the payment of the principal of or the interest on such bonds. (1975, c. 800, s. 1.)

§ 159C-18. Bonds eligible for investment.

Bonds issued by an authority under the provisions of this Chapter are hereby made securities in which all public officers and agencies of the State and all political subdivisions, all insurance companies, trust companies, banking associations, investment companies, executors, administrators, trustees and other fiduciaries may properly and legally invest funds, including capital in their control or belonging to them. (1975, c. 800, s. 1.)

§ 159C-19. Revenue refunding bonds.

(a) Each authority is authorized to provide by resolution for the issuance of refunding bonds of the authority for the purpose of refunding any bonds then outstanding that have been issued under the provisions of this Chapter, including the payment of any redemption premium on them and any interest accrued or to accrue to the date of redemption of the bonds, and, if deemed advisable by the authority, for either or both of the following additional purposes:

(1) Constructing improvements, additions, extensions or enlargements of the project or projects in connection with which the bonds to be refunded have been issued, and

(2) Paying all or any part of the cost of any additional project or projects.

(a1) The issuance of these bonds, their maturities and other details, the rights of their holders, and the rights, duties, and obligations of the authority in respect to them shall be governed by the provisions of this Chapter that relate to the issuance of bonds, to the extent appropriate, including that the bonds may have a single maturity within the limit prescribed by G.S. 159C-6.

The approvals required by G.S. 159C-7 and 159C-8 shall be obtained prior to the issuance of any refunding bonds, except that if the refunding bonds of all or a portion of an issue are to be issued solely for the purpose of refunding outstanding bonds issued under this Chapter, the approval required by G.S. 159C-7 is not required as to the project financed with the bonds to be refunded.

(b) Refunding bonds issued under this section may be sold or exchanged for outstanding bonds issued under this Chapter and, if sold, their proceeds may be applied, in addition to any other authorized purposes, to the purchase, redemption, or payment of the outstanding bonds. Refunding bonds may be issued, in the determination of the authority, at any time before the date of maturity or maturities or the date selected for the redemption of the bonds being refunded by them. Pending the application of the proceeds of the refunding bonds, with any other available funds, to the payment of the principal of and accrued interest and any redemption premium on the bonds being refunded, and, if so provided or permitted in the security document securing them, to the payment of any interest on the refunding bonds and any expenses in connection with the refunding, the proceeds may be invested in direct obligations of, or obligations the principal of and the interest on which are unconditionally guaranteed by, the United States of America that mature or are subject to redemption by the holder, at the option of such holder, not later than the respective dates when the proceeds, together with the interest accruing on them, will be required for the purposes intended. (1975, c. 800, s. 1; 1997-463, s. 4; 2000-179, s. 9.)

§ 159C-20. No power of eminent domain.

No authority shall have any right or power to acquire any property through the exercise of eminent domain or any proceedings in the nature of eminent domain. (1975, c. 800, s. 1.)

§ 159C-21. Dissolution of authorities.

Whenever the board of commissioners of an authority and the governing body of the county for which such authority was created shall by joint resolution determine that the purposes for which the authority was formed have been substantially fulfilled and that all bonds theretofore issued and all other obligations theretofore incurred by the authority have been fully paid or satisfied, such board of commissioners and governing body may declare the authority to be dissolved. On the effective date of such joint resolution, the title to all funds and other property owned by the authority at the time of such dissolution shall vest in the county or in such other political subdivisions as the county shall direct, and possession of such funds and other property shall forthwith be delivered to the county or to such other political subdivisions in accordance with the direction of the county. (1975, c. 800, s. 1.)

§ 159C-22. Annual reports; application of Article 3, Subchapter III of Chapter 159.

Each authority shall, promptly following the close of each calendar year, submit an annual report of its activities for the preceding year to the governing body of the county for which the authority was created. Each such report shall set forth a complete operating and financial statement covering the operations of the authority during such year.

The provisions of Article 3, Subchapter III of Chapter 159 of the General Statutes of North Carolina entitled: "The Local Government Budget and Fiscal Control Act" shall have no application to authorities created pursuant to this Chapter. (1975, c. 800, s. 1; 1977, c. 719, s. 8.)

§ 159C-23. Officers not liable.

No commissioner of any authority shall be subject to any personal liability or accountability by reason of his execution of any bonds or the issuance thereof. (1975, c. 800, s. 1.)

§ 159C-24. Additional method.

The foregoing sections of this Chapter shall be deemed to provide an additional and alternative method for the doing of the things authorized thereby and shall be regarded as supplemental and additional to powers conferred by other laws, and shall not be regarded as in derogation of any powers now existing; provided, however, that the issuance of bonds or refunding bonds under the provisions of this Chapter need not comply with the requirements of any other law applicable to the issuance of bonds. (1975, c. 800, s. 1.)

§ 159C-25. Liberal construction.

This Chapter, being necessary for the prosperity and welfare of the State and its inhabitants, shall be liberally construed to effect the purposes hereof. (1975, c. 800, s. 2.)

§ 159C-26. Inconsistent laws inapplicable.

Insofar as the provisions of this Chapter are inconsistent with the provisions of any general, special or local laws, or parts thereof, the provisions of this Chapter shall be controlling. (1975, c. 800, s. 3.)

§ 159C-27. Creation, etc., of prior authorities ratified.

The creation, formation and organization of all authorities heretofore [prior to June 24, 1977] purported to have been created, formed and organized are hereby ratified, confirmed and validated. (1977, c. 719, s. 9.)

§ 159C-28: Repealed by Session Laws 2001-218, s. 5.

Chapter 159D

The North Carolina Capital Facilities Financing Act.

Article 1.

Industrial And Pollution Control Facilities Financing.

§ 159D-1. Short title.

This Article may be referred to as "The North Carolina Industrial and Pollution Control Facilities Financing Act." (1977, 2nd Sess., c. 1198, s. 1; 1987, c. 517, s. 1; 2000-179, s. 2.)

§ 159D-2. Legislative findings and purposes.

(a) The General Assembly finds and determines that there exists in the State a critical condition of unemployment and a scarcity of employment opportunities; that the economic insecurity which results from such unemployment and scarcity of employment opportunities constitutes a serious menace to the safety, morals and general welfare of the entire State; that such unemployment and scarcity of employment opportunities have caused many workers and their families, including young adults upon whom future economic prosperity is dependent, to migrate elsewhere to find employment and establish homes; that such emigration has resulted in a reduced rate of growth in the tax base of the counties and other local governmental units of the State which impairs the financial ability of such counties and other local governmental units to support education and other local governmental services; that such unemployment results in obligations to grant public assistance and to pay unemployment compensation; that the aforesaid conditions can best be remedied by the attraction, stimulation, expansion and rehabilitation and revitalization of industrial and manufacturing facilities for industry in the State; and that there is a need to stimulate a larger flow of private investment funds into industrial building programs in the State.

(b) The General Assembly further finds and determines that the development and expansion of industry within the State, which are essential to the economic growth of the State, and to the full employment and prosperity of its people, are accompanied by the increased production and discharge of gaseous, liquid, and solid pollution and wastes which threaten and endanger the health, welfare and safety of the inhabitants of the State by polluting the air, land and waters of the State; that in order to reduce, control, and prevent such environmental pollution, it is imperative that action be taken at various levels of government to require the provision of devices, equipment and facilities for the collection, reduction, treatment, and disposal of such pollution and wastes; that the assistance provided in this Article, especially with respect to financing, is therefore in the public interest and serves a public purpose of the State in promoting the health, welfare and safety of the inhabitants of the State not only physically by collecting, reducing, treating and preventing environmental pollution but also economically by securing and retaining private industry thereby maintaining a higher level of employment and economic activity and stability.

(c)   Repealed by Session Laws 2000, c. 179, s. 2.

(c1)   Repealed by Session Laws 2000, c. 179, s. 2.

(d)   Repealed by Session Laws 2000, c. 179, s. 2. (1977, 2nd Sess., c. 1198, s. 1; 1987, c. 517, ss. 2, 3; 2000-179, s. 2.)

§ 159D-3. Definitions.

The following terms, whenever used or referred to in this Article, shall have the following respective meanings, unless a different meaning clearly appears from the context:

(1)   "Agency" means the North Carolina Capital Facilities Finance Agency, an agency of the State created pursuant to G.S. 159D-38 of the North Carolina Capital Facilities Finance Act, codified as Article 2 of this Chapter.

(2)   "Air pollution control facility" shall mean any structure, equipment or other facility for, including any increment in the cost of any structure, equipment or facility attributable to, the purpose of treating, neutralizing or reducing gaseous industrial waste and other air pollutants, including recovery, treatment, neutralizing or stabilizing plants and equipment and their appurtenances, which shall have been certified by the agency having jurisdiction to be in furtherance of the purpose of abating or controlling atmospheric pollutants or contaminants.

(3) "Authority" shall mean The North Carolina Industrial and Pollution Control Facilities Financing Authority, a political subdivision and body politic of the State, created pursuant to the provisions of this Article.

(4) "Bonds" shall mean revenue bonds issued under the provisions of this Article.

(4a) "Code" means the Internal Revenue Code of 1986, as amended.

(5) "Cost" as applied to any project shall embrace all capital costs thereof, including the cost of construction, the cost of acquisition of all property, including rights in land and other property, both real and personal and improved and unimproved, the cost of demolishing, removing or relocating any buildings or structures on lands so acquired, including the cost of acquiring any lands to which such buildings or structures may be moved or relocated, the cost of all machinery and equipment, installation, start-up expenses, financing charges, interest prior to, during and for a period not exceeding one year after completion of construction, the cost of engineering and architectural surveys, plans and specifications, the cost of consultants and legal services, other expenses necessary or incident to determining the feasibility or practicability of such project, administrative and other expenses necessary or incident to the acquisition or construction of such project and the financing of the acquisition and construction thereof, including a reserve for debt services.

(6) Repealed by Session Laws 2000, c. 179, s. 2, effective July 1, 2000.

(7) "Financing agreement" shall mean a written instrument establishing the rights and responsibilities of the agency and the operator with respect to a project financed by the issue of bonds.

(8) "Governing body" shall mean the board, commission, council or other body in which the general legislative powers of any county or other political subdivision are vested.

(9) "Obligor" shall mean collectively the operator and any others (including, but not by way of limitation, any other person, collateral device or fund that shall be obligated to pay) who or which shall be obligated under a financing agreement or guaranty agreement or other contract or agreement to make payments to, or for the benefit of, the holders of bonds of the agency. Any requirement of an obligor may be satisfied by any one or more persons who are defined collectively by this Article as the obligor.

(10) "Operator" shall mean the person entitled to the use or occupancy of a project.

(11) "Political subdivision" shall mean any county, city, town, other unit of local government or any other governmental corporation, entity, authority or instrumentality of the State now or hereafter existing.

(12) "Pollution and pollutants" shall mean any noxious or deleterious substances in any air or waters of or adjacent to the State of North Carolina or affecting the physical, chemical or biological properties of any air or waters of or adjacent to the State of North Carolina in a manner and to an extent which renders or is likely to render such air or waters harmful or inimical to the public health, safety or welfare, or to animal, bird or aquatic life, or to the use of such air or waters for domestic, industrial or agricultural purposes or recreation.

(13) "Project" means any land, equipment or any one or more buildings or other structures, whether or not on the same site or sites, and any rehabilitation, improvement, renovation or enlargement of, or any addition to, any building or structure for use as or in connection with (i) any industrial project, which may be an industrial or manufacturing factory, mill, assembly plant, fabricating plant, freight terminal, industrial research, development or laboratory facility, industrial processing facility for industrial or manufactured products, a facility used in the manufacturing or production of tangible personal property, a facility used in the creation or production of intangible property as described in section 197(d)(1)(C)(iii) of the Code, or a distribution facility for industrial or manufactured products, or (ii) any pollution control project for industry which project may be any air pollution control facility, water pollution control facility, or solid waste disposal facility in connection with any factory, mill, plant, terminal or facility described in clause (i) of this subdivision, or (iii) any combination of projects mentioned in clauses (i) and (ii) of this subdivision. Any project may include all appurtenances and incidental facilities such as land, headquarters or office facilities, warehouses, distribution centers, access roads, sidewalks, utilities, railway sidings, trucking and similar facilities, parking facilities, landing strips and other facilities for aircraft, waterways, docks, wharves and other improvements necessary or convenient for the construction, maintenance and operation of any building or structure, or addition thereto.

(14) "Revenues" shall mean, with respect to any project, the rents, fees, charges, payments, proceeds and other income or profit derived therefrom or from the financing agreement or security document in connection therewith.

(15) "Security document" shall mean a written instrument or instruments establishing the rights and responsibilities of the agency and the holders of bonds issued to finance a project, and may provide for, or be in the form of an agreement with, a trustee for the benefit of such bondholders. A security document may contain an assignment, pledge, mortgage or other encumbrance of all or part of the agency's interest in, or right to receive revenues with respect to, a project and any other property provided by the operator or other obligor under a financing agreement and may bear any appropriate title. A financing agreement and a security document may be combined as one instrument.

(16) "Solid waste" shall mean solid waste materials resulting from any industrial or manufacturing activities or from any pollution control facility.

(17) "Solid waste disposal facility" shall mean a facility for the purpose of treating, burning, compacting, composting, storing or disposing of solid waste.

(18) "Water pollution control facility" shall mean any structure, equipment or other facility for, including any increment in the cost of any structure, equipment or facility attributable to, the purpose of treating, neutralizing or reducing liquid industrial waste and other water pollution, including collecting, treating, neutralizing, stabilizing, cooling, segregating, holding, recycling, or disposing of liquid industrial waste and other water pollution, including necessary collector, interceptor, and outfall lines and pumping stations, which has been certified by the entity exercising jurisdiction to be in furtherance of the purpose of abating or controlling water pollution. (1977, 2nd Sess., c. 1198, s. 1; 1987, c. 517, ss. 4, 4.1; 2000-179, s. 2; 2009-140, s. 8.)

§ 159D-4: Repealed by Session Laws 2000-179, s. 2.

§ 159D-4.1. Jurisdiction of the agency.

All actions taken by counties, local officials, the Secretary of State, the State Treasurer, and other interested parties to create and organize The North Carolina Industrial Facilities and Pollution Control Financing Authority are ratified and confirmed. All duties, powers, jurisdiction, and responsibilities vested by statute or by contract in the authority are transferred to and vested in the North Carolina Capital Facilities Finance Agency, subject to the provisions of this Article. Upon this transfer, the agency is responsible for all duties and obligations of the authority entered into or incurred, by contract or otherwise, before the transfer. Particularly, the agency is responsible for all matters relating to any outstanding bonds of the authority to the same extent that the authority was responsible for them before the date of transfer. The agency for all purposes assumes the role and is the legal successor of the authority. Upon this transfer, the authority is dissolved. (2000-179, s. 2.)

§ 159D-5. General powers.

The agency shall have all of the powers necessary or convenient to carry out and effectuate the purposes and provisions of this Article, including all of the following:

(1)   To adopt bylaws for the regulation of its affairs and the conduct of its business and to prescribe rules, regulations and policies in connection with the performance of its functions and duties;

(2)   To adopt an official seal and alter the same at pleasure;

(3)   To maintain an office at such place or places as it may determine;

(4)   To sue and be sued in its own name, plead and be impleaded;

(5)   To receive, administer and comply with the conditions and requirements respecting any gift, grant or donation of any property or money;

(6)   To make and execute financing agreements, security documents and other contracts and instruments necessary or convenient in the exercise of the powers and functions of the agency under this Article;

(7)   To acquire by purchase, lease, gift or otherwise, but not by eminent domain, or to obtain options for the acquisition of any property, real or personal, improved or unimproved, and interests in land less than the fee thereof, for the construction, operation or maintenance of any project;

(8)   To sell, lease, exchange, transfer or otherwise dispose of, or to grant options for any such purposes with respect to, any real or personal property or interest therein;

(9)   To pledge or assign revenues of the agency;

(10) To construct, acquire, own, repair, maintain, extend, improve, rehabilitate, renovate, furnish and equip one or more projects and to pay all or any part of the costs thereof from the proceeds of bonds of the agency or from any contribution, gift or donation or other funds made available to the agency for such purpose;

(11) To fix, charge and collect revenues with respect to any project;

(12) To employ consulting engineers, architects, attorneys, real estate counselors, appraisers and such other consultants and employees as may be required in the judgment of the agency and to fix and pay their compensation from funds available to the agency therefor and to select and retain subject to approval of the Local Government Commission the financial consultants, underwriters and bond attorneys to be associated with the issuance of any bonds and to pay for services rendered by underwriters, financial consultants or bond attorneys out of the proceeds of any such issue with regard to which the services were performed; and

(13) To do all acts and things necessary, convenient or desirable to carry out the purposes, and to exercise the powers granted in this Article. (1977, 2nd Sess., c. 1198, s. 1; 1985, c. 723, s. 3; 2000-179, s. 2.)

§ 159D-6. Bonds.

(a) The agency is authorized to provide for the issuance, at one time or from time to time, of bonds of the agency for the purpose of paying all or any part of the cost of any project. The principal of, the interest on and any premium payable under the redemption of such bonds shall be payable solely from the funds herein authorized for such payment. The bonds of each issue shall bear interest as may be determined by the Local Government Commission of North Carolina with the approval of the agency and the obligor irrespective of the limitations of G.S. 24-1.1, as amended, and successor provisions. The bonds of each issue shall be dated, shall mature at such time or times not exceeding 30 years from the date of their issuance, and may be made redeemable before maturity at such price or prices and under such terms and conditions, as may be fixed by the agency prior to the issuance of the bonds. The agency shall determine the form and the manner of execution of the bonds, including any interest coupons to be attached thereto, and shall fix the denomination or denominations of the bonds and the place or places of payment of principal and interest. In case any officer whose signature or a facsimile of whose signature appears on any bonds or coupons ceases to be that officer before the delivery of the bonds, the signature or the facsimile shall nevertheless be valid and sufficient for all purposes the same as if the officer had remained in office until such delivery. The agency may also provide for the authentication of the bonds by a trustee or fiscal agent.

(b) The proceeds of the bonds of each issue shall be used solely for the payment of the cost of the project or projects, or a portion thereof, for which the bonds were issued, and shall be disbursed in such manner and under such restrictions, if any, as the agency may provide in the financing agreement and the security document. If the proceeds of the bonds of any issue, by reason of increased construction costs or error in estimates or otherwise, are less than such cost, additional bonds may in like manner be issued to provide the amount of such deficiency.

(c) The proceeds of bonds issued pursuant to this Article shall not be used to refinance the cost of a project. For the purposes of this section, a cost of a project is considered refinanced if both of the following conditions are met:

(1) The cost is initially paid from sources other than bond proceeds, and the original expenditure is to be reimbursed from bond proceeds.

(2) The original expenditure was paid more than 60 days before the agency took some action indicating its intent that the expenditure would be financed or reimbursed from bond proceeds.

(d) Notwithstanding subsection (c) of this section, preliminary expenditures that are incurred prior to the commencement of the acquisition, construction, or rehabilitation of a project, such as architectural costs, engineering costs, surveying costs, soil testing costs, bond issuance costs, and other similar costs, may be reimbursed from bond proceeds even if these costs are incurred or paid more than 60 days prior to the agency's action. This exception that allows preliminary expenditures to be reimbursed from bond proceeds, whether or not they are incurred or paid within 60 days of the agency's action, does not include costs that are incurred incident to the commencement of the construction of a project, such as expenditures for land acquisition and site preparation. In any event, an expenditure originally paid before the agency took some action indicating its intent that the expenditures would be financed or reimbursed from bond proceeds may be reimbursed from bond proceeds only if the agency finds that reimbursing those costs from bond proceeds will promote the purposes of this Article.

(e)   Bonds may be issued under the provisions of this Article without obtaining, except as otherwise expressly provided in this Article, the consent of the State or of any political subdivision and without any other proceedings or the happening of any conditions or things other than those proceedings, conditions or things specifically required by this Article and the provisions of the financing agreement and security document authorizing the issuance of such bonds and securing the same. (1977, 2nd Sess., c. 1198, s. 1; 2000-179, s. 2.)

§ 159D-7. Approval of project by Secretary of Commerce.

(a)   Approval Required. - No bonds may be issued by the agency pursuant to this Article unless the project for which their issuance is proposed is first approved by the Secretary of Commerce. The agency shall file an application for approval of its proposed project with the Secretary of Commerce, and shall notify the Local Government Commission of such filing.

(b)   Findings. - The Secretary shall not approve any proposed project unless the Secretary makes all of the following, applicable findings:

(1)   In the case of a proposed industrial project, that the proposed project will not have a materially adverse effect on the environment.

(2)   In the case of a proposed pollution control project, that such project will have a materially favorable impact on the environment or will prevent or diminish materially the impact of pollution which would otherwise occur.

(2a)   In the case of a hazardous waste facility or low-level radioactive waste facility that is used as a reduction, recovery or recycling facility, that such project will further the waste management goals of North Carolina and will not have an adverse effect upon public health or a significant adverse effect on the environment.

(3)   In any case (whether the proposed project is an industrial or a pollution control project),

a. That the jobs to be generated or saved, directly or indirectly, by the proposed project will be large enough in number to have a measurable impact on the area immediately surrounding the proposed project and will be commensurate with the size and cost of the proposed project,

b. That the proposed operator of the proposed project has demonstrated or can demonstrate the capability to operate such project, and

c. That the financing of such project by the agency will not cause or result in the abandonment of an existing industrial or manufacturing facility of the proposed operator or an affiliate elsewhere within the State unless the facility is to be abandoned because of obsolescence, lack of available labor in the area, or site limitations.

(c) Initial Operator. - If the initial proposed operator of a project is not expected to be the operator for the term of the bonds proposed to be issued, the Secretary may make the findings required pursuant to subdivisions (b)(1)a. and (3)b. of this section only with respect to the initial operator. The initial operator shall be identified in the application for approval of the proposed project.

(d) Public Hearing, Generally. - The Secretary of Commerce shall not approve any proposed project pursuant to this section unless the governing body of the county in which the project is located has first conducted a public hearing and, at or after the public hearing, approved in principle the issuance of bonds under this Article for the purpose of paying all or part of the cost of the proposed project. Notice of the public hearing shall be published at least once in at least one newspaper of general circulation in the county not less than 14 days before the public hearing. The notice shall describe generally the bonds proposed to be issued and the proposed project, including its general location, and any other information the governing body considers appropriate or the Secretary of Commerce prescribes for the purpose of providing the Secretary with the views of the community. The notice shall also state that following the public hearing the agency intends to file an application for approval of the proposed project with the Secretary of Commerce.

(d1) Public Hearing, Multiple Projects. - Notwithstanding subsection (d) of this section, in the event the bonds proposed to be issued are to finance more than one project, the public hearing shall be conducted by the agency or by a hearing officer designated by the agency to conduct public hearings. The public hearing may be held at any location designated by the agency. Notice of the public hearing shall be published at least once in at least one newspaper of general circulation in each county in which a proposed project is to be located not less than 14 days before the public hearing. The notice shall describe generally the bonds proposed to be issued and any proposed project in that county, including its general location, and any other information the agency considers appropriate or the Secretary of Commerce prescribes for the purpose of providing the Secretary with the views of the community. A copy of the notice of public hearing must be mailed to the board of county commissioners of any county in which a proposed project is to be located and to the governing body of any municipality in which a proposed project is to be located.

(e) Certificate of Department of Environment and Natural Resources. - The Secretary of Commerce shall not make the findings required by subdivisions (b)(1)b and (2) of this section unless the Secretary has first received a certification from the Department of Environment and Natural Resources that, in the case of a proposed industrial project, the proposed project will not have a materially adverse effect on the environment and that, in the case of a proposed pollution control project, the proposed project will have a materially favorable impact on the environment or will prevent or diminish materially the impact of pollution which would otherwise occur. The Secretary shall not make the findings required by subdivision (b)(2a) of this section unless the Secretary has first received a certification from the Department of Environment and Natural Resources that the proposed project is environmentally sound, will not have an adverse effect on public health and will further the waste management goals of North Carolina. The Secretary of Commerce shall deliver a copy of the application to the Department of Environment and Natural Resources. The Department of Environment and Natural Resources shall provide each certification to the Secretary of Commerce within seven days after the applicant satisfactorily demonstrates to it that all permits, including environmental permits, necessary for the construction of the proposed project have been obtained, unless the agency consents to a longer period of time.

(f) Waiver of Wage Requirement. - If the Secretary of Commerce has made all of the required findings respecting a proposed industrial project, except that prescribed in subdivision (b)(1)a of this section, the Secretary may, in the Secretary's discretion, approve the proposed project if the Secretary has received (i) a resolution of the governing body of the county in which the proposed project is to be located requesting that the proposed project be approved notwithstanding that the operator will not pay an average weekly manufacturing wage above the average weekly manufacturing wage in the county and (ii) a letter from an appropriate State official, selected by the Secretary, to the effect that unemployment in the county is especially severe.

(g) Rules. - To facilitate the Secretary's review of each proposed project, the Secretary may require the agency to obtain and submit such data and information about such project as the Secretary may prescribe. The Secretary may also prescribe such forms and such rules as the Secretary considers reasonably necessary to implement the provisions of this section.

(h) Certificate of Approval. - If the Secretary approves the proposed project, the Secretary shall prepare a certificate of approval evidencing such approval and setting forth the findings and shall cause the certificate of approval to be published in a newspaper of general circulation within the county in which the proposed project is to be located. Any such approval shall be reviewable as provided in Article 4 of Chapter 150B of the General Statutes only by an action filed, within 30 days after notice of such findings and approval shall have been so published, in the Superior Court of Wake County. The superior court is hereby vested with jurisdiction to hear such action, but if no such action is filed within the 30 days herein prescribed, the validity of such approval shall be conclusively presumed, and no court shall have authority to inquire into such approval. Copies of the certificate of approval of the proposed project will be given to the agency, the governing body of the county in which the proposed project is to be located and the secretary of the Local Government Commission.

The certificate of approval shall become effective immediately following the expiration of the 30-day period or the expiration of any appeal period after a final determination by any court of any action timely filed pursuant to this section. The certificate shall expire one year after its date unless extended by the Secretary who shall not extend the certificate unless the Secretary again approves the proposed project as provided in this section. If bonds are issued within that year pursuant to the authorization of this Article or Chapter 159C of the General Statutes to pay all or part of the costs of the project, however, the certificate expires three years after the date of the first issuance of the bonds.

(i) Certificate Issued Under Chapter 159C Effective. - Any certificate of approval with respect to a project which has become effective pursuant to G.S. 159C-7 satisfies the requirements of this section to the extent that the findings made by the Secretary pursuant to G.S. 159C-7 are consistent with the findings required to be made by the Secretary pursuant to this section. (1977, 2nd Sess., c. 1198, s. 1; 1987, c. 517, s. 6; c. 827, s. 1; 1989, c. 727, ss. 218(162), 219(39); c. 751, s. 8(30); 1991 (Reg. Sess., 1992), c. 959, s. 82; 1997-443, s. 11A.123; 2000-179, s. 2; 2002-172, s. 5.2; 2003-416, s. 2; 2004-132, s. 2.)

§ 159D-8. Approval of bonds.

(a) No bonds may be issued by the agency pursuant to this Article unless the issuance is first approved by the Local Government Commission.

The agency shall file an application for approval of its proposed bond issue with the secretary of the Local Government Commission, and shall notify the Secretary of the Department of Commerce of such filing.

(b) In determining whether a proposed bond issue should be approved, the Local Government Commission may consider, without limitation, the following:

(1) Whether the proposed operator and obligor have demonstrated or can demonstrate the financial responsibility and capability to fulfill their obligations with respect to the financing agreement. In making such determination, the commission may consider the operator's experience and the obligor's ratio of current assets to current liabilities, net worth, earnings trends and coverage of fixed charges, the nature of the industry or business involved and its stability and any additional security such as credit enhancement, insurance, guaranties or property to be pledged or secure such bonds.

(2) Whether the political subdivisions in or near which the proposed project is to be located have the ability to cope satisfactorily with the impact of such project and to provide, or cause to be provided, the public facilities and services, including utilities, that will be necessary for such project and on account of any increase in population which are expected to result therefrom.

(3) Whether the proposed date and manner of sale will have an adverse effect upon any scheduled or anticipated sale of obligations by the State or any political subdivision or any agency of either of them.

(c) To facilitate the review of the proposed bond issue by the commission, the Secretary may require the agency to obtain and submit such financial data and information about the proposed bond issue and the security therefor, including the proposed prospectus or offering circular, the proposed financing agreement and security document and annual and other financial reports and statements of the obligor, as the Secretary may prescribe. The Secretary may also prescribe forms and rules that the Secretary considers reasonably necessary to implement the provisions of this section. (1977, 2nd Sess., c. 1198, s. 1; 1989, c. 751, s. 7(52); 1991 (Reg. Sess., 1992), c. 959, s. 83; 2000-179, s. 2; 2002-172, s. 5.3.)

§ 159D-9. Sale of bonds.

Bonds issued under this Article may be sold in such manner, either at public or private sale, and for such price as the Local Government Commission determines to be for the best interests of the agency and effectuate best the purposes of this Article irrespective of the interest limitations set forth in G.S. 24-1.1, as amended, and successor provisions, as long as the sale is approved by the agency and the obligor. (1977, 2nd Sess., c. 1198, s. 1; 2000-179, s. 2.)

§ 159D-10. Location of projects.

Any project of the agency shall be located within the boundaries of the State. Bonds may not be issued to finance any project or group of projects in any county of the State unless the board of commissioners for the county in which the project is located has consented to the location of the project within the county. (1977, 2nd Sess., c. 1198, s. 1; 1993, c. 130, s. 2; 2000-179, s. 2.)

§ 159D-11. Financing agreements.

(a) Every financing agreement shall provide that:

(1) Repealed by Session Laws 1987, c. 517, s. 7.

(2) The amounts payable under the financing agreement shall be sufficient to pay all of the principal of and interest and redemption premium, if any, and interest on the bonds issued by the agency to pay the cost of the project as they respectively become due;

(3) The obligor shall pay all costs incurred by the agency in connection with the financing and administration of the project, except as may be paid out of the proceeds of bonds or otherwise, including, but without limitation, insurance costs, the cost of administering the financing agreement and the security document and the fees and expenses of the fiscal agent or trustee, paying agents, attorneys, consultants and others;

(4) The obligor shall pay all the costs and expenses of operation, maintenance and upkeep of the project; and

(5) The obligor's obligation to provide for the payment of the bonds in full shall not be subject to cancellation, termination or abatement until payment of the bonds or provision for payment has been made.

(b) The financing agreement may be in the nature of:

(1) A sale and leaseback,

(2) A lease purchase,

(3) A conditional sale,

(4) An installment sale,

(5) A secured or unsecured loan,

(6) A loan and mortgage, or

(7) Another similar transaction.

(c) The financing agreement, if in the nature of a lease agreement, shall either provide that the obligor has an option to purchase, or require that the obligor purchase, the project upon the expiration or termination of the financing agreement subject to the condition that payment in full of the principal of, and the interest and any redemption premium on, the bonds, or provision for payment has been made.

(d) The financing agreement may provide the agency with rights and remedies in the event of a default by the obligor under it including, without limitation, any one or more of the following:

(1) Acceleration of all amounts payable under the financing agreement;

(2) Reentry and repossession of the project;

(3) Termination of the financing agreement;

(4) Leasing or sale or foreclosure of the project to others; and

(5) Taking whatever actions at law or in equity may appear necessary or desirable to collect the amounts payable under, and to enforce covenants made in, the financing agreement.

(e) The agency's interest in a project under a financing agreement may be that of owner, lessor, lessee, conditional or installment vendor, mortgagor, mortgagee, secured party or otherwise, but the agency need not have any ownership or possessory interest in the project.

(f) The agency may assign all or any of its rights and remedies under the financing agreement to the trustee or bondholders under the security document.

(g) The financing agreement may contain any additional provisions the agency considers necessary or convenient to effectuate the purposes of this Article. (1977, 2nd Sess., c. 1198, s. 1; 1987, c. 517, s. 7; 2000-179, s. 2.)

§ 159D-12. Security documents.

(a) Bonds issued under the provisions of this Article may be secured by a security document which may be a trust instrument between the agency and a bank or trust company or individual within the State, or a bank or a trust company without the State, as trustee. Such security document may pledge and assign the revenues provided for the security of the bonds, including proceeds from the sale of any project, or part thereof, insurance proceeds and condemnation awards, and may convey or mortgage the project and other property to secure a bond issue.

The revenues and other funds derived from the project, except any part necessary to provide reserves shall be set aside at such regular intervals as may be provided in such security document in a sinking fund which may be pledged to, and charged with, the payment of the principal of and the interest on such bonds as they become due and the redemption price or the purchase price of bonds retired by call or purchase as therein provided. Such pledge shall be valid and binding from the time when the pledge is made. The revenues so pledged and thereafter received by the agency shall immediately be subject to the lien of such pledge without any physical delivery thereof or further act, and the lien of any such pledge shall be valid and binding as against all parties having claims of any kind in tort, contract or otherwise against the agency, irrespective of whether such parties have notice thereof. The use and disposition of money to the credit of such sinking fund shall be subject to the provisions of the security document. Such security document may contain such provisions for protecting and enforcing the rights and remedies of the bondholders as may be reasonable and proper and not in violation of law, including, without limitation, any one or more of the following:

(1)   Acceleration of all amounts payable under the security document;

(2)   Appointment of a receiver to manage the project and any other property mortgaged or assigned as security for the bonds;

(3)   Foreclosure and sale of the project and any other property mortgaged or assigned as security for the bonds; and

(4)   Rights to bring and maintain such other actions at law or in equity as may appear necessary or desirable to collect the amounts payable under, or to enforce the covenants made in, the security document.

(b)   It is lawful for any bank or trust company incorporated under the laws of this State which may act as depositary of the proceeds of bonds, revenues or other funds provided under this Article to furnish such indemnifying bonds or to pledge such securities as may be required by the agency. All expenses incurred in carrying out the provisions of such security document may be treated as a part of the cost of the project in connection with which bonds are issued or as an expense of administration of such project.

The agency may subordinate the bonds or its rights under the financing agreement or otherwise to any prior, contemporaneous or future securities or obligations or lien, mortgage or other security interest.

Any such security document may contain such additional provisions as in the determination of the agency are necessary or convenient or effectuate the purposes of this Article. (1977, 2nd Sess., c. 1198, s. 1; 2000-179, s. 2.)

§ 159D-13. Trust funds.

Notwithstanding any other provisions of law to the contrary, all money received pursuant to the authority of this Article, whether as proceeds from the sale of bonds or as revenues, are trust funds to be held and applied solely as provided in this Article. The security document may provide that any of the money may be temporarily invested and reinvested pending its disbursement in any securities and other investments as provided in such security document, and shall provide that any officer with whom, or any bank or trust company with which, the money is deposited shall act as trustee and shall hold and apply it for the purpose of this Article, subject to any regulations this Article and the security document provide. (1977, 2nd Sess., c. 1198, s. 1; 2000-179, s. 2.)

§ 159D-14. Tax exemption.

The agency is not required to pay any taxes on any project or on any other property owned by the agency under the provisions of this Article or upon the income from the property.

The interest on bonds issued by the agency is exempt from all income taxes within the State.

All projects and all transactions for them are subject to taxation to the extent they would be subject to taxation if no public body were involved with them. (1977, 2nd Sess., c. 1198, s. 1; 2000-179, s. 2.)

§ 159D-15. Construction contracts.

The agency may agree with the prospective operator that all contracts relating to the acquisition, construction, installation and equipping of a project shall be solicited, negotiated, awarded and executed by the prospective operator and its agents subject only to such approval by the agency as the agency may require in such agreement. Such agreement may provide that the agency may, out of the proceeds of bonds, make advances to or reimburse the operator for all or a portion of its costs incurred in connection with such contracts. (1977, 2nd Sess., c. 1198, s. 1; 2000-179, s. 2.)

§ 159D-16. Conflict of interest.

If any officer, commissioner or employee of the agency is interested either directly or indirectly in any contract with the agency, such interest shall be disclosed to the agency and shall be set forth in the minutes of the agency, and the officer, commissioner, employee or member having such interest shall not participate on behalf of the agency in the authorization of the project. This section does not apply to the ownership of less than one percent (1%) of the stock of any operator or obligor. Failure to take any or all actions necessary to carry out the purposes of this section does not affect the validity of bonds issued pursuant to the provisions of this Article. (1977, 2nd Sess., c. 1198, s. 1; 2000-179, s. 2.)

§ 159D-17. Credit of State not pledged.

Bonds issued under the provisions of this Article do not constitute a debt of the State or any political subdivision or a pledge of the faith and credit of the State or any political subdivisions, but shall be payable solely from the revenues and other funds provided for payment. Each bond issued under this Chapter shall contain on its face a statement to the effect that the agency shall not be obligated to pay the bonds or the interest on it except from the revenues and other funds pledged for payment and that neither the faith and credit nor the taxing power of the State or any political subdivision is pledged to the payment of the principal of or the interest on the bonds. (1977, 2nd Sess., c. 1198, s. 1; 2000-179, s. 2.)

§ 159D-18. Bonds eligible for investment.

Bonds issued by the agency under the provisions of this Article are securities in which all public officers and agencies of the State and all political subdivisions, and all insurance companies, trust companies, banking associations, investment companies, executors, administrators, trustees and other fiduciaries may properly and legally invest funds, including capital in their control or belonging to them. (1977, 2nd Sess., c. 1198, s. 1.; 2000-179, s. 2.)

§ 159D-19. Revenue refunding bonds.

(a) The agency is authorized to provide by resolution for the issuance of refunding bonds of the agency for the purpose of refunding any bonds then outstanding that have been issued under the provisions of this Article, or under the provisions of Chapter 159C of the General Statutes, including the payment of any redemption premium and any interest accrued or to accrue to the date of redemption of such bonds, and, if considered advisable by the agency, for either or both of the following additional purposes:

(1) Constructing improvements, additions, extensions or enlargements of the project or projects in connection with which the bonds to be refunded shall have been issued; and

(2) Paying all or any part of the cost of any additional project or projects.

(a1) The issuance of bonds, the maturities and other details thereof, the rights of the holders thereof, and the rights, duties and obligations of the agency in respect to the bonds are governed by the provisions of this Article that relate to the issuance of bonds.

The approvals required by G.S. 159D-7 and G.S. 159D-8 shall be obtained prior to the issuance of any refunding bonds, except that in the case where the refunding bonds of all or a portion of an issue are to be issued solely for the purpose of refunding outstanding bonds issued under this Article, the approval required by G.S. 159D-7 is not required as to the project financed with the bonds to be refunded.

(b) Refunding bonds issued under this section may be sold or exchanged for outstanding bonds issued under this Article and, if sold, the proceeds may be applied, in addition to any other authorized purposes, to the purchase, redemption or payment of such outstanding bonds. Refunding bonds may be issued, in the determination of the agency, at any time not more than five years prior to the date of maturity or maturities or the date selected for the redemption of the bonds being refunded thereby. Pending the application of the proceeds of such refunding bonds, with any other available funds, to the payment of the principal of and accrued interest and any redemption premium on the bonds being refunded, and, if so provided or permitted in the security document securing the bonds to the payment of any interest on such refunding bonds, such proceeds may be invested in direct obligations of, or obligations the principal of and the interest on which are unconditionally guaranteed by, the United States of America if these obligations mature or are subject to redemption by the holder, at the holder's option not later than the respective dates when the proceeds, together with the interest accruing on them will be required for the purposes intended. (1977, 2nd Sess., c. 1198, s. 1; 1987, c. 517, s. 8; 2000-179, s. 2.)

§ 159D-20. No power of eminent domain.

The agency shall not have any right or power to acquire any property through the exercise of eminent domain or any proceedings in the nature of eminent domain. (1977, 2nd Sess., c. 1198, s. 1; 2000-179, s. 2.)

§ 159D-21: Repealed by Session Laws 2000-179, s. 2.

§ 159D-22: Repealed by Session Laws 2000-179, s. 2.

§ 159D-23: Repealed by Session Laws 2001-218, s. 5.

§ 159D-24. Officers not liable.

No member of the Board of Directors of the agency shall be subject to any personal liability or accountability by reason of the issuance or execution of any bonds. (1977, 2nd Sess., c. 1198, s. 1; 2000-179, s. 2.)

§ 159D-25. Additional method.

The foregoing sections of this Article provide an additional and alternative method for the doing of the things authorized and are supplemental and additional to powers conferred by other laws. They do not derogate any other powers. The issuance of bonds or refunding bonds under the provisions of this Article need not comply with the requirements of any other law applicable to the issuance of bonds. (1977, 2nd Sess., c. 1198, s. 1; 2000-179, s. 2.)

§ 159D-26. Liberal construction.

This Article, being necessary for the prosperity and welfare of the State and its inhabitants, shall be liberally construed to effect its purposes. (1977, 2nd Sess., c. 1198, s. 1; 2000-179, s. 2.)

§ 159D-27. Inconsistent laws inapplicable.

Insofar as the provisions of this Article are inconsistent with the provisions of any general, special or local laws, or parts thereof, the provisions of this Article shall be controlling. (1977, 2nd Sess., c. 1198, s. 1; 2000-179, s. 2.)

§§ 159D-28 through 159D-34. Reserved for future codification purposes.

Article 2.

Private Capital Facilities Finance Act.

§ 159D-35. Short title.

This Article shall be known, and may be cited, as the "Private Capital Facilities Finance Act." (1985 (Reg. Sess., 1986), c. 794, s. 1; 1998-124, s. 2; 2000-179, s. 2.)

§ 159D-36. Legislative findings.

It is declared that for the benefit of the people of the State of North Carolina, the increase of their commerce, welfare and prosperity and the improvement of their health and living conditions it is essential that they be given the fullest opportunity to learn and to develop their intellectual capacities; that it is essential for institutions for higher education and institutions for elementary and secondary education within the State to be able to construct and renovate facilities to assist its citizens in achieving the fullest development of their intellectual capacities; and that it is the purpose of this Article to provide a measure of assistance and an alternative method to enable private institutions for higher education and institutions for elementary and secondary education in the State to provide the facilities and the structures that are needed to accomplish the purposes of this Article, all to the public benefit and good, to the extent and in the manner provided in this Article.

It is further declared that this purpose will benefit the people as a way to improve student learning, increase learning opportunities for all students, encourage the use of different and innovative teaching methods, create new professional opportunities for teachers, provide parents and students with expanded choices in the types of educational opportunities that are available, and lower the overall cost of education to the State and to parents and students.

The General Assembly also finds that the private sector often provides services and opportunities to the people of the State of North Carolina in activities that constitute a public purpose, and that these activities by the private sector are to be fostered and encouraged. The people of the State of North Carolina will benefit from the enactment of laws and creation of programs that assist the private sector in obtaining financing for capital improvements of facilities that will be used in conducting these activities. (1985 (Reg. Sess., 1986), c. 794, s. 2; 1998-124, s. 3; 2000-179, s. 2.)

§ 159D-37. Definitions.

As used or referred to in this Article, the following words and terms have the following meanings, unless the context clearly indicates otherwise:

(1)   "Agency" means the North Carolina Capital Facilities Finance Agency or, should this agency be abolished or otherwise divested of its functions under this Article, the public body succeeding it in its principal functions, or upon which are conferred by law the rights, powers and duties given by this Article to the agency.

(1a)   "Bonds" or "notes" means the revenue bonds or bond anticipation notes, respectively, authorized to be issued by the agency under this Article, including revenue refunding bonds, notwithstanding that they may be secured by a deed of trust or the full faith and credit of a participating institution or any other lawfully pledged security of a participating institution.

(2) "Cost", as applied to any project or any portion of a project financed under the provisions of this Article, means all or any part of the cost of construction, acquisition, alteration, enlargement, reconstruction and remodeling of a project, including all lands, structures, real or personal property, rights, rights-of-way, franchises, easements and interests acquired or used for or in connection with a project, the cost of demolishing or removing any buildings or structures on land so acquired, including the cost of acquiring any lands to which such buildings or structures may be moved, the cost of all machinery and equipment, financing charges, interest prior to and during construction and, if deemed advisable by the agency, for a period not exceeding two years after the estimated date of completion of construction, the cost of engineering and architectural surveys, plans and specifications, the cost of consulting and legal services and other expenses necessary or incident to determining the feasibility or practicability of constructing or equipping a project, the cost of administrative and other expenses necessary or incident to the construction or acquisition of a project and the financing of the construction or acquisition thereof, including reasonable provision for working capital and a reserve for debt service, and the cost of reimbursing any participating institution for any payments made for any cost described above or the refinancing of any cost described above, including any evidence of indebtedness incurred to finance such cost; provided, however, that no payment shall be reimbursed or any cost or indebtedness be refinanced if such payment was made or such cost or indebtedness was incurred before November 25, 1981.

(3), (4) Repealed by Session Laws 2000, c. 179. s. 2, effective July 1, 2000.

(4a) "Institution for elementary and secondary education" means a nonprofit institution within the State of North Carolina authorized by law and engaged or to be engaged in the providing of kindergarten, elementary, or secondary education, or any combination of these.

(5) "Institution for higher education" means a nonprofit private educational institution within the State of North Carolina authorized by law to provide a program of education beyond the high school level.

(6) "Participating institution" means an institution for higher education, an institution for elementary and secondary education, or a special purpose institution that, pursuant to the provisions of this Article, undertakes the financing, refinancing, acquiring, constructing, equipping, providing, owning, repairing, maintaining, extending, improving, rehabilitating, renovating, or

furnishing of a project or undertakes the refunding or refinancing of obligations or of a deed of trust or a mortgage or of advances as provided in this Article.

(6a) "Project" means any one or more buildings, structures, equipment, improvements, additions, extensions, enlargements, or other facilities comprising any of the following:

a. Educational facilities used by an institution for higher education or an institution for elementary and secondary education, including dormitories and other housing facilities, housing facilities for student nurses, dining halls and other food preparation and food service facilities, student unions, administration buildings, academic buildings, libraries, laboratories, research facilities, classrooms, athletic facilities, health care facilities, laundry facilities, and other structures or facilities related to these facilities or required or useful for the instruction of students, the conducting of research, or the operation of the institution.

b. Student housing facilities to be owned or operated by an owner or operator other than an institution for higher education or an institution for elementary and secondary education.

c. A special purpose project as defined in G.S. 159C-3.

The term "project" includes landscaping, site preparation, furniture, equipment and machinery, and other similar items necessary or convenient for operation of a particular facility in the manner for which its use is intended. The term also includes all appurtenances and incidental facilities, such as headquarters or office facilities, maintenance, storage, or utility facilities, parking facilities, and other facilities related to, required, or useful for the operation of the project or essential or convenient for the orderly conduct of the facility. The term "project" does not include the cost of items that customarily result in a current operating charge, such as books, fuel, or supplies. The term does not include any facility used or to be used for sectarian instruction or as a place of religious worship nor any facility that is used or to be used primarily in connection with any part of the program of a school or department of divinity for any religious denomination.

(6b) "Special purpose institution" means a for-profit or not-for-profit corporation or similar entity that undertakes any of the activities set forth in sub-subdivisions (6a)b. and (6a)c. of this section.

(7) "State" means the State of North Carolina. (1985 (Reg. Sess., 1986), c. 794, s. 3; 1998-124, s. 4; 2000-179, s. 2; 2007-128, s. 2.)

§ 159D-38. Capital facilities finance agency.

(a) There is created a body politic and corporate to be known as "North Carolina Capital Facilities Finance Agency" which shall be constituted a public agency and an instrumentality of the State for the performance of essential public functions. The agency shall be governed by a board of directors composed of seven members. Two of the members of the board shall be the State Treasurer and the State Auditor, both of whom shall serve ex officio. The remaining directors of the agency shall be residents of the State and shall not hold other public office. The General Assembly upon the recommendation of the President Pro Tempore of the Senate shall appoint one director in accordance with G.S. 120-121, the General Assembly upon the recommendation of the Speaker of the House of Representatives shall appoint one director in accordance with G.S. 120-121, and the Governor shall appoint three directors of the agency. The five appointive directors of the agency shall be appointed for staggered four-year terms, two being appointed initially for one year by the President of the Senate and the Speaker of the House, respectively, and one for two years, one for three years and one for four years, respectively, as designated by the Governor. Each director shall continue in office until a successor is duly appointed and qualified, except that any person appointed to fill a vacancy shall serve only for the unexpired term. Any vacancy in a position held by an appointive member shall be filled by a new appointment made by the officer who originally made the appointment. Any member of the board of directors is eligible for reappointment. Each appointive member of the board of directors may be removed by the Governor for misfeasance, malfeasance or neglect of duty after reasonable notice and a public hearing, unless the notice and hearing are in writing expressly waived. Each appointive member of the board of directors shall take an oath of office to administer the duties of office faithfully and impartially and a record of the oath shall be filed in the office of the Secretary of State. The Governor shall designate from among the members of the board of directors a chair and a vice-chair, whose terms extend to the earlier of either two years or the date of expiration of their then current terms as members of the board of directors of the agency. The board of directors shall elect and appoint and prescribe the duties of a secretary-treasurer and any other officers it considers necessary or advisable, which officers need not be members of the board of directors.

(b) No part of the revenues or assets of the agency shall inure to the benefit of or be distributable to its members or officers or other private persons. The members of the agency shall receive no compensation for their services but shall be entitled to receive, for attendance at meetings of the agency or any committee thereof and for other services for the agency, reimbursement for such actual expenses as may be incurred for travel and subsistence in the performance of official duties and such per diem as is allowed by law for members of other State boards, commissions and committees.

(c) The secretary-treasurer of the agency shall keep a record of the proceedings of the agency and shall be custodian of all books, documents and papers filed with the agency, the minute book or journal of the agency and its official seal. The secretary-treasurer shall have authority to cause copies to be made of all minutes and other records and documents of the agency and to give certificates under the official seal of the agency to the effect that such copies are true copies, and all persons dealing with the agency may rely upon such certificates.

(d) Four members of the board of directors of the agency shall constitute a quorum and the affirmative vote of a majority of the members present at a meeting of the board of directors duly called and held shall be necessary for any action taken by the board of directors of the agency. The board of directors may, however, appoint an executive committee to act on behalf of the board during the period between regular meetings of said board, and said committee shall have full power to act upon the vote of a majority of its members. No vacancy in the membership of the agency impairs the rights of a quorum to exercise all the rights and to perform all the duties of the agency.

(e) The North Carolina Capital Facilities Finance Agency shall be contained within the Department of State Treasurer as if it had been transferred to that department by a Type II transfer as defined in G.S. 143A-6(b). (1985 (Reg. Sess., 1986), c. 794, s. 4; 1995, c. 490, s. 17(a); 2000-179, s. 2.)

§ 159D-39. General powers.

The agency shall have all of the powers necessary or convenient to carry out and effectuate the purposes and provisions of this Article, including all of the following:

(1) To make and execute contracts and agreements necessary or incidental to the exercise of its powers and duties under this Article, Including loan agreements and agreements of sale or leases with, mortgages and deeds of trust and conveyances to participating institutions, persons, firms, corporations, governmental agencies and others and including credit enhancement agreements.

(2) To acquire by purchase, lease, gift or otherwise, or to obtain options for the acquisition of any property, real or personal, improved or unimproved, including interests in land in fee or less than fee for any project, upon such terms and at such cost as shall be agreed upon by the owner and the agency.

(3) To arrange or contract with any county, city, town or other political subdivision or instrumentality of the State for the opening or closing of streets or for the furnishing of utility or other services to any project.

(4) To sell, convey, lease as lessor, mortgage, exchange, transfer, grant a deed of trust in, or otherwise dispose of, or to grant options for these purposes with respect to, any real or personal property or interest in property.

(5) To pledge or assign any money, purchase price payments, rents, loan repayments, charges, fees or other revenues, including any federally guaranteed securities and moneys received from them whether the securities are initially acquired by the agency or a participating institution, and any proceeds derived by the agency from sales of property, insurance, condemnation awards or other sources.

(6) To pledge or assign the revenues and receipts from any project and from any loan agreement, agreement of sale, or lease, including any loan repayments, purchase price payments, rent, or other income received under a loan agreement, agreement of sale, or lease.

(7) To borrow money as provided in this Article to carry out and effectuate its corporate purposes and to issue bonds and notes for the purpose of providing funds to pay all or any part of the cost of any project, to lend money to any participating institution for the acquisition of any federally guaranteed securities, and to issue revenue refunding bonds.

(8) To finance, refinance, acquire, construct, equip, provide, operate, own, repair, maintain, extend, improve, rehabilitate, renovate and furnish any project and to pay all or any part of the cost thereof from the proceeds of bonds or

notes or from any contribution, gift or donation or other funds available to the agency for this purpose.

(9)   To fix, revise, charge and collect or cause to be fixed, revised, charged and collected purchase price payments, rents, loan repayments, fees, rates and charges for the use of, or services rendered by, any project.

(10)   To employ fiscal consultants, consulting engineers, architects, attorneys, feasibility consultants, appraisers and any other consultants and employees as may be required in the judgment of the agency and to fix and pay their compensation from funds available to the agency.

(11)   To conduct studies and surveys respecting the need for projects and their location, financing and construction.

(12)   To apply for, accept, receive and agree to and comply with the terms and conditions governing grants, loans, advances, contributions, interest subsidies and other aid with respect to any project from federal and State agencies or instrumentalities.

(13)   To sue and be sued in its own name, plead and be impleaded.

(14)   To acquire and enter into commitments to acquire any federally guaranteed security or federally insured mortgage note and to pledge or otherwise use the federally guaranteed security or federally insured mortgage note as the agency considers in its best interest to secure or otherwise provide a source of repayment on any of its bonds or notes issued on behalf of any participating institution to finance or refinance the cost of any project.

(15)   To make loans to any participating institution for the cost of a project in accordance with an agreement between the agency and the participating institution.

(16)   To make loans to a participating institution to refund outstanding loans, obligations, deeds of trust or advances issued, made or given by the participating institutions for the cost of a project.

(17)   To charge and to apportion among participating institutions its administrative costs and expenses incurred in the exercise of its powers and duties conferred by this Article.

(18) To adopt an official seal and alter it at pleasure.

(19) To do all other things necessary or convenient to carry out the purposes of this Article. (1985 (Reg. Sess., 1986), c. 794, s. 5; 1998-124, s. 5; 2000-179, s. 2.)

§ 159D-40. Criteria and requirements.

(a) In undertaking any project pursuant to this Article, the agency shall be guided by and shall observe the following criteria and requirements listed below. The determination of the agency as to its compliance with these criteria and requirements is conclusive.

(1) No project shall be sold or leased nor any loan made to any participating institution that is not financially responsible and capable of fulfilling its obligations, including its obligations under an agreement of sale or lease or a loan agreement to make purchase price payments, to pay rent, to make loan repayments, to operate, repair and maintain at its own expense the project and to discharge any other responsibilities imposed under the agreement of sale or lease or loan agreement.

(2) Adequate provision shall be made for the payment of the principal of and the interest on the bonds and any necessary reserves for payment and for the operation, repair and maintenance of the project at the expense of the participating institution.

(3) The public facilities, including utilities, and public services necessary for the project will be made available.

(4) The projects shall be operated to serve and benefit the public and there shall be no discrimination against any person based on race, creed, color, or national origin.

(b) In making these determinations, the agency may consider the participating institution's experience and ratio of current assets to current liabilities; the participating institution's net worth, earnings trends, and coverage of fixed charges; the nature of the project involved; and any additional security for payment of the bonds and performance of the participating institution's obligations under the agreement of sale or lease or loan agreement, such as credit enhancement, insurance, guaranties, or property pledged to secure the payment and performance. (1985 (Reg. Sess., 1986), c. 794, s. 6; 1998-124, s. 6; 2000-179, s. 2.)

§ 159D-41. Procedural requirements.

Any participating institution may submit to the agency, and the agency may consider, a proposal for financing a project using forms and following instructions prescribed by the agency. The proposal shall set forth the type and location of the project and may include other information and data respecting the project and the extent to which the project conforms to the criteria and requirements set forth in this Article. The agency may request the applicant to provide additional information and data respecting the project. The agency is authorized to make or cause to be made any investigation, surveys, studies, reports and reviews as in its judgment are necessary and desirable to determine the feasibility and desirability of the project, the extent to which the project will contribute to the health and welfare of the area in which it will be located, the powers, experience, background, financial condition, record of service and capability of the management of the applicant, the extent to which the project otherwise conforms to the criteria and requirements of this Article, and any other factors the agency considers relevant or convenient in carrying out the purposes of this Article. (1985 (Reg. Sess., 1986), c. 794, s. 7; 1998-124, s. 7; 2000-179, s. 2.)

§ 159D-42. Operations of projects; agreements of sale on leases; conveyance of interest in projects.

(a) The agency may sell or lease any project to a participating institution for operation and maintenance or lend money to any participating institution to effectuate the purposes of this Article, under a loan agreement or an agreement of sale or lease in form and substance not inconsistent with this Article. The loan agreement or agreement of sale or lease may include provisions that:

(1) The participating institution shall, at its own expense, operate, repair and maintain the project covered by the agreement.

(2) The purchase price payments to be made under the agreement of sale, the rent payable under the agreement of lease or the loan repayments under the loan agreement shall in the aggregate be not less than an amount sufficient to pay all of the interest, principal and any redemption premium on the bonds or

notes issued by the agency to pay the cost of the project sold or leased or with respect to which the loan was made.

(3)   The participating institution shall pay all other costs incurred by the agency in connection with the providing of the project covered by any agreement, except costs paid out of the proceeds of bonds or notes or otherwise, including insurance costs, the cost of administering the resolution authorizing the issuance of, or any trust agreement securing, the bonds or notes and the fees and expenses of trustees, paying agents, attorneys, consultants, and others.

(4)   The loan agreement or the agreement of sale or lease shall terminate not earlier than the date on which all bonds and all other obligations incurred by the agency in connection with the project covered by the agreement are retired or provision for their retirement is made.

(5)   The obligation of the participating institution to make loan repayments or purchase price payments or to pay rent shall not be subject to cancellation, termination or abatement by the participating institution until the bonds have been retired or provision has been made for their retirement.

(b)   If the agency has acquired a possessory or ownership interest in any project it has undertaken on behalf of a participating institution, it shall promptly convey, without the payment of any consideration, all its right, title and interest in the project to that participating institution upon the retirement or provision for the retirement of all bonds or notes issued and obligations incurred by the agency in connection with that project. (1985 (Reg. Sess., 1986), c. 794, s. 8; 1998-124, s. 8; 2000-179, s. 2.)

§ 159D-43. Construction contracts.

If the agency determines that the purposes of this Article will be more effectively served, the agency in its discretion may award or cause to be awarded contracts for the construction of any project on behalf of a participating institution upon a negotiated basis as determined by the agency. The agency shall prescribe any bid security requirements and other procedures in connection with the award of the contracts as in its judgment will protect the public interest. The agency may by written contract engage the services of the participating institution in the construction of the project and may provide in the contract that the participating institution, subject to any conditions and requirements consistent with the provisions of this Article prescribed in the contract, may act as an agent of, or an independent contractor for, the agency for the performance of the functions described in the contract including the acquisition of the site and other real property for the project, the preparation of plans, specifications and contract documents, the award of construction and other contracts upon a competitive or negotiated basis, the construction of the project directly by the participating institution, the inspection and supervision of construction, the employment of engineers, architects, builders and other contractors and the provision of money to pay the cost of these functions pending reimbursement by the agency. The contract may provide that the agency may, out of proceeds of bonds or notes, make advances to or reimburse the participating institution for its costs incurred in the performance of these functions, and shall set forth the supporting documents required to be submitted to the agency and the reviews, examinations and audits that are required in connection to assure compliance with the provisions of this Article and the contract. (1985 (Reg. Sess., 1986), c. 794, s. 9; 1998-124, s. 9; 2000-179, s. 2.)

§ 159D-44. Credit of State not pledged.

Bonds or notes issued under the provisions of this Article shall not be secured by a pledge of the faith and credit of the State or of any political subdivision of the State, or create an indebtedness of the State, or of any political subdivision of the State requiring any voter approval, but shall be payable solely from the revenues and other funds provided for payment. Each bond or note issued under this Article shall contain on its face a statement to the effect that the agency is not obligated to pay it nor the interest on it except from the revenues and other funds pledged for its payment and that neither the faith and credit nor the taxing power of the State or of any political subdivision of the State is pledged as security for the payment of the principal of or the interest on the bond or note.

Expenses incurred by the agency in carrying out the provisions of this Article may be made payable from funds provided pursuant to, or made available for use under, this Article and no liability shall be incurred by the agency under this Article beyond the extent to which moneys have been so provided. (1985 (Reg. Sess., 1986), c. 794, s. 10; 2000-179, s. 2.)

§ 159D-45. Bonds and notes.

(a)   The agency is authorized to provide for the issuance, at one time or from time to time, of bonds, or notes in anticipation of the issuance of bonds, of the agency to carry out and effectuate its corporate purposes. The principal of and the interest on such bonds or notes shall be payable solely from funds provided under this Article for such payment. Any such notes may be made payable from the proceeds of bonds or renewal notes or, in the event bond or renewal note proceeds are not available, such notes may be paid from any available revenues or other funds provided therefor. The bonds or notes of each issue shall be dated and may be made redeemable before maturity at the option of the agency at such price or prices and upon such terms and conditions as may be determined by the agency. The bonds may also be made payable from time to time on demand or tender for purchase by the owner upon such terms and conditions as may be determined by the agency. Any such bonds or notes shall bear interest at such rate or rates (including variable rates) as may be determined by the Local Government Commission with the approval of the agency. Notes shall mature at such time or times not exceeding 10 years from their date or dates and bonds shall mature at such time or times not exceeding 40 years from their date or dates, as may be determined by the agency. The agency shall determine the form and manner of execution of the bonds or notes, including any interest coupons to be attached thereto, and shall fix the denomination or denominations and the place or places of payment of principal and interest, which may be any bank or trust company within or without the State. In case any officer whose signature or a facsimile of whose signature appears on any bonds or notes or coupons attached to them ceases to be that officer before their delivery, the signature or facsimile shall nevertheless be valid and sufficient for all purposes the same as if the officer had remained in office until delivery. The agency may also provide for the authentication of the bonds or notes by a trustee or fiscal agent. The bonds or notes may be issued in coupon or in registered form, or both, as the agency may determine, and provision may be made for the registration of any coupon bonds or notes as to principal alone and also as to both principal and interest, and for the reconversion into coupon bonds or notes of any bonds or notes registered as to both principal and interest, and for the interchange of registered and coupon bonds or notes. No bonds or notes may be issued by the agency under this Article unless the issuance thereof is approved by the Local Government Commission.

(b)   The agency shall file with the Secretary of the Local Government Commission an application requesting approval of the issuance of the bonds or notes. The application must include any information and documents concerning the proposed financing and prospective borrower, vendee or lessee required by the Secretary.

In determining whether a proposed bond or note issue should be approved, the Local Government Commission may consider, in addition to the criteria and requirements in this Article, the effect of the proposed financing upon any scheduled or proposed sale of tax-exempt obligations by the State or any of its agencies or departments or by any unit of local government in the State.

The Local Government Commission shall approve the issuance of the bonds or notes if, upon the information and evidence it receives, it finds that the proposed financing will effectuate the purposes of this Article.

Upon the filing with the Local Government Commission of a resolution of the agency requesting that its bonds or notes be sold, the bonds or notes may be sold in such manner, either at public or private sale, and for such price as the Local Government Commission determines to be for the best interests of the agency and to effectuate best the purposes of this Article, as long as the sale is approved by the agency.

(c)   The proceeds of any bonds or notes shall be used solely for the purposes for which issued and shall be disbursed in such manner and under such restrictions, if any, as the agency may provide in the resolution authorizing the issuance of, or any trust agreement securing, the bonds or notes.

(d)   Prior to the preparation of definitive bonds, the agency may, under like restrictions, issue interim receipts or temporary bonds, with or without coupons, exchangeable for definitive bonds, when the bonds have been executed and are available for delivery. The agency may also provide for the replacement of any bonds or notes which become mutilated or are destroyed or lost.

(e)   Bonds or notes may be issued under the provisions of this Article without obtaining, except as otherwise expressly provided in this Article, the consent of any department, division, commission, board, body, bureau or agency of the State, and without any other proceedings or the happening of any conditions or things other than those proceedings, conditions or things specifically required by this Article and the provisions of the resolution authorizing the issuance of, or any trust agreement securing, the bonds or notes.

(f) Before the issuance of bonds pursuant to this Article to finance a project, the Agency shall hold a public hearing with respect to the proposed project and the issuance of the bonds to finance the proposed project. The public hearing may be held at any location designated by the Agency, including at the offices of the Agency in Raleigh, North Carolina.

The public hearing may be conducted by the Agency or by a hearing officer designated by the Agency to conduct public hearings. Notice of the public hearing must be published at least once in at least one newspaper of general circulation in the county where the proposed project is to be located not less than 14 days before the public hearing. The notice must describe generally the bonds proposed to be issued and the proposed project, including its general location, and any other information the Agency considers appropriate. A copy of the notice of public hearing must be mailed to the clerk of the Board of Commissioners of the county in which the proposed project is to be located and to the governing body of any city or town in which the proposed project is to be operated.

(g) A county or city that receives an allocation to issue recovery zone facility bonds within the meaning of the American Recovery and Reinvestment Tax Act of 2009 to finance recovery zone property may designate the agency as the governmental entity authorized to issue recovery zone facility bonds. (1985 (Reg. Sess., 1986), c. 794, s. 11; 2000-179, s. 2; 2009-140, s. 9.)

§ 159D-46. Trust agreement or resolution.

In the discretion of the agency any bonds or notes issued under the provisions of this Article may be secured by a trust agreement by and between the agency and a corporate trustee, which may be any trust company or bank having the powers of a trust company within or without the State. Such trust agreement or the resolution authorizing the issuance of such bonds or notes may pledge or assign all or any part of the revenues of the agency received pursuant to this Article, including, without limitation, fees, loan repayments, purchase price payments, rents, charges, insurance proceeds, condemnation awards and any other revenues and funds received in connection with any project and may grant a deed of trust or a mortgage on any project. Such trust agreement or resolution may contain such provisions for protecting and enforcing the rights and remedies of the holders of any such bonds or notes as may be reasonable and proper and not in violation of law, including covenants setting forth the duties of the agency in relation to the purposes to which bond or note proceeds may be applied, the disposition or pledging of the revenues of the agency, including any payments in respect of any federally guaranteed security or any federally insured mortgage note, the duties of the agency with respect to the acquisition, construction, maintenance, repair and operation of any project, the fees, loan repayments, purchase price payments, rents and charges to be fixed and collected in connection therewith, the terms and conditions for the issuance of additional bonds or notes, and the custody, safeguarding and application of all moneys. All bonds issued under this Article shall be equally and ratably secured by a pledge, charge, and lien upon revenues provided for in such trust agreement or resolution, without priority by reason of number, or of dates of bonds, execution, or delivery, in accordance with the provisions of this Article and of such trust agreement or resolution; except that the agency may provide in such trust agreement or resolution that bonds issued pursuant thereto shall to the extent and in the manner prescribed in such trust agreement or resolution be subordinated and junior in standing, with respect to the payment of principal and interest and the security thereof, to any other bonds. It shall be lawful for any bank or trust company incorporated under the laws of the State which may act as depositary of the proceeds of bonds or notes, revenues or other money hereunder to furnish such indemnifying bonds or to pledge such securities as may be required by the agency. Any such trust agreement or resolution may set off the rights and remedies, including foreclosure of any deed of trust or mortgage, of the holders of any bonds or notes and of the trustee, and may restrict the individual right of action by any such holders. In addition to the foregoing, any such trust agreement or resolution may contain such other provisions as the agency considers reasonable and proper for the security of the holders of any bonds or notes. Expenses incurred in carrying out the provisions of such trust agreement or resolution may be treated as a part of the cost of any project or paid from the revenues pledged or assigned to the payment of the principal of and the interest on bonds or notes or from any other funds available to the agency. (1985 (Reg. Sess., 1986), c. 794, s. 12; 2000-179, s. 2.)

§ 159D-47. Revenues; pledges of revenues.

(a) The agency is authorized to fix and to collect fees, loan repayments, purchase price payments, rents and charges for the use of any project, and any part or section of the project and to contract with any participating institution for its use. The agency may require that the participating institution operate, repair or maintain such project and bear the cost and other costs of the agency in connection with the project all as may be provided in the agreement of sale or lease, loan agreement or other contract with the agency, in addition to other obligations imposed under the agreement or contract.

(b) The fees, loan repayments, purchase price payments, rents and charges shall be fixed so as to provide a fund sufficient, with any other available funds, (i) to pay the costs of operating, repairing and maintaining the project to the extent that adequate provision for the payment of such costs has not otherwise been provided for, (ii) to pay the principal of and the interest on all bonds or notes as they become due and payable and (iii) to create and maintain any reserves provided for in the resolution authorizing the issuance of, or any trust agreement securing, the bonds. The fees, loan repayments, purchase price payments, rents and charges may be applied or pledged to the payment of debt service on the bonds prior to the payment of the costs of operating, repairing and maintaining the project.

(c) All pledges of fees, loan repayments, purchase price payments, rents, charges and other revenues under the provisions of this Article are valid and binding from the time when they are made. All revenues so pledged and thereafter received by the agency are immediately subject to the lien of the pledge without any physical delivery or further act, and the lien of the pledge is valid and binding as against all parties having claims of any kind in tort, contract or otherwise against the agency, irrespective of whether the parties have notice of it. The resolution or any trust agreement by which a pledge is created or any loan agreement, agreement of sale or lease need not be filed or recorded except in the records of the agency.

(d) The State of North Carolina pledges to and agrees with the holders of any bonds or notes issued by the agency that so long as any of the bonds or notes are outstanding and unpaid the State will not limit or alter the rights vested in the agency at the time of issuance of the bonds or notes to fix, revise, charge, and collect or cause to be fixed, revised, charged and collected loan repayments, purchase price payments, rents, fees and charges for the use of or services rendered by any project in connection with which the bonds or notes were issued, so as to provide a fund sufficient, with any other available funds to pay the costs of operating, repairing and maintaining the project, to pay the principal of and the interest on all bonds and notes as they become due and payable, to create and maintain any reserves provided for their payment, and to fulfill the terms of any agreements made with the bondholders or noteholders. The State will not in any way impair the rights and remedies of the bondholders or noteholders until the bonds or notes and all costs and expenses in connection with any action or proceedings by or on behalf of the bondholders or noteholders, are fully paid, met and discharged. (1985 (Reg. Sess., 1986), c. 794, s. 13; 1998-124, s. 10; 2000-179, s. 2.)

§ 159D-48. Trust funds.

Notwithstanding any other provisions of law to the contrary, all moneys received pursuant to the authority of this Article, including fees, loan repayments, purchase price payments, rents, charges, insurance proceeds, condemnation awards and any other revenues and funds received in connection with any project, are trust funds to be held and applied solely as provided in this Article. The resolution authorizing the issuance of, or any trust agreement securing, any bonds or notes may provide that any of these moneys may be temporarily invested pending their disbursement and shall provide that any officer with whom, or any bank or trust company with which, such moneys are deposited shall act as trustee of such moneys and shall hold and apply them for the purposes of this Article, subject to any limitations provided in this Article and in the resolution or trust agreement. The moneys may be invested as provided in G.S. 159-30, as it may from time to time be amended. (1985 (Reg. Sess., 1986), c. 794, s. 14; 2000-179, s. 2.)

§ 159D-49. Remedies.

Any holder of bonds or notes issued under the provisions of this Article or any coupons appertaining thereto, and the trustee under any trust agreement or resolution authorizing the issuance of such bonds or notes, except to the extent the rights herein given may be restricted by such trust agreement or resolution, may, either at law or in equity, by suit, action, mandamus or other proceeding, protect and enforce any and all rights under the laws of the State or granted hereunder or under such trust agreement or resolution, or under any other contract executed by the agency pursuant to this Article, and may enforce and compel the performance of all duties required by this Article or by such trust agreement or resolution to be performed by the agency or by any officer of the agency. (1985 (Reg. Sess., 1986), c. 794, s. 15; 2000-179, s. 2.)

§ 159D-50. Investment securities.

All bonds, notes and interest coupons issued under this Article are investment securities within the meaning of and for all the purposes of Article 8 of the Uniform Commercial Code as enacted in this State, whether or not they are of such form and character as to be investment securities under that Article, subject only to the provisions of the bonds and notes pertaining to registration. (1985 (Reg. Sess., 1986), c. 794, s. 16; 2000-179, s. 2.)

§ 159D-51. Bonds or notes eligible for investment.

Bonds or notes issued under the provisions of this Article are securities in which all public officers and public bodies of the State and its political subdivisions, and all insurance companies, trust companies, banking associations, investment companies, executors, administrators, trustees and other fiduciaries may properly and legally invest funds, including capital in their control or belonging to them. These bonds or notes are securities which may properly and legally be deposited with and received by any State or municipal officer or any agency or political subdivision of the State for any purpose for which the deposit of bonds, notes or obligations of this State is authorized by law. (1985 (Reg. Sess., 1986), c. 794, s. 17; 2000-179, s. 2.)

§ 159D-52. Refunding bonds or notes.

(a)   The agency is authorized to provide for the issuance of refunding bonds or notes for the purpose of refunding any bonds or notes then outstanding which have been issued under the provisions of this Article, including the payment of any redemption premium and any interest accrued or to accrue to the date of redemption of the bonds or notes and, if considered advisable by the agency, for any corporate purpose of the agency, including, without limitation:

(1)   Constructing improvements, additions, extensions or enlargements of the project in connection with which the bonds or notes to be refunded shall have been issued, and

(2)   Paying all or any part of the cost of any additional project.

(b) The issuance of refunding bonds or notes, their maturities and other details the rights of their holders, and the rights, duties and obligations of the agency are governed by the provisions of this Article which relate to the issuance of bonds or notes, as appropriate.

Refunding bonds may be sold or exchanged for outstanding bonds issued under this Article and, if sold, their proceeds, and investment earnings on them, may be applied, with any other available funds, to the purchase, redemption, or payment of the bonds being refunded, to the payment of any interest on the refunding bonds, and to the payment of any expenses in connection with the refunding. The proceeds may be invested in direct obligations of, or obligations the principal of and the interest on which are unconditionally guaranteed by, the United States of America if the obligations mature or are subject to redemption by the holders, at their option not later than the respective dates when the proceeds, together with the interest accrued thereon, will be required for the purposes intended. (1985 (Reg. Sess., 1986), c. 794, s. 18; 2000-179, s. 2.)

§ 159D-53. Annual report.

The agency shall, promptly following the close of each fiscal year, submit an annual report of its activities under this Article for the preceding year to the Governor, the State Auditor, the General Assembly, and the Local Government Commission. The agency shall cause an audit of its books and accounts relating to its activities under this Article to be made at least once in each year by an independent certified public accountant and the cost of the audit may be paid from any available moneys of the agency. (1985 (Reg. Sess., 1986), c. 794, s. 19; 2000-179, s. 2; 2010-96, s. 34.)

§ 159D-54. Officers not liable.

No member or officer of the agency shall be subject to any personal liability or accountability by reason of the issuance or execution of any bonds or notes. (1985 (Reg. Sess., 1986), c. 794, s. 20; 2000-179, s. 2.)

§ 159D-55. Tax exemption.

The exercise of the powers granted by this Article will bo in all respects for the benefit of the people of the State and will promote their health and welfare.

Any bonds or notes issued by the agency under the provisions of this Article are at all times be free from taxation by the State or any local unit or political subdivision or other instrumentality of the State, excepting inheritance or gift taxes, income taxes on the gain from the transfer of the bonds and notes, and franchise taxes. The interest on the bonds and notes is not subject to taxation as income. (1985 (Reg. Sess., 1986), c. 794, s. 21; 1995, c. 46, s. 5; 2000-179, s. 2.)

§ 159D-56. Conflict of interest.

If any member, officer or employee of the agency is interested either directly or indirectly, or is an officer or employee of or has an ownership interest in any firm or corporation interested directly or indirectly, in any contract with the agency, this interest shall be disclosed to the agency and shall be set forth in the minutes of the agency, and the member, officer or employee having an interest in a contract shall not participate on behalf of the agency in the authorization of the contract. (1985 (Reg. Sess., 1986), c. 794, s. 22; 2000-179, s. 2.)

§ 159D-57. Additional method.

The foregoing sections of this Article provide an additional and alternative method for the doing of the things authorized and are supplemental and additional to powers conferred by other laws. This Article does not derogate any existing powers. The issuance of bonds or notes under the provisions of this Article need not comply with the requirements of any other law applicable to the issuance of bonds or notes. (1985 (Reg. Sess., 1986), c. 794, s. 23; 2000-179, s. 2.)

§§ 159D-58 through 159D-64: Reserved for future codification purposes.

Article 3.

Life Sciences Revenue Bond Authority.

§ 159D-65: Repealed by Session Laws 2007-527, s. 40, effective August 31, 2007.

§ 159D-66: Repealed by Session Laws 2007-527, s. 40, effective August 31, 2007.

§ 159D-67: Repealed by Session Laws 2007-527, s. 40, effective August 31, 2007.

§ 159D-68: Repealed by Session Laws 2007-527, s. 40, effective August 31, 2007.

§ 159D-69: Repealed by Session Laws 2007-527, s. 40, effective August 31, 2007.

Chapter 159E.

Registered Public Obligations Act.

§ 159E-1. Short title.

This Chapter may be cited as the "Registered Public Obligations Act." (1983, c. 322, s. 1.)

§ 159E-2. Definitions.

As used in this Chapter, the following terms have the following meanings, unless the context otherwise requires:

(1) "Authorized officer" means any individual required or permitted, alone or with others, by any provision of law or by the issuing public entity, to execute on behalf of the public entity a certificated registered public obligation or a writing relating to an uncertificated registered public obligation.

(2) "Certificated registered public obligation" means a registered public obligation which is represented by an instrument.

(3) "Code" means the Internal Revenue Code of 1954, as amended.

(4) "Commission" means the Local Government Commission,

(5) "Facsimile seal" means the reproduction by engraving, imprinting, stamping, or other means of the seal of the issuer, official or official body.

(6) "Facsimile signature" means the reproduction by engraving, imprinting, stamping, or other means of the manual signature.

(7) "Financial intermediary" means a bank, broker, clearing corporation or other person or the custodian for or nominee of any of them which in the ordinary course of its business maintains registered public obligation accounts for its customers, when so acting.

(8) "Issuer" means a public entity which issues an obligation.

(9) "Obligation" means an agreement of a public entity issuer to pay principal and any interest thereon, whether in the form of a contract to repay borrowed money, a lease, an installment purchase agreement or otherwise, and includes a share, participation, or other interest in any such agreement.

(10) "Official actions" means the actions by statute, order, ordinance, resolution, contract, or other authorized means by which the issuer provides for issuance of a registered public obligation.

(11) "Official or official body" means the officer or board that is empowered under the laws applicable to an issuer to provide for original issuance of an obligation of the issuer, by defining the obligation and its terms, conditions and other incidents, the successor or successors of any such official or official body, and such other person or group of persons as shall be assigned duties of such official or official body with respect to a registered public obligation under applicable law from time to time. Unless otherwise provided by law, the State Treasurer shall be the "official" for the issuance of all State obligations.

(12) "Public entity" means any entity, department, or agency which is empowered under the laws of this State, to issue obligations any interest with respect to which may, under any provision of law, be provided an exemption from the income tax referred to in the Code. The term "public entity" may thus include, without limitation, this State, an entity deriving powers from and acting pursuant to the State Constitution or a special legislative act, a political subdivision, a municipal corporation, a State university or college, a special district, a public authority and other similar entities.

(13)   "Registered public obligation" means an obligation issued by a public entity pursuant to a system of registration.

(14)   "System of registration" and its variants means a plan that provides:

a.   With respect to a certificated registered public obligation, that (i) the certificated registered public obligation specify a person entitled to the registered public obligation or the rights it represents, and (ii) transfer of the certificated registered public obligation and the rights it represents may be registered upon books maintained for that purpose by or on behalf of the issuer; and

b.   With respect to an uncertificated registered public obligation, that (i) books maintained by or on behalf of the issuer for the purpose of registration of the transfer of a registered public obligation specify a person entitled to the registered public obligation and the rights evidenced thereby, and (ii) transfer of the uncertificated registered public obligation and the rights evidenced thereby be registered upon such books.

(15)   "Uncertificated registered public obligation" means a registered public obligation which is not represented by an instrument. (1983, c. 322, s. 1.)

§ 159E-3. Declaration of State interest; purposes.

(a)   The Code provides that interest with respect to certain obligations may not be exempt from federal income taxation unless they are in registered form. It is therefore a matter of State concern that public entities be authorized to provide for the issuance of obligations in such form. It is a purpose of this Chapter to empower all public entities to establish and maintain a system pursuant to which obligations may be issued in registered form within the meaning of the applicable provisions of the Code.

(b)   Obligations have traditionally been issued predominantly in bearer rather than in registered form, and a change from bearer to registered form may affect the relationships, rights and duties of issuers of and the persons that deal with obligations, and by such effect, the costs. Such effects will impact the various issuers and varieties of obligations differently depending on their legal and financial characteristics, their markets and their adaptability to recent and prospective technological and organizational developments. It is therefore a matter of State concern that public entities be provided flexibility in the development of such systems and control over system incidents, so as to accommodate such differing impacts. It is a purpose of this Chapter to empower the establishment and maintenance, and amendment from time to time, of differing systems of registration of obligations, including system incidents, so as to accommodate the differing impacts upon issuers and varieties of obligations. It is further a purpose of this Chapter to authorize systems that will facilitate the prompt and accurate transfer of registered public obligations and the development of practices with regard to the registration and transfer of registered public obligations in order to maintain market acceptance for obligations of public entities. (1983, c. 322, s. 1.)

§ 159E-4. Systems of registration.

(a) Each issuer, with the approval of the Commission, is authorized to establish and maintain a system of registration with respect to each obligation which it issues. The system may either be (i) a system pursuant to which only certificated registered public obligations are issued, or (ii) a system pursuant to which only uncertificated registered public obligations are issued, or (iii) a system pursuant to which both certificated and uncertificated registered public obligations are issued. The issuer may amend, discontinue and reinstitute any system, from time to time, subject to covenants.

(b) The system shall be established, amended, discontinued, or reinstituted, for the issuer by the official or official body.

(c) The system shall be described in the registered public obligation or in the official actions which provide for original issuance of the registered public obligation, and in subsequent official actions providing for amendments and other matters from time to time. Such description may be by reference to a program of the issuer which is established by the official or official body.

(d) The system shall define the method or methods by which transfer of the public obligations shall be effective with respect to the issuer, and by which payment of principal and any interest shall be made. The system may permit the issuance of registered public obligations in any denomination to represent several registered public obligations of smaller denominations. The system may also provide for the form of any certificated registered public obligation, or of any writing relating to an uncertificated registered public obligation, for identifying numbers or other designations, for a sufficient supply of certificates for subsequent transfers, for record and payment dates, for varying denominations, for communications to holders or owners of obligations, and for accounting, cancelled certificate destruction and other incidental matters. Unless the issuer otherwise provides, the record date for interest payable on the first or fifteenth day of a month shall be the fifteenth day or the last business day of the preceding month, respectively, and for interest payable on other than the first or fifteenth day of a month, shall be the fifteenth calendar day before the interest payment date.

(e) Under a system pursuant to which both certificated and uncertificated registered public obligations are issued, both types of registered public obligations may be regularly issued, or one type may be regularly issued and the other type issued only under described circumstances or to particular described categories of owners.

(f) The system may include covenants of the issuer as to amendments, discontinuances, and reinstitutions of the system and the effect of such on the exemption of interest from the income tax provided for by the Code.

(g) Whenever an issuer shall issue an uncertificated registered public obligation, the system of registration may provide that a true copy of the official actions of the issuer relating to such uncertificated registered public obligation be maintained by the issuer or by the person, if any, maintaining such system on behalf of the issuer, so long as the uncertificated registered public obligation remains outstanding and unpaid. A copy of such official actions, verified to be such by an authorized officer, shall be admissible before any court of record, administrative body or arbitration panel without further authentication.

(h) Nothing in this Chapter shall preclude a conversion from one of the forms of registered public obligations provided for by this Chapter to a form of obligation not provided for by this Chapter if interest on the obligation so converted will continue to be exempt from the income tax provided for by the Code.

(i) The rights provided by other laws with respect to obligations in forms not provided for by this Chapter shall, to the extent not inconsistent with this Chapter, apply with respect to registered public obligations issued in forms authorized by this Chapter. This includes Subchapter IV of Chapter 159 of the General Statutes and the "State Debt" provisions of Chapter 142 of the General Statutes. (1983, c. 322, s. 1.)

§ 159E-5. Certificated registered public obligations; execution; authentication.

(a) A certificated registered public obligation shall be executed by the issuer by the manual or facsimile signature or signatures of authorized officers. Any signature of an authorized officer may be attested by the manual or facsimile signature of another authorized officer.

(b) In addition to the signatures referred to in (a) of this section any certificated registered public obligation or any writing relating to an uncertificated registered public obligation may include a certificate or certificates signed by the manual or facsimile signature of an authenticating agent, registrar, transfer agent or the like. (1983, c. 322, s. 1; 1987, c. 282, s. 29.)

§ 159E-6. Certificated registered public obligation; signatures.

(a) Any certificated registered public obligation signed by the authorized officers at the time of the signing thereof shall remain valid and binding, notwithstanding that before the issuance thereof any or all of such officers shall have ceased to fill their respective offices.

(b) Any authorized officer empowered to sign any certificated registered public obligation may adopt as and for the signature of such officer the signature of a predecessor in office in the event that such predecessor's signature appears on such certificated registered public obligation. An unauthorized officer incurs no liability by adoption of a predecessor's signature that would not be incurred by such authorized officer if the signature were that of such authorized officer. (1983, c. 322, s. 1.)

§ 159E-7. Certificated registered public obligation; seal.

When a seal is required or permitted in the execution of any certificated registered public obligation, an authorized officer may cause the seal to be printed, engraved, stamped, or otherwise placed in facsimile thereon. The facsimile seal has the same legal effect as the impression of the seal. (1983, c. 322, s. 1.)

§ 159E-8. Agents; depositories.

(a) An issuer, with the approval of the Commission, may appoint for such term as may be agreed, including for so long as a registered public obligation may be outstanding, corporate or other authenticating agents, transfer agents, registrars, paying or other agents and specify the terms of their appointment, including their rights, their compensation and duties, limits upon their liabilities and provision for their payment of liquidated damages in the event of breach of certain of the duties imposed, which liquidated damages may be made payable to the issuer, the owner or a financial intermediary. None of such agents need have an office or do business within this State.

(b) An issuer may agree with financial intermediaries in connection with the establishment and maintenance by others of a depository system for the transfer or pledge of registered public obligations or any interest therein. Any such financial intermediaries may, if qualified and acting as fiduciaries, also serve as authenticating agents, transfer agents, registrars, paying or other agents of the issuer with respect to the same issue of public obligations.

(c) Nothing in this Chapter shall preclude the issuer from itself performing, either alone or jointly with others, any transfer, registration, authentication, payment, depository or other function described in this section. (1983, c. 322, s. 1.)

§ 159E-9. Costs; collection.

(a) An issuer, prior to or at original issuance of registered public obligations, may provide as a part of a system of registration that the transferor or transferee of the registered public obligations pay all or a designated part of the costs of the system as a condition precedent to transfer, that costs be paid out of proceeds of the registered public obligations, or that both methods be used. The portion of the costs of the system not provided to be paid for by the transferor or transferee or out of proceeds shall be the responsibility of the issuer. Moneys for the discharge of this responsibility may be appropriated annually.

(b) The issuer may as a part of the system of registration provide for reimbursement or for satisfaction of its responsibility for costs by others. The issuer may enter into agreements with others respecting such reimbursement or satisfaction, may establish fees and charges pursuant to such agreements or otherwise, and may provide that the amount or estimated amount of such fees and charges shall be reimbursed or satisfied from the same sources and by means of the same collection and enforcement procedures and with the same priority and effect as with respect to the obligation. (1983, c. 322, s. 1.)

§ 159E-10. Security for deposits.

Obligations issued by public entities under the laws of one or more states, territories, or possessions of the United States, the Commonwealth of Puerto Rico, or the District of Columbia, which are in registered form, whether or not represented by an instrument, and which, except for their form, satisfy the requirements with regard to security for deposits of moneys of public agencies prescribed pursuant to any law of this State, shall be deemed to satisfy all such requirements even though they are in registered form if a security interest in such obligations is perfected under the laws of this State on behalf of the public agencies whose moneys are so deposited. (1983, c. 322, s. 1.)

§ 159E-11. Public records; locations.

(a) Records, with regard to the ownership of or security interests in registered public obligations, are not subject to inspection or copying under any law of this State relating to the right of the public to inspect or copy public records, notwithstanding any law to the contrary. This provision shall not exempt from public inspection records of ownership of a public entity's own holdings in this type of security.

(b) Registration records of the issuer may be maintained at such locations within or without this State as the issuer shall determine. (1983, c. 322, s. 1.)

§ 159E-12. Applicability; determination.

(a) Unless at any time prior to or at original issuance of a registered public obligation the official or official body of the issuer determines otherwise, this Chapter shall be applicable to such registered public obligation notwithstanding any provision of law to the contrary. When this Chapter is applicable, no contrary provision shall apply.

(b) Nothing in this Chapter limits or prevents issuance of obligations in any other form or manner authorized by law.

(c) Unless determined otherwise pursuant to subsection (a) of this section, the provisions of this Chapter shall be applicable with respect to obligations which have heretofore been approved by vote, referendum or hearing authorizing or permitting the authorization of obligations in bearer and registered form, or in bearer form only, and such obligations need not be resubmitted for a further vote, referendum or hearing for the purpose of authorizing or permitting the authorization of registered public obligations pursuant to this Chapter. (1983, c. 322, s. 1.)

§ 159E-13. Construction.

This Chapter shall be construed in conjunction with the Uniform Commercial Code and the principles of contract law relative to the registration and transfer of obligations. (1983, c. 322, s. 1.)

§ 159E-14. Amendment or repeal; effect.

The State hereby covenants with the owners of any registered public obligations that it will not amend or repeal this Chapter if the effect may be to impair the exemption from income taxation of interest on registered public obligations. (1983, c. 322, s. 1.)

§ 159E-15. Severability.

If any provision or the application of any provision of this Chapter shall be invalid, such shall not affect the validity of other provisions or other applications, it hereby being declared that the provisions or the applications of this Chapter are separable and this Chapter would have been enacted with the invalid provision omitted or without the invalid application in any event. (1983, c. 322, s. 1.)

Chapter 159F.

North Carolina Energy Development Authority.

§§ 159F-1 through 159F-9: Repealed by Session Laws 1993, c. 16, s. 1.

Chapter 159G.

Water Infrastructure.

Article 1.

General Provisions.

§§ 159G-1 through 159G-18: Repealed by Session Laws 2005-454, s. 2, effective January 1, 2006.

§ 159G-19. Reserved for future codification purposes.

§ 159G-20. Definitions.

The following definitions apply in this Chapter:

(1) Asset management plan. - The strategic and systematic application of management practices applied to the infrastructure assets of a local government unit in order to minimize the total costs of acquiring, operating, maintaining, improving, and replacing the assets while at the same time maximizing the efficiency, reliability, and value of the assets.

(1a) Construction costs. - The costs of planning, designing, and constructing a project for which a loan or grant is available under this Chapter. The term includes the following:

a. Excess or reserve capacity costs attributable to no more than 20-year projected domestic growth plus ten percent (10%) unspecified industrial growth.

b. Legal, fiscal, administrative, and contingency costs.

c. The fee imposed under G.S. 159G-24 to obtain a loan or grant for a project.

d. A fee payable to the Department for a permit to implement a project for which a loan or grant is obtained.

e. The cost to acquire real property or an interest in real property.

(2)   CWSRF. - The Clean Water State Revolving Fund established in G.S. 159G-22 as an account in the Water Infrastructure Fund.

(3)   Department. - The Department of Environment and Natural Resources.

(4)   Repealed by Session Laws 2011-145, s. 13.3(ggg), effective July 1, 2011.

(5)   Repealed by Session Laws 2013-360, s. 14.21(d), effective July 1, 2013 and Repealed by Session Laws 2013-413, s. 57(q), effective August 23, 2013.

(5a)   Repealed by Session Laws 2013-360, s. 14.21(d), effective July 1, 2013.

(5b)   Division. - Division of Water Infrastructure.

(6)   Drinking Water Reserve. - The Drinking Water Reserve established in G.S. 159G-22 as an account in the Water Infrastructure Fund.

(7)   DWSRF. - The Drinking Water State Revolving Fund established in G.S. 159G-22 as an account in the Water Infrastructure Fund.

(8)   Grant. - A sum of money given to an applicant without any obligation on the part of the applicant to repay the sum.

(9)   High-unit-cost project. - A project that results in an estimated average household user fee for water and sewer service in the area served by the project in excess of the high-unit-cost threshold. The average household user fee is calculated for a continuous 12-month period.

(10)   High-unit-cost threshold. - Either of the following amounts determined on the basis of data from the most recent federal decennial census and updated by the U.S. Department of Housing and Urban Development's annual estimated income adjustment factors:

a.   One and one-half percent (1.5%) of the median household income in an area that receives both water and sewer service.

b.   Three-fourths of one percent (3/4%) of the median household income in an area that receives only water service or only sewer service.

(10a) Investor-owned drinking water corporation. - A corporation owned by investors and incorporated solely for the purpose of providing drinking water services for profit.

(11) Loan. - A sum of money loaned to an applicant with an obligation on the part of the applicant to repay the sum.

(12) Local Government Commission. - The Local Government Commission of the Department of the State Treasurer, established in G.S. 159-3.

(13) Local government unit. - Any of the following:

a. A city as defined in G.S. 160A-1.

b. A county.

c. A consolidated city-county as defined in G.S. 160B-2.

d. A county water and sewer district created pursuant to Article 6 of Chapter 162A of the General Statutes.

e. A metropolitan sewerage district or a metropolitan water district created pursuant to Article 4 of Chapter 162A of the General Statutes.

f. A water and sewer authority created under Article 1 of Chapter 162A of the General Statutes.

g. A sanitary district created pursuant to Part 2 of Article 2 of Chapter 130A of the General Statutes.

h. A joint agency created pursuant to Part 1 of Article 20 of Chapter 160A of the General Statutes.

i. A joint agency that was created by agreement between two cities and towns to operate an airport pursuant to G.S. 63-56 and that provided drinking water and wastewater services off the airport premises before 1 January 1995.

(14) Nonprofit water corporation. - A nonprofit corporation that is incorporated under Chapter 55A of the General Statutes solely for the purpose of providing drinking water or wastewater services and is an eligible applicant

for a federal loan or grant from the Rural Utility Services Division, U.S. Department of Agriculture.

(15) Public water system. - Defined in G.S. 130A-313.

(16) Reserved.

(17) Reserved.

(18) Secretary. - The Secretary of Environment and Natural Resources.

(19) State. - The State of North Carolina.

(20) Stormwater quality project. - A project whose primary purpose is to prevent or remove pollution from stormwater rather than collect, store, or convey stormwater for drainage or flood control purposes.

(21) Targeted interest rate project. - Either of the following types of projects:

a. A high-unit-cost project that is awarded a loan.

b. A project that is awarded a loan from the CWSRF or the DWSRF and is in a category for which federal law encourages a special focus.

(22) Treasurer. - The Treasurer of the State elected pursuant to Article III, Section 7, of the Constitution.

(23) Wastewater collection system. - A unified system of pipes, conduits, pumping stations, force mains, and appurtenances for collecting and transmitting water-carried human wastes and other wastewater from residences, industrial establishments, or any other buildings.

(24) Wastewater Reserve. - The Wastewater Reserve established in G.S. 159G-22 as an account in the Water Infrastructure Fund.

(25) Wastewater system. - A wastewater collection system, wastewater treatment works, stormwater quality project, or nonpoint source pollution project.

(26) Wastewater treatment works. - The various facilities and devices used in the treatment of sewage, industrial waste, or other wastes of a liquid nature, including the necessary interceptor sewers, outfall sewers, nutrient removal

equipment, pumping equipment, power and other equipment, and their appurtenances.

(27) Water Infrastructure Fund. - The fund established in G.S. 159G-22. (2005-454, s. 3; 2010-151, s. 1; 2011-145, ss. 13.3(ggg), 13.11A(a), 2013 360, s. 14.21(d); 2013-413, s. 57(q).)

§ 159G-21. Revenue for water projects.

This Chapter governs the use of the following revenue:

(1) Revenue appropriated to the Department to match federal funds received for loans and grants for wastewater and drinking water projects and revenue received by the Department from the repayment of loans made with the use of the federal funds.

(2) Revenue appropriated to the Department to provide a source of State funds to make loans and grants for wastewater and drinking water projects and revenue received by the Department from the repayment of loans made with the use of these funds. (2005-454, s. 3.)

§ 159G-22. Water Infrastructure Fund.

(a) Fund Established. - The Water Infrastructure Fund is established as a special revenue fund. The Fund is comprised of the accounts set out in this section. The Fund provides revenue through its accounts for loans and grants as provided in this Chapter to meet the water infrastructure needs of the State. The Treasurer is responsible for distributing and investing all revenue received by the Fund. Interest and other investment income earned by the Fund accrues to it and must be allocated to the account to which the income is attributable. Accounts to which federal funds are credited must be kept separate from accounts that do not receive federal funds. A payment of the principal of or interest on a loan made from an account of the Fund must be credited to the account from which the loan was made.

(b) CWSRF. - The Clean Water State Revolving Fund is established as an account within the Water Infrastructure Fund. The account receives federal funds for wastewater projects and the State funds required to match the federal funds. The account is established under and must be managed in accordance with Title VI of the Federal Water Quality Act of 1987, Pub. L. 100-4, to achieve the purposes of that act and the Federal Water Pollution Control Act of 1972, 33 U.S.C. §§ 1251 through 1387. The account must comply with these federal acts and the federal regulations adopted to implement the acts. Revenue credited to the account is available in perpetuity and must be used only to provide construction loans and other assistance allowed under federal law. Grants are available from this account only to the extent allowed under federal law.

(c)   DWSRF. - The Drinking Water State Revolving Fund is established as an account within the Water Infrastructure Fund. The account receives federal funds for public water systems and the State funds required to match the federal funds. The account is established under and must be managed in accordance with section 130 of Title 1 of the federal Safe Drinking Water Act of 1996 as amended, 42 U.S.C. § 300J-12, to achieve the purposes of that act. The account must comply with that act and the federal regulations adopted to implement the act. Revenue credited to the account is available in perpetuity and must be used only to provide construction loans and other assistance allowed under federal law. Grants are available from this account only to the extent allowed under federal law.

(d)   Wastewater Reserve. - The Wastewater Reserve is established as an account within the Water Infrastructure Fund. The account is established to receive State funds that are to be used for loans and grants for wastewater systems. Revenue credited to the Reserve is neither received from the federal government nor provided as a match for federal funds.

(e)   Wastewater Accounts. - The Department is directed to establish accounts within the Wastewater Reserve to administer loans and grants for wastewater collection systems, wastewater treatment works, stormwater quality projects, and nonpoint source pollution projects. The wastewater accounts must include an account for each type of loan or grant set out in G.S. 159G-33.

(f)   Drinking Water Reserve. - The Drinking Water Reserve is established as an account within the Water Infrastructure Fund. The account is established to receive State funds that are to be used for loans and grants for public water systems. Revenue credited to the Reserve is neither received from the federal government nor provided as a match for federal funds.

(g)   Drinking Water Accounts. - The Department is directed to establish accounts within the Drinking Water Reserve to administer loans and grants for public water systems. The drinking water accounts must include an account for each type of loan or grant set out in G.S. 159G-34. (2005-454, s. 3.)

§ 159G-23. Common criteria for loan or grant from Wastewater Reservo or Drinking Water Reserve.

The criteria in this section apply to a loan or grant from the Wastewater Reserve or the Drinking Water Reserve. The Division of Water Infrastructure must establish a system of assigning points to applications based on the following criteria:

(1) Public necessity. - An applicant must explain how the project promotes public health and protects the environment. A project that improves a system that is not in compliance with permit requirements or is under orders from the Department, enables a moratorium to be lifted, or replaces failing septic tanks with a wastewater collection system has priority.

(2) Effect on impaired waters. - A project that improves designated impaired waters of the State has priority.

(3) Efficiency. - A project that achieves efficiencies in meeting the State's water infrastructure needs or reduces vulnerability to drought consistent with Part 2A of Article 21 and Article 38 of Chapter 143 of the General Statutes by one of the following methods has priority:

a. The combination of two or more wastewater or public water systems into a regional wastewater or public water system by merger, consolidation, or another means.

b. Conservation or reuse of water, including bulk water reuse facilities and waterlines to supply reuse water for irrigation and other approved uses.

c. Construction of an interconnection between water systems intended for use in drought or other water shortage emergency.

d. Repair or replacement of leaking waterlines to improve water conservation and efficiency or to prevent contamination.

e. Replacement of meters and installation of new metering systems.

(4) Comprehensive land-use plan. - A project that is located in a city or county that has adopted or has taken significant steps to adopt a comprehensive land-use plan under Article 18 of Chapter 153A of the General Statutes or Article 19 of Chapter 160A of the General Statutes has priority over a project located in a city or county that has not adopted a plan or has not taken steps to do so. The existence of a plan has more priority than steps taken to adopt a plan, such as adoption of a zoning ordinance. A plan that exceeds the minimum State standards for protection of water resources has more priority than one that does not. A project is considered to be located in a city or county if it is located in whole or in part in that unit. A land-use plan is not considered a comprehensive land-use plan unless it has provisions that protect existing water uses and ensure compliance with water quality standards and classifications in all waters of the State affected by the plan.

(5) Flood hazard ordinance. - A project that is located in a city or county that has adopted a flood hazard prevention ordinance under G.S. 143-215.54A has priority over a project located in a city or county that has not adopted an ordinance. A plan that exceeds the minimum standards under G.S. 143-215.54A for a flood hazard prevention ordinance has more priority than one that does not. A project is considered to be located in a city or county if it is located in whole or in part in that unit. If no part of the service area of a project is located within the 100-year floodplain, the project has the same priority under this subdivision as if it were located in a city or county that has adopted a flood hazard prevention ordinance. The most recent maps prepared pursuant to the National Flood Insurance Program or approved by the Department determine whether an area is within the 100-year floodplain.

(6) Sound management. - A project submitted by a local government unit that has demonstrated a willingness and ability to meet its responsibilities through sound fiscal policies and efficient operation and management has priority.

(6a) Asset management plan. - A project submitted by a local government unit with more than 1,000 service connections that has developed and is implementing an asset management plan has priority over a project submitted by a local government unit with more than 1,000 service connections that has not developed or is not implementing an asset management plan.

(7) Capital improvement plan. - A project that implements the applicant's capital improvement plan for the wastewater system or public water system it manages has priority over a project that does not implement a capital

improvement plan. To receive priority, a capital improvement plan must set out the applicant's expected water infrastructure needs for at least 10 years.

(8) Coastal habitat protection. - A project that implements a recommendation of a Coastal Habitat Protection Plan adopted by the Environmental Management Commission, the Coastal Resources Commission, and the Marine Fisheries Commission pursuant to G.S. 143B-279.8 has priority over other projects that affect counties subject to that Plan.

(9) High-unit-cost threshold. - A high-unit-cost project has priority over projects that are not high-unit-cost projects. The priority given to a high-unit-cost project shall be set using a sliding scale based on the amount by which the applicant exceeds the high-unit-cost threshold.

(10) Regionalization. - A project to provide for the planning of regional public water and wastewater systems, to provide for the orderly coordination of local actions relating to public water and wastewater systems, or to help realize economies of scale in regional public water and wastewater systems through consolidation, management, merger, or interconnection of public water and wastewater systems has priority. If an applicant demonstrates that it is not feasible for the project to include regionalization, the funding agency shall assign the project the same priority as a project that includes regionalization.

(11) State water supply plan. - A project that addresses a potential conflict between local plans or implements a measure in which local water supply plans could be better coordinated, as identified in the State water supply plan pursuant to G.S. 143-355(m), has priority.

(12) Water conservation measures for drought. - A project that includes adoption of water conservation measures by a local government unit that are more stringent than the minimum water conservation measures required pursuant to G.S. 143-355.2 has priority.

(13) Low-income residents. - A project that is located in an area annexed by a municipality under Article 4A of Chapter 160A of the General Statutes in order to provide water or sewer services to low-income residents has priority. For purposes of this section, low-income residents are those with a family income that is eighty percent (80%) or less of median family income. (2005-454, s. 3; 2008-143, s. 15; 2010-151, s. 2; 2011-145, s. 13.3(hhh); 2011-396, s. 11.2; 2013-360, s. 14.21(e); 2013-413, s. 57(r).)

§ 159G-24. Fee imposed on a loan or grant from Water Infrastructure Fund.

(a) A loan awarded from the Water Infrastructure Fund is subject to a fee of two percent (2%) of the loan. A grant awarded from the Water Infrastructure Fund is subject to a fee of one and one-half percent (1 1/2%) of the grant. The fee is payable when a loan or grant is awarded.

(b) Departmental Receipt. - The fee on a loan from the Water Infrastructure Fund is a departmental receipt and must be applied to the Department's and the Local Government Commission's costs in administering loans from these Reserves. The Department and the Local Government Commission must determine how to allocate the fee receipts between their agencies. The fee on a grant from the Water Infrastructure Fund is a departmental receipt of the Department and must be applied to the Department's costs in administering grants from these Reserves. (2005-454, s. 3; 2012-142, s. 12.01.)

§ 159G-25. Expenditure for emergency corrective action at a wastewater treatment works.

(a) The Department may use revenue in any account of the Wastewater Reserve to provide funds for emergency corrective action at a wastewater treatment works under the circumstances set out in this section. The amount expended in a fiscal year for corrective action under this section may not exceed two hundred thousand dollars ($200,000). An expenditure for emergency corrective action is authorized only under the following circumstances:

(1) A person holding a wastewater discharge or nondischarge permit issued under Article 21 of Chapter 143 of the General Statutes is violating the terms of the permit.

(2) The wastewater treatment works operated under the permit has a design flow capacity of no more than 100,000 gallons a day.

(3) The Department has given the permit holder written notice of the violation.

(4) The permit holder refuses to take the action required to comply with the permit.

(5) The inaction by the permit holder poses a threat to public health.

(6) The Department has informed the permit holder in writing that the Department plans to take emergency corrective action and then bring a civil action against the permit holder to recover the cost of the emergency corrective action.

(b) The Department may bring a civil action against the holder of the permit for the wastewater treatment works to recover the amount expended from the Wastewater Reserve for the emergency corrective action. The amount recovered in a civil action must be credited to the account in the Wastewater Reserve from which the funds were expended. (2005-454, s. 3.)

§ 159G-26. Annual reports on Water Infrastructure Fund.

(a) Requirement. - The Department must publish a report each year on the accounts in the Water Infrastructure Fund that are administered by the Division of Water Infrastructure. The report must be published by 1 November of each year and cover the preceding fiscal year. The Department must make the report available to the public and must give a copy of the report to the Environmental Review Commission and the Fiscal Research Division of the Legislative Services Commission.

(b) Content. - The report required by this section must contain the following information concerning the accounts of the Water Infrastructure Fund:

(1) The beginning and ending balance of the account for the fiscal year.

(2) The amount of revenue credited to the account during the fiscal year, by source.

(3) The total amount of loans and grants awarded from the account, by type, and the amount of any expenditure for emergency corrective action made from the account.

(4) For each loan or grant awarded, the recipient of the award, the amount of the award, the amount of the award that was disbursed, and the amount of the award remaining to be disbursed in a subsequent fiscal year.

(5) The amount disbursed for loans and grants awarded but not disbursed in a prior fiscal year and the amount remaining to be disbursed in a subsequent fiscal year.

(6) An assessment of the expected impact on water quality and water supply of the projects for which the loans and grants were awarded. (2005-454, s. 3; 2011-145, s. 13.3(iii); 2013-360, s. 14.21(f); 2013-413, s. 57(s).)

§ 159G-27. Reserved for future codification purposes.

§ 159G-28. Reserved for future codification purposes.

§ 159G-29. Reserved for future codification purposes.

Article 2.

Water Infrastructure Loans and Grants Administered by Department.

§ 159G-30. Department's responsibility.

The Department, through the Division of Water Infrastructure, administers loans and grants made from the CWSRF, the DWSRF, the Wastewater Reserve, and the Drinking Water Reserve. (2005-454, s. 3; 2011-145, s. 13.3(jjj); 2013-360, s. 14.21(g); 2013-413, s. 57(t).)

§ 159G-31. Entities eligible to apply for loan or grant.

A local government unit or a nonprofit water corporation is eligible to apply for a loan or grant from the CWSRF, the DWSRF, the Wastewater Reserve, or the Drinking Water Reserve. An investor-owned drinking water corporation is also eligible to apply for a loan or grant from the DWSRF. Other entities are not eligible for a loan or grant from these accounts. (2005-454, s. 3; 2011-145, s. 13.11A(b).)

§ 159G-32. Projects eligible for loan or grant.

(a) CWSRF and DWSRF. - Federal law determines whether a project is eligible for a loan or grant from the CWSRF and the DWSRF. A project must meet the eligibility requirements set under federal law.

(b) Wastewater Reserve. - The Department is authorized to make loans and grants from the Wastewater Reserve for the following types of projects:

(1) Wastewater collection system

(2) Wastewater treatment works.

(3) Stormwater quality projects, including innovative stormwater management projects and pilot projects.

(4) Nonpoint source pollution project.

(c) Drinking Water Reserve. - The Department is authorized to make loans and grants from the Drinking Water Reserve for public water system projects. (2005-454, s. 3; 2013-360, s. 14.21(h).)

§ 159G-33. Loans and grants available from Wastewater Reserve.

(a) Types. - The Department is authorized to make the types of loans and grants listed in this subsection from the Wastewater Reserve. Each type of loan or grant must be administered through a separate account within the Wastewater Reserve.

(1) General. - A loan or grant is available for a project authorized in G.S. 159G-32(b).

(2) High-unit-cost grant. - A high-unit-cost grant is available for the portion of the construction costs of a wastewater collection system project or a wastewater treatment works project that results in an estimated average household user fee for water and sewer service in the area served by the project that exceeds the high-unit-cost threshold.

(3) Technical assistance grant. - A technical assistance grant is available to determine the best way to correct the deficiencies in a wastewater collection system or wastewater treatment works that either is not in compliance with its permit limits or, as identified in the most recent inspection report by the Department under G.S. 143-215.3, is experiencing operational problems and is at risk of violating its permit limits.

(4)   Emergency loan. - An emergency loan is available in the event the Secretary certifies that a serious public health hazard related to the inadequacy of an existing wastewater collection system or wastewater treatment works is present or imminent in a community.

(b)   Interaccount Transfer. - The Secretary may use revenue in any account in the Wastewater Reserve to provide funds for an emergency loan. (2005-454, s. 3.)

§ 159G-34. Loans and grants available from Drinking Water Reserve.

(a)   Types. - The Department is authorized to make the types of loans and grants listed in this section from the Drinking Water Reserve. Each type of loan or grant must be administered through a separate account within the Drinking Water Reserve.

(1)   General. - A loan or grant is available for a project for a public water system.

(2)   High-unit-cost grant. - A grant is available for the portion of the construction costs of a public water system project that results in an estimated average household user fee for water and sewer service in the area served by the project that exceeds the high-unit-cost threshold.

(3)   Technical assistance grant. - A technical assistance grant is available to determine the best way to correct the deficiencies in a public water system that does not comply with State law or the rules adopted to implement that law.

(4)   Emergency loan. - An emergency loan is available to an applicant in the event the Secretary certifies that either a serious public health hazard or a drought emergency related to the water supply system is present or imminent in a community.

(b)   Interaccount Transfer. - The Secretary may use revenue in any account in the Drinking Water Reserve to provide funds for an emergency loan. (2005-454, s. 3.)

§ 159G-35. Criteria for loans and grants.

(a) CWSRF and DWSRF. - Federal law determines the criteria for awarding a loan or grant from the CWSRF or the DWSRF. An award of a loan or grant from one of these accounts must meet the criteria set under federal law. The Department is directed to establish through negotiation with the United States Environmental Protection Agency the criteria for evaluating applications for loans and grants from the CWSRF and the DWSRF and the priority assigned to the criteria. The Department must incorporate the negotiated criteria and priorities in the Capitalization Grant Operating Agreement between the Department and the United States Environmental Protection Agency. The criteria and priorities incorporated in the Agreement apply to a loan or grant from the CWSRF or the DWSRF. The common criteria in G.S. 159G-23 do not apply to a loan or grant from the CWSRF or the DWSRF.

(b) Reserves. - The common criteria in G.S. 159G-23 apply to a loan or grant from the Wastewater Reserve or the Drinking Water Reserve. The Department may establish by rule other criteria that apply to a loan or grant from the Wastewater Reserve or the Drinking Water Reserve. (2005-454, s. 3.)

§ 159G-36. Limits on loans and grants.

(a) CWSRF and DWSRF. - Federal law governs loans and grants from the CWSRF and the DWSRF. An award of a loan or grant from one of these accounts must be consistent with federal law.

(b) Reserve Cost Limit. - The amount of a loan or grant from the Wastewater Reserve or the Drinking Water Reserve may not exceed the construction costs of a project. A loan or grant from one of these Reserves is available only to the extent that other funding sources are not reasonably available to the applicant.

(c) Reserve Recipient Limit. - The following limits apply to a loan or grant made from the Wastewater Reserve or the Drinking Water Reserve to the same local government unit or nonprofit water corporation:

(1) The amount of loans awarded for a fiscal year may not exceed three million dollars ($3,000,000).

(2) The amount of loans awarded for three consecutive fiscal years for targeted interest rate projects may not exceed three million dollars ($3,000,000).

(3) The amount of high-unit-cost grants awarded for three consecutive fiscal years may not exceed three million dollars ($3,000,000).

(4) The amount of technical assistance grants awarded for three consecutive fiscal years may not exceed fifty thousand dollars ($50,000). (2005-454, s. 3.)

§ 159G-37. Application to CWSRF, Wastewater Reserve, DWSRF, and Drinking Water Reserve.

An application [for a loan or grant from the] CWSRF, the Wastewater Reserve, the DWSRF, or the Drinking Water Reserve must be filed with the Division of Water Infrastructure [of the Department. An application must] be submitted on a form prescribed by the Division and must contain the information required by the Division. An applicant must submit to the Division any additional information requested by the Division to enable the Division to make a determination on the application. An application that does not contain information required on the application [or] requested by the Division is incomplete and is not eligible for consideration. An applicant may submit an application in as many categories as it is eligible for consideration under this Article. (2005-454, s. 3; 2011-145, s. 13.3(kkk); 2013-360, s. 14.21(i); 2013-413, s. 57(u).)

§ 159G-38. Environmental assessment and public hearing.

(a) Required Information. - An application submitted under this Article for a loan or grant for a project must state whether the project requires an environmental assessment. If the application indicates that an environmental assessment is not required, it must identify the exclusion in the North Carolina Environmental Policy Act, Article 1 of Chapter 113A of the General Statutes, that applies to the project. If the application does not identify an exclusion in the North Carolina Environmental Policy Act, it must include an environmental assessment of the project's probable impacts on the environment.

(b) Division Review. - If, after reviewing an application, the Division of Water Infrastructure determines that a project requires an environmental assessment, the assessment must be submitted before the Division continues its review of the application. If, after reviewing an environmental assessment, the Division concludes that an environmental impact statement is required, the Division may not continue its review of the application until a final environmental impact statement has been completed and approved as provided in the North Carolina Environmental Policy Act.

(c) Hearing. - The Division of Water Infrastructure may hold a public hearing on an application for a loan or grant under this Article if it determines that holding a hearing will serve the public interest. An individual who is a resident of any county in which a proposed project is located may submit a written request for a public hearing. The request must set forth each objection to the proposed project or other reason for requesting a hearing and must include the name and address of the individual making the request. The Division may consider all written objections to the proposed project, any statement submitted with the hearing request, and any significant adverse effects the proposed project may have on the environment. The Division's decision on whether to hold a hearing is conclusive. The Division must keep all written requests for a hearing on an application as part of the records pertaining to the application. (2005-454, s. 3; 2011-145, s. 13.3(lll), (mmm); 2013-360, s. 14.21(j); 2013-413, s. 57(v).)

§ 159G-39. Review of applications and award of loan or grant.

(a) Point Assignment. - The Division of Water Infrastructure must review all applications filed for a loan or grant under this Article for an application period. The Division must rank each application in accordance with the points assigned to the evaluation criteria. The Division must make a written determination of an application's rank and attach the determination to the application for the Authority's review. The Authority must consider the Division's determination of rank when the Authority determines an application's rank. The Authority's determination of rank is conclusive.

(b) Initial Consideration. - The Division may consider an application for an emergency loan from the Wastewater Reserve or the Drinking Water Reserve at any time. The Division must consider all other loan applications and all grant applications filed during an application period at the same time in order to rank the applications. The Division shall forward all applications received for the application period to the State Water Infrastructure Authority.

(c) Reconsideration. - When the Authority determines an application's rank is too low to receive an award of a loan or grant for an application period, the Division must include the application with those considered for the next application period. If the application's rank is again too low to receive an award, the application is not eligible for consideration in a subsequent application period. An applicant whose application does not receive an award after review in two application periods may file a new application.

(d) Notification of Decision. - When the Authority determines that an application's rank makes it eligible for an award of a loan or grant, the Division must send the applicant a letter of intent to award the loan or grant. The notice must set out any conditions the applicant must meet to receive an award of a loan or grant. When the applicant satisfies the conditions set out in the letter of intent, the Division must send the applicant an offer to award a loan or grant. The applicant must give the Division written notice of whether it accepts or rejects the offer. A loan or grant is considered awarded when an offer to award the loan or grant is issued. (2005-454, s. 3; 2011-145, s. 13.3(nnn); 2013-360, s. 14.21(k); 2013-413, s. 57(w).)

§ 159G-40. Terms of loan and execution of loan documents.

(a) Approval by Local Government Commission. - The Department may not award a loan under this Article unless the Local Government Commission approves the award of the loan and the terms of the loan. The terms of a loan awarded from the CWSRF and the DWSRF must be consistent with federal law. In reviewing a proposed loan to a local government unit, the Local Government Commission must consider the loan as if it were a bond proposal and review the proposed loan in accordance with the factors set out in G.S. 159-52 for review of a proposed bond issue. The Local Government Commission must review a proposed loan to a nonprofit water corporation and to an investor-owned drinking water corporation in accordance with the factors set out in G.S. 159-153.

(b) Interest Rate and Maturity. - The interest rate payable on and the maximum maturity of a loan are subject to the following limitations:

(1) Interest rate. - The interest rate for a loan may not exceed the lesser of four percent (4%) or one half the prevailing national market rate for tax-exempt general obligation debt of similar maturities derived from a published indicator. When recommended by the Department, the Local Government Commission may set an interest rate for a loan for a targeted interest rate project at a rate that is lower than the standard rate to achieve the purpose of the target.

(2) Maturity. - The maximum maturity for a loan for a project that is not a high-unit-cost project may not exceed 20 years or the project's expected life,

whichever is shorter. The maximum maturity for a loan for a high-unit-cost project is 30 years or the project's expected life, whichever is shorter.

(c) Security for Loan. A local government unit may pledge any of the following, alone or in combination, as security for an obligation to repay the principal of and interest on a loan awarded under this Article:

(1) User fee revenues derived from operation of the wastewater system or public water system that benefits from the project for which the loan is awarded.

(2) A mortgage, deed of trust, security interest, or similar lien on part or all of the real and personal property comprising the wastewater system or public water system that benefits from the project for which the loan is awarded.

(3) Its full faith and credit if it meets the requirements of Article 4 of Chapter 159 of the General Statutes.

(4) Nontax revenue not included in subdivision (1) of this subsection.

(d) Debt Instrument. - A local government unit, a nonprofit water corporation, and an investor-owned drinking water corporation may execute a debt instrument payable to the State to evidence an obligation to repay the principal of and interest on a loan awarded under this Article. The Treasurer, with the assistance of the Local Government Commission, must develop debt instruments for use by local government units, nonprofit water corporations, and investor-owned drinking water corporations under this section. The Local Government Commission must develop procedures for loan recipients to deliver debt instruments to the State without public bidding. (2005-454, s. 3; 2011-145, s. 13.11A(c).)

§ 159G-41. Withdrawal of loan or grant.

A letter of intent to offer an award for a loan or grant for a project is withdrawn if the applicant fails to enter into a construction contract for the project within two years after the date of the letter, unless the Department finds that the applicant has good cause for the failure. An award for a loan or grant for a project is withdrawn if the applicant fails to enter into a construction contract for the project within one year after the date of the award, unless the Department finds that the applicant has good cause for the failure. If the Department finds good cause for an applicant's failure, the Department must set a date by which the applicant must take action or forfeit the loan or grant. (2005-454, s. 3.)

§ 159G-42. Disbursement of loan or grant.

The Department must disburse the proceeds of a loan or grant to a recipient in a series of payments based on the progress of the project for which the loan or grant was awarded. To obtain a payment, a loan or grant recipient must submit a request for payment to the Department and document the expenditures for which the payment is requested. (2005-454, s. 3.)

§ 159G-43. Inspection of project.

(a) Authority. - The Department may inspect a project for which it awards a loan or grant under this Article to determine the progress made on the project and whether the construction of the project is consistent with the project described in the loan or grant application. The inspection may be performed by personnel of the Department or by a professional engineer licensed under Chapter 89C of the General Statutes.

(b) Disqualification. - An individual may not perform an inspection of a project under this section if the individual meets any of the following criteria:

(1) Is an officer or employee of the local government unit, nonprofit water corporation, or investor-owned drinking water corporation that received the loan or grant award for the project.

(2) Is an owner, officer, employee, or agent of a contractor or subcontractor engaged in the construction of the project for which the loan or grant was made. (2005-454, s. 3; 2011-145, s. 13.11A(d).)

§ 159G-44. Rules.

The Department may adopt rules to implement this Chapter. Chapter 150B of the General Statutes, the Administrative Procedure Act, governs the adoption of rules by the Department. A rule adopted to administer a loan or grant from the

CWSRF or the DWSRF must be consistent with federal law. The Department must give a copy of the rules adopted to implement this Article without charge to a person who requests a copy. (2005-454, s. 3.)

§ 159G-45. Reserved for future codification purposes.

§ 159G-46. Reserved for future codification purposes.

§ 159G-47. Reserved for future codification purposes.

§ 159G-48. Reserved for future codification purposes.

§ 159G-49. Reserved for future codification purposes.

§ 159G-50. Reserved for future codification purposes.

Article 3.

[Reserved.]

§§ 159G-51 through 159G-64: Reserved for future codification purposes.

Article 4.

State Water Infrastructure Commission.

§§ 159G-65 through 159G-67: Repealed by Session Laws 2013-360, s. 14.21(c), effective July 1, 2013.

§ 159G-68: Reserved for future codification purposes.

§ 159G-69: Reserved for future codification purposes.

Article 5.

State Water Infrastructure Authority.

§ 159G-70. State Water Infrastructure Authority created.

(a)   Authority Established. - The State Water Infrastructure Authority is created within the Department of Environment and Natural Resources.

(b)   Membership. - The Authority consists of nine members as follows:

(1)   The Director of the Division of Water Infrastructure of the Department or the Director's designee who is familiar with the water infrastructure financing, regulatory, and technical assistance programs of the Department.

(2)   The Secretary of Commerce or the Secretary's designee who is familiar with the State programs that fund water or other infrastructure improvements for the purpose of promoting economic development.

(3)   The Director of the Local Government Commission or the Director's designee who is familiar with the functions of the Commission.

(4)   One member who is a professional engineer in the private sector and is familiar with the development of infrastructure necessary for wastewater systems, to be appointed by the Governor to a term that expires on July 1 of even-numbered years.

(5)   One member who is knowledgeable about, and has experience related to, direct federal funding programs for wastewater and public water systems, to be appointed by the Governor to a term that expires on July 1 of odd-numbered years.

(6)   One member who is knowledgeable about, and has experience related to, urban local government wastewater systems or public water systems, to be appointed by the General Assembly upon the recommendation of the President Pro Tempore of the Senate to a term that expires on July 1 of even-numbered years.

(7)   One member who is knowledgeable about, and has experience related to, rural local government wastewater systems or public water systems, to be appointed by the General Assembly upon the recommendation of the President Pro Tempore of the Senate to a term that expires on July 1 of odd-numbered years.

(8) One member who either (i) is a county commissioner of a rural county or (ii) resides in a rural county and is knowledgeable about, and has experience related to, public health services, to be appointed by the General Assembly upon the recommendation of the Speaker of the House of Representatives to a term that expires on July 1 of even-numbered years.

(9) One member who is familiar with wastewater, drinking water, and stormwater issues and related State funding sources, to be appointed by the General Assembly upon the recommendation of the Speaker of the House of Representatives to a term that expires on July 1 of odd-numbered years.

(c) Terms. - The members appointed by the Governor, the President Pro Tempore of the Senate, and the Speaker of the House of Representatives shall serve two-year terms. The other members, who are ex officio members or designees of those members, shall serve until they are no longer in office or are replaced with another designee.

(d) Chair. - The Director of the Division of Water Infrastructure, or the Director's designee, shall serve as Chair of the Authority. The Chair must call the first meeting. The Chair shall serve as a nonvoting member, provided, however, that the Chair shall vote to break a tie.

(e) Meetings. - The Authority shall meet at least four times a year and may meet as often as needed. A majority of the members of the Authority constitutes a quorum for the transaction of business. The affirmative vote of a majority of the members present at a meeting of the Authority is required for action to be taken by the Authority.

(f) Vacancies. - A vacancy in the Authority or as Chair of the Authority resulting from the resignation of a member or otherwise is filled in the same manner in which the original appointment was made. The term of an appointment to fill a vacancy is for the balance of the unexpired term.

(g) Compensation. - Each member of the Authority shall receive no salary as a result of serving on the Authority but shall receive per diem, subsistence, and travel expenses in accordance with the provisions of G.S. 120-3.1, 138-5, and 138-6, as applicable. (2013-360, s. 14.21(b); 2013-363, s. 5.12.)

§ 159G-71. State Water Infrastructure Authority; powers and duties.

The Authority has the following additional duties:

(1)   After reviewing the recommendations for grants and loans submitted to it by the Division, to determine the rank of applications and to select the applications that are eligible to receive grants and loans, consistent with federal law.

(2)   To establish priorities for making loans and grants under this Chapter, consistent with federal law.

(3)   To review the criteria for making loans and grants under G.S. 159G-23 and make recommendations, if any, to the Department for additional criteria or changes to the criteria, consistent with federal law.

(4)   To develop guidelines for making loans and grants under this Chapter, consistent with federal law.

(5)   To develop a master plan to meet the State's water infrastructure needs.

(6)   To assess and make recommendations on the role of the State in the development and funding of wastewater, drinking water, and stormwater infrastructure in the State.

(7)   To analyze the adequacy of projected funding to meet projected needs over the next five years.

(8)   To make recommendations on ways to maximize the use of current funding resources, whether federal, State, or local, and to ensure that funds are used in a coordinated manner.

(9)   To review the application of management practices in wastewater, drinking water, and stormwater utilities and to determine the best practices.

(10)   To assess the role of public-private partnerships in the future provision of utility service.

(11)   To assess the application of the river basin approach to utility planning and management.

(12)   To assess the need for a "troubled system" protocol. (2013-360, s. 14.21(b).)

§ 159G-72. State Water Infrastructure Authority; reports.

No later than November 1 of each year, the Authority shall submit a report of its activity and findings, including any recommendations or legislative proposals, to the Senate Appropriations Committee on Natural and Economic Resources, the House of Representatives Appropriations Subcommittee on Natural and Economic Resources, and the Fiscal Research Division of the Legislative Services Commission. (2013-360, s. 14.21(b).)

Chapter 159I.

Solid Waste Management Loan Program and Local Government Special Obligation Bonds.

§ 159I-1. Short title.

This Chapter may be cited as the Solid Waste Management Loan Program and Local Government Special Obligation Bond Act. (1989, c. 756, s. 1; 2002-72, s. 21.)

§ 159I-2. Findings and purpose.

The General Assembly finds that units of local government need a source of funds to implement solid waste management programs. Units of local government will confront a crisis in solid waste management in the near future. Within five years of the creation of this program, one-third of all the landfills in this State will have reached their capacity. Many local governments do not have the funds to meet:

(1)   The increased costs of constructing new landfills that meet current standards for the protection of the environment; or

(2)   The cost of constructing a local or regional incinerator that would serve to reduce the volume of waste to be landfilled; or

(3)   The costs of implementing alternative programs to reduce the amount of waste generated, to decrease the volume of waste that is generated, or to recover or to recycle that part of the waste stream that can be recovered or used for another purpose.

The General Assembly finds that comprehensive solid waste management programs at a local or regional level are needed in order to preserve the quality of North Carolina's groundwater. It is the purpose of the General Assembly to facilitate the implementation of local and regional solid waste management programs by establishing a loan fund for financing the capital expenses of these programs. The General Assembly seeks to encourage and assist units of local government to continue to voluntarily provide solid waste collection and disposal for their citizens, thereby maintaining a clean and healthful environment and an adequate supply of clean water. (1989, c. 756, s. 1.)

§ 159I-3. Definitions.

(a) Unless a different meaning is required by the context, the following definitions shall apply throughout this Chapter:

(1), (2) Repealed by Session Laws 2011-266, s. 1.26(a), effective July 1, 2011.

(3) "Board" means the Clean Water Management Trust Fund Board of Trustees.

(4) "Bonds" means the revenue bonds authorized to be issued by the Board under this Chapter. As used in this Chapter, the term "bonds" does not include any loan agreement.

(5) "Costs" means the capital cost of acquiring or constructing any project, including, without limitation, the following:

a. The costs of doing any or all of the following deemed necessary or convenient by a unit of local government:

1. Acquiring, constructing, erecting, providing, developing, installing, furnishing, and equipping;

2. Reconstructing, remodeling, altering, renovating, replacing, refurnishing, and re-equipping;

3. Enlarging, expanding, and extending; and

4. Demolishing, relocating, improving, grading, draining, landscaping, paving, widening, and resurfacing.

b. The costs of all property, both real and personal and both improved and unimproved, and of plants, works, appurtenances, structures, facilities, furnishings, machinery, equipment, vehicles, easements, water rights, air rights, franchises, and licenses used or useful in connection with the purpose authorized;

c. The costs of demolishing or moving structures from land acquired and acquiring any lands to which such structures thereafter are to be moved;

d. Financing charges, including estimated interest during the acquisition or construction of such project and for six months thereafter;

e. The costs of services to provide and the cost of plans, specifications, studies and reports, surveys, and estimates of costs and revenues;

f. The costs of paying any interim financing, including principal, interest, and premium, related to the acquisition or construction of a project;

g. Administrative and legal expenses and administrative charges;

h. The costs of obtaining bond and reserve fund insurance and investment contracts, of credit-enhancement facilities, liquidity facilities and interest-rate agreements, and of establishing and maintaining debt service and other reserves; and

i. Any other services, costs, and expenses necessary or incidental to the purpose authorized.

(6) "Division" means the Division of Waste Management of the Department of Environment and Natural Resources and any successor of the Division of Waste Management.

(7) "Loan" means moneys loaned by the Board to a unit of local government for a project authorized by this Chapter.

(8) "Loan agreement" means any bond, note, contract, loan agreement, or other written agreement of a unit of local government delivered to the Board and evidencing the unit's receipt of loan proceeds from the sale of all or a portion of

the Board's bonds or from other available money of the Board and setting forth the terms of the unit's agreement to make payments to the Board in respect of such loan.

(9) "Local Government Commission" means the Local Government Commission of the Department of the State Treasurer, established by Article 2 of Chapter 159 of the General Statutes and any successor of said Commission.

(10) "Notes" means the revenue notes or revenue bond anticipation notes authorized to be issued by the Board under this Chapter. As used in this Chapter, the term "notes" does not include any loan agreement.

(11) "Project" means any capital project authorized to be financed in G.S. 159I-8.

(12) "Revenues" means all moneys received by the Board, other than the proceeds received by the Board from the sale of bonds or notes and moneys appropriated by the State for the Solid Waste Management Loan Fund, in connection with the providing of financing to units of local government, including without limitation:

a. The payments received by the Board of the principal of and premium, if any, and interest on loan agreements;

b. Administrative charges, but only to the extent determined by the Board; and

c. Investment earnings on all revenues, funds, and other moneys of the Board.

(13) "Unit of local government" or "unit" means:

a. A unit of local government as defined in G.S. 159-44(4);

b. Any combination of units, as defined in G.S. 160A-460(2), entering into a contract or agreement with each other under G.S. 160A-461;

c. Any joint agency established under G.S. 160A-462; as any such section may be amended from time to time;

d. Any regional solid waste management authority created pursuant to G.S. 153A-421; or

e. A consolidated city-county as defined by G.S. 160B-2(1), including such a consolidated city-county acting with respect to an urban service district defined by a consolidated city-county.

(b) Unless a different meaning is required by the context, the definitions set out in G.S. 130A-290, as such section may be amended from time to time, shall apply throughout this Chapter. (1989, c. 756, s. 1; 1989 (Reg. Sess., 1990), c. 888, s. 2; c. 1004, ss. 20, 47.1; c. 1024, s. 48; 1995, c. 461, s. 12; 1995 (Reg. Sess., 1996), c. 743, s. 24; 1997-443, s. 11A.123; 2011-266, s. 1.26(a), (c).)

§ 159I-4: Repealed by Session Laws 2011-266, s. 1.26(b), effective July 1, 2011.

§ 159I-5. General powers of the Board.

The Board shall have all of the powers necessary or convenient to carry out and to effect the purposes and provisions of this Chapter, including, without limitation, the powers:

(1) To make and execute contracts and agreements necessary or incidental to the exercise of its powers and duties under this Chapter, including, without limitation, agreements in respect of loan agreements and agreements with issuers of credit-enhancement facilities, liquidity facilities, bond insurance policies, reserve fund insurance policies and investment contracts, and interest-rate agreements;

(2) To contract with any unit of local government with respect to any of the matters covered by this Chapter;

(3) To establish a debt service reserve fund or funds, from moneys in the Solid Waste Management Loan Fund or from other available moneys, and other reserve funds and to borrow money to purchase insurance and investment contracts to establish, maintain, or increase such funds;

(4) To agree to apply and assign any money, loan agreements, and other revenues;

(5) To borrow money as herein provided to carry out and effect its corporate purposes and to issue in evidence thereof bonds, notes, or bond anticipation notes for the purpose of providing funds therefor, including funds for the financing and refinancing of the cost of the acquisition or construction of projects, including the payment or advance on behalf of units of local government of the costs of such projects;

(6) To apply any payments, or prepayments, or principal of or interest on any loan agreement, to the extent such payment or prepayment is not necessary to pay debt service on the Board's bonds or notes, to the financing of the cost of the acquisition or construction of projects for units of local government to the same extent as provided in G.S. 159I-6;

(7) To fix, revise, charge and collect, or cause to be fixed, revised, charged, and collected, and to apportion administrative charges among units of local government participating in any program of the Board.

(8) To employ an administrator to administer the operations of the Board, fiscal and financial consultants, underwriters, attorneys, trustees, remarketing agents, and such other consultants, agents, and employees as may be required in the judgment of the Board and to fix and pay their compensation from funds available to the Board;

(9) To apply for, accept, receive and agree to, and to comply with the terms and conditions governing grants, loans, advances, contributions, gifts, and other aid from any source whatsoever, including federal and State sources;

(10) To sue and be sued in its own name, to plead and be impleaded;

(11) To adopt an official seal and to alter the same at its pleasure;

(12) To establish and revise from time to time minimum financial standards and criteria for determining the eligibility of specific units of local government to obtain financing and to make loans as provided in this Chapter;

(13) To deposit, disburse, and invest, pursuant to the provisions of this Chapter, the proceeds of any fund established in accordance with this Chapter and to determine the application of the proceeds of any earnings thereon, subject to the specific provisions of this Chapter; and

(14) To act as otherwise necessary or convenient to carry out the purposes of this Chapter. (1989, c. 756, s. 1; 2011-266, s. 1.26(c).)

§ 159I-6. Specific powers of the Board.

(a) The Board shall have the discretion to enter into one or more loan agreements with a unit of local government, providing for the making of a loan by the Board to the unit of local government, to finance or refinance the cost of the acquisition or construction of a project; and

(b) Any loan agreement entered into by the Board with a unit of local government shall be in writing and shall set forth the terms and conditions agreed to between the Board and the unit of local government for the Board's loan to such unit of local government including, without limitation, the following:

(1) The term of such loan agreement;

(2) The payment provisions and prepayment provisions, if any, required:

a. To enable the Board to administer its programs;

b. To pay when due the principal of and premium, if any, and interest on bonds or notes or other obligations of the Board incurred to make such loan; and

c. To pay or reimburse the Board for such unit's administration charges and the cost of establishing and maintaining any reserves;

(3) The security for payment by the unit of local government of the loan; and

(4) Such other provisions and covenants as the Board may require.

(c) Nothing in this Chapter shall be deemed to change the application of the provisions of Article 8 of Chapter 143 of the General Statutes, relating to competitive bidding for public contracts, or the application of the provisions of Article 3 of Chapter 143 of the General Statutes specifically including the provisions of G.S. 143-49(6), as it applies to units of local government financing projects under this Chapter. To the extent that units comply with such competitive bidding requirements, there shall be no further requirements in respect of the Board. (1989, c. 756, s. 1; 2011-266, s. 1.26(c).)

§ 159I-7. Solid Waste Management Loan Fund.

(a)   A Fund to be known as the Solid Waste Management Loan Fund is established. Moneys appropriated to, paid to, or earned by this Fund shall be deposited with the State Treasurer or a corporate trustee as provided for in G.S. 159I-16, as may be determined by the Board.

(b)   Moneys in the Solid Waste Management Loan Fund may be invested in the same manner as permitted for investments of funds belonging to the State or held in the State treasury. Interest earnings derived from such investments shall be credited to the Fund, credited to such other use as may be provided in a trust agreement or resolution securing any bonds or notes issued under the provisions of this Chapter, or credited to such other use, including the payment of administrative expenses of the Board, the costs of research for solid waste management programs and the making of grants for such research, as may be directed by the Board.

(b1)   In connection with solid waste research to be contracted for by the Division, the Secretary of Environment and Natural Resources shall negotiate, with the Board of the Board, a memorandum of agreement which shall contain necessary rules and provisions for certifying that proper competitive bid procedures, and when appropriate, proper sole source bid procedures, for contracts have been executed in connection with a Request for Proposals (RFP); and, which shall state that a previously determined one-to-one match requirement from private sector sources has been met in accordance with rules and provisions set out in the memorandum of agreement, and that the Secretary is ready to award a contract for a specified amount. The Treasurer, at the direction of the Board, shall certify that funds are available and that the purpose of the contract is consistent with provisions for the use of solid waste loan program proceeds.

(c)   Moneys in the Solid Waste Management Loan Fund may be used, as shall be determined by the Board, for any one or more of the following purposes:

(1)   The establishment of one or more debt service reserve funds;

(2)   The obtaining of one or more credit facilities as hereinafter defined in this Chapter;

(3) The making of loans to units of local government, which loans may be evidenced by debt instruments; and

(4) The subsidization of interest rates on loans to units of local government.

In addition, any investment income or profit on moneys in the Solid Waste Management Loan Fund or on any moneys transferred from the Fund to a debt service reserve fund may be used, as shall be determined by the Board, to pay administrative expenses of the Board.

(d) As used in this section, "debt instrument" means an instrument in the nature of a promissory note executed by a unit of local government to evidence a debt to the Board in respect of a loan made to the unit from the Solid Waste Management Loan Fund and obligation to repay the principal, plus interest, under stated terms. (1989, c. 756, s. 1; 1989 (Reg. Sess., 1990), c. 1004, s. 21; c. 1024, s. 49; 1997-443, s. 11A.119(a); 2011-266, s. 1.26(c).)

§ 159I-8. Eligible purpose.

(a) Loans may be made by the Board to finance the cost of acquisition or construction of projects. Projects shall include solid waste management projects and capital expenditures to implement such projects, including, without limitation, the purchase of equipment or facilities, construction costs of an incinerator; land to be used for recycling facilities or landfills; leachate collection and treatment systems; liners for landfills; monitoring wells; recycling equipment and facilities; volume reduction equipment; and financing charges.

(b) Projects may not include:

(1) The operational and maintenance costs of solid waste management facilities or programs;

(2) General planning or feasibility studies; or

(3) The purchase of land, unless the land is to be used for a recycling facility or a landfill. (1989, c. 756, s. 1; 1995, c. 384, s. 1; 2011-266, s. 1.26(c).)

§ 159I-9. Application.

(a)   All applications for loans shall be filed with the Division. The information required in the application shall be sufficient to permit the Division to determine the eligibility of the applicant pursuant to G.S. 159I-10 and to establish the priority of the application pursuant to G.S. 159I-11. An applicant shall furnish information in addition or supplemental to the information contained in its application upon written request.

(b)   Applicants may apply for a loan prior to arranging for repayment. (1989, c. 756, s. 1.)

§ 159I-10. Eligible applicant.

(a)   In determining the eligibility of a unit of local government for financing a project with a loan from the Board, the Board may consider:

(1)   The type and useful life of and the need for the project to be financed or refinanced;

(2)   The amount of financing or the cost of the project sought;

(3)   The credit rating, if any, of the unit of local government;

(4)   The future financing and capital needs of the unit of local government;

(5)   The availability and cost to the unit of local government of other methods of financing;

(6)   The construction, disbursement, and management procedures in effect in the unit of local government; and

(7)   Such other factors as the Board may, in its discretion, determine to be relevant in the providing of such financing.

(b)   As a condition of determining eligibility for participating in one or more financing programs, the Board may establish:

(1)   Procedures requiring compliance by units of local government with such construction, disbursement and accounting procedures, and programs as the Board may determine;

(2) Minimum credit ratings or criteria;

(3) Minimum and maximum amounts with respect to the cost of the projects to be financed under this Chapter;

(4) Procedures that may be employed by the Board in respect of units of local government that default in their obligations under loan agreements; and

(5) Such other procedures, conditions, and requirements as the Board determines to be necessary or desirable in establishing its programs.

Nothing in this Chapter shall be deemed to restrict or limit the powers otherwise available to a unit of local government except to the extent restricted by the terms of any loan agreements or other agreements between a unit and the Board, to obtain financing or refinancing for projects from a source other than the Board or to establish or continue its own financing program or to enter into any other financing program.

(c) A unit of local government is not eligible to finance a project with a loan from the Board unless the unit holds a public hearing on the issue of obtaining a loan from the Board before it applies for the loan. The unit must publish notice of the hearing in a newspaper that is qualified for legal advertising in the unit at least ten days before the date fixed for the hearing. (1989, c. 756, s. 1; 2011-266, s. 1.26(c).)

§ 159I-11. Priority factors.

(a) The Commission for Public Health shall adopt, pursuant to Chapter 150B of the General Statutes, rules for the assignment of a priority to each application for a loan under this Chapter.

(b) An application for a loan under this Chapter shall be assigned a priority by the Division. Factors to be taken into consideration in assigning such priorities shall include, but are not limited to, projects identified by the Division as addressing emergency solid waste management situations, current implementation by the unit of local government of a recycling program or a waste stream reduction program; financial need; multi-county solid waste management projects; groundwater protection needs; local effort; public health needs; and the proposed purpose of the applicant's loan is to implement a method of disposal that is an alternative to landfilling.

(c) A written statement of each priority assigned shall be prepared by the Division and shall be attached to the application. The priority assigned shall be conclusive.

(d) Any application that does not qualify for a loan for the period in which the application was eligible for consideration by reason of the priority assigned shall be considered for a loan during the next period upon written request of the applicant. If the second application should fail to qualify for a loan during the period for consideration by reason of the priority assigned, the application shall receive no further consideration. An applicant may file a new or amended application at any time. (1989, c. 756, s. 1; 2007-182, s. 2.)

§ 159I-12. Units of local government authorized to borrow money from the Board by loans.

(a) Any unit of local government determined by the Board to be eligible pursuant to G.S. 159I-10 may borrow money from the Board for the purpose of financing or refinancing the cost of the acquisition or construction of a project by a unit. The unit shall enter into a loan agreement with the Board. The loan agreement shall set forth the terms and conditions of the loan, including the terms and conditions described in G.S. 159I-6(b), as determined and approved by the governing body of the unit.

(b) The obligation of a unit of local government under any loan agreement entered into with the Board pursuant to this section shall be payable and otherwise secured as provided in G.S. 159I-13.

(c) In connection with entering into a loan obligation, any unit of local government may enter into a credit facility, as defined in G.S. 159I-13(g), and the obligation of a unit of local government under the credit facility to repay any drawing thereunder may be made payable and otherwise secured, to the extent applicable, as provided in G.S. 159I-13.

(d) The Board or a unit of local government may propose an amendment, including an amendment restructuring or otherwise relating to the principal repayment schedule and the interest payment schedule set forth in such loan agreement, upon a determination by the Board that such amendment is:

(1) Consistent with the then existing financial condition of the unit of local government and its ability to meet its agreement under the loan agreement; and

(2) Consistent with the then existing financial condition of the Board and the administration of the Board's duties and responsibilities under this Chapter.

Nothing in this Chapter shall be deemed as restricting the power of the Board or the unit of local government to agree to any amendment to a loan agreement.

(e) No loan agreement or amendment to a loan agreement may become effective without the approval of the Local Government Commission. In determining whether a loan agreement or any amendment thereto should be approved, the Local Government Commission may consider, to the extent applicable as shall be determined by the Local Government Commission, the criteria set forth in G.S. 159-52 and G.S. 159-86. The Local Government Commission shall approve any such loan agreement, or any amendment thereto, if, upon the information and evidence it receives, it finds and determines that such loan agreement, or amendment thereto, will satisfy its criteria and is consistent with the purposes of this Chapter. After considering a loan agreement or an amendment thereto, the Local Government Commission shall enter its order either approving or disapproving such agreement or amendment. An order of approval may not be regarded as an approval of the legality of such agreement or amendment. The order of the Local Government Commission disapproving such agreement or amendment is final. (1989, c. 756, s. 1; 2011-266, s. 1.26(c).)

§ 159I-13. Sources and security for units of local government.

(a) The source or sources of and the security for payment of each loan agreement shall be determined by the governing body of such unit of local government and shall be set forth in the loan agreement.

(b) In the event that, under the provisions of The Local Government Bond Act a bond order authorizing the issuance of bonds that pledge the faith and credit of a unit of local government, that is otherwise authorized to issue bonds under the act, for the purpose of providing funds for one or more purposes that constitute eligible projects within the meaning of this Chapter has taken effect, then, in lieu of issuing any bonds authorized or any bond anticipation note in anticipation of such bonds, but not sold and delivered pursuant to such order, the governing body of any unit of local government may enter into a loan agreement authorized by this Chapter and may pledge the faith and credit of such unit to secure its obligation to make the payments required under such loan agreement or a credit facility in support of such loan agreement, provided the following conditions are met:

(1) The aggregate principal amount due under such loan agreement does not exceed the aggregate amount of authorized but unissued bonds, or any bond anticipation notes in anticipation of such bonds, under the bond order; and

(2) The project to be acquired is a purpose for which proceeds of bonds or bond anticipation notes may be expended under the bond order.

(c) Each unit of local government may agree to apply to the payment of a loan agreement any available source or sources of revenues of such unit and, to the extent the generation of such revenues is within the power of such unit, to enter into covenants to take action in order to generate such revenues, provided such agreement to use such sources to make payments or such covenant to generate revenues does not constitute a pledge of the unit's taxing power.

(d) Each unit of local government otherwise having the power of taxation may enter into loan agreements constituting a continuing contract and providing for the making of payments in ensuing fiscal years from any available source or sources of revenues, including the proceeds of taxes realized from the exercise of the unit's power of taxation, appropriated by the unit in its annual budget provided:

(1) The governing body of such unit shall have appropriated sufficient funds to pay any amount to be paid under the loan agreement in the fiscal year in which such contract is entered into, this appropriation to be made prior to the entering into of the loan agreement;

(2) There is included in the loan agreement a provision automatically cancelling the loan agreement in the event the governing body of the unit decides not to appropriate funds to make payment in an ensuing fiscal year in which event the obligation of the unit to make any future payments in any ensuing fiscal year shall cease;

(3) No deficiency judgment requiring the exercise of the unit's power of taxation may be entered against the unit in any action for breach of a contractual obligation authorized by this subsection; and

(4) The taxing power of the unit is not pledged to secure any payments to be made pursuant to the loan agreement and the Board shall have agreed that it has no right to require the exercise of a unit's power of taxation to secure such loan agreement.

No loan agreement may contain a nonsubstitution clause which restricts the right of a unit to replace or provide a substitute for any project financed pursuant to the loan agreement.

(e) The obligation of a unit of local government with respect to the sources of revenues authorized by subsections (c) and (d) of this section shall be specifically identified in the proceedings of the governing body authorizing the unit to enter into a loan agreement. This loan agreement shall be valid and binding from the date the unit enters into the loan agreement. The sources of payment so specifically identified and then held or thereafter received by a unit, any fiduciary, or the Board shall immediately be subject to the lien of the loan agreement without any physical delivery of such sources or further act. This lien shall be valid and binding as against all parties having claims of any kind in tort, contract, or otherwise against a unit without regard to whether such parties have notice thereof. The proceedings, the loan agreement, or any other document or action by which the lien on a source of payment is created need not be filed or recorded in any manner other than as provided in the Chapter.

Any loan agreement secured by a source or sources of revenue authorized by subsection (b), (c) or (d) of this section may provide additional security by the granting of a security interest in the project financed to secure payment of the purchase money provided by the loan agreement, including a deed of trust on any real property so acquired.

(f) The interest payable by a unit to the Board on any loan agreement may be at such rate or rates, including variable rates, as may be determined by the Local Government Commission with the approval of the governing body of such unit. Such approval may be given as the governing body of such unit may direct, including without limitation, a certificate signed by a representative of the unit designated by the governing body of such unit. The Board may determine that it is necessary that certain provisions in the Board's bonds or notes be reflected, in similar terms, in loan agreements, so that if it is necessary to vary the interest rate or call the principal prior to maturity of certain of the Board's bonds or notes the Board will have the power to effect a similar variation in interest rate or a similar call prior to maturity of certain loan agreements. Accordingly, in fixing the details of a loan agreement, the governing body of such unit may provide that a loan agreement be:

(1) Made payable from time to time on demand or tender for purchase by the Board, provided a credit facility supports such a loan agreement. A credit facility is not required if the governing body of such unit specifically determines that a credit facility is not required upon a finding and determination by the governing body that the absence of a credit facility will not affect the unit's ability to make payments on demand or tender, and will not materially and adversely affect the financial position of the unit and the entering into of the loan agreement at a reasonable interest cost to the unit;

(2) Additionally supported by a credit facility;

(3) Made subject to redemption or a mandatory tender for purchase by the unit prior to maturity; and

(4) Bear interest at a rate or rates that may vary for such period or periods of time, all as may be provided in the proceedings of the governing body providing for the entering into of the loan agreement, including, without limitation, such variation as may be permitted pursuant to a par formula.

(g) As used in this section:

(1) "Credit facility" means an agreement entered into by the unit of local government with a bank, savings and loan association, or other banking institution; an insurance company, reinsurance company, surety company or other insurance institution; a corporation, investment banking firm or other investment institution; or any financial institution providing for prompt payment of all or any part of the principal or purchase price (whether at maturity, presentment, or tender for purchase, redemption, or acceleration), redemption premium, if any, and interest on any loan agreement payable on demand or tender by the Board, in consideration of the unit agreeing to repay the provider of such credit facility in accordance with the terms and provisions of the agreement; the provider of any credit facility may be located either within or without the United States of America.

(2) "Par formula" shall mean any provision or formula adopted by the unit to provide for the adjustment from time to time, of the interest rate or rates borne by any loan agreement, including:

a. A provision for such adjustment so that the purchase price of such loan agreement in the open market would be as close to par as possible.

b. A provision providing for such adjustment based upon a percentage or percentages of a prime rate or base rate, which percentage or porcentages may vary or be applied for different periods of time.

c. A provision providing for such adjustment based upon the adjustments of the interest rate or rates of the Board's bonds and notes, or

d. Such other provision as the unit may determine to be consistent with this Chapter and will not affect the unit's ability to pay the principal of and the interest on any loan agreement, and will not materially and adversely affect the financial position of the unit and the entering into of the loan agreement at a reasonable interest cost to the unit.

(h) Any loan agreement may provide for an acceleration of the repayment schedule. (1989, c. 756, s. 1; 2011-266, s. 1.26(c).)

§ 159I-14. Credit of State not pledged.

Bonds or notes issued by the Board under the provisions of this Chapter shall not be secured by a pledge of the faith and credit of the State or of any political subdivision thereof or be deemed to create an indebtedness of the State, or of any such political subdivision thereof, requiring any voter approval, but shall be payable solely from Board revenues and other funds provided therefor. Each bond or note issued by the Board under this Chapter shall contain on its face a statement to the effect that the Board shall not be obligated to pay the same, the interest, or the premium thereon except from Board revenues and other funds pledged therefor and that neither the faith and credit nor the taxing power of the State or of any political subdivision thereof is pledged as security for the payment of the principal of or the interest or premium on such Board bond or note.

Expenses incurred by the Board in carrying out the provisions of this Chapter shall be payable from revenues and other funds provided pursuant to, or available for use under, this Chapter. No liability may be incurred by the Board beyond the extent to which moneys shall have been so provided. (1989, c. 756, s. 1; 2011-266, s. 1.26(c).)

§ 159I-15. Bonds and notes.

(a) The Board may provide for the issuance at one time or from time to time of bonds and notes, including bond anticipation notes and renewal notes, of the Board to carry out and effectuate its corporate purposes. The principal of and interest on such bonds or notes shall be payable solely from funds provided under this Chapter for such payment. Any bond anticipation notes may be made payable from the proceeds of bonds or renewal notes or, in the event bond or renewal note proceeds are not available, notes may be paid from any available Board revenues or other funds provided for this purpose. Bonds and notes may also be paid from the proceeds of any credit facility. The bonds and notes of each issue shall be dated and may be made redeemable prior to maturity at the option of the Board or otherwise, at such price or prices, on such date or dates, and upon such terms and conditions as may be determined by the Board. The bonds or notes may also be made payable from time to time on demand or tender for purchase by owner, all upon such terms and conditions as may be determined by the Board. Any such bonds or notes shall bear interest at such rate or rates, including variable rates, as may be determined by the Local Government Commission with the approval of the Board.

The Board may also issue one or more series of bonds and notes, including bond anticipation notes and renewal notes, from time to time, to make loans to an individual unit of local government upon a determination, by resolution, of the Board as follows:

(1) The issuance of a series of bonds or notes by the Board in order to make a loan to an individual unit of local government, as distinct from the proceeds of such series of bonds or notes being used to provide a pool of money to make a number of such loans, does not materially adversely affect the ability of the Board to effect its general policy of making loans on a pooled basis.

(2) The issuance of the series of bonds or notes will not economically disadvantage the Board and will provide an economic benefit to the individual unit of local government.

(3) The use, if any, of any of the proceeds of the Solid Waste Management Loan Fund in connection with the Board financing for an individual unit of local government is consistent with the Board's use of any proceeds in connection with loans made on a pooled basis.

All of the provisions of this Chapter, including, without limitation, G.S. 159I-13 relating to the sources and security that may be used by units of local government in making loans, shall apply to any Board financing for an individual unit of local government.

(b) In fixing the details of bonds or notes, the Board may provide that any of the bonds or notes may:

(1) Be made payable from time to time on demand or tender for purchase by the owner thereof provided a credit facility supports such bonds or notes, unless the Local Government Commission specifically determines that a credit facility is not required upon a finding and determination by the Local Government Commission that the absence of a credit facility will not materially and adversely affect the financial position of the Board and the marketing of the bonds or notes at a reasonable interest cost to the Board;

(2) Be additionally supported by a credit facility;

(3) Be made subject to redemption or a mandatory tender for purchase prior to maturity;

(4) Bear interest at a rate or rates that may vary for such period or periods of time, all as may be provided in the proceedings providing for the issuance of such bonds or notes including, without limitation, such variations as may be permitted pursuant to a par formula; and

(5) Be made the subject of a remarketing agreement whereby an attempt is made to remarket the bonds or notes to new purchasers prior to their presentment for payment to the provider of the credit facility or to the Board.

(c) As used in this section:

(1) "Credit facility" means an agreement entered into by the Board with a bank, savings and loan association or other banking institution, an insurance company, reinsurance company, surety company or other insurance institution, a corporation, investment banking firm or other investment institution, or any financial institution providing for prompt payment of all or any part of the principal or purchase price (whether at maturity, presentment or tender for purchase, redemption or acceleration), redemption premium, if any, and interest on any bonds or notes payable on demand or tender by the owner, in consideration of the Board agreeing to repay the provider of such credit facility

in accordance with the terms and provisions of such agreement; the provider of any credit facility may be located either within or without the United States of America.

(2) "Par formula" means any provision or formula adopted by the Board to provide for the adjustment, from time to time, of the interest rate or rates borne by any bonds or notes including:

a. A provision providing for the adjustment so that the purchase price of the bonds or notes in the open market would be as close to par as possible;

b. A provision providing for the adjustment based upon a percentage or percentages of a prime rate or base rate, which percentage or percentages may vary or be applied for different periods of time; or

c. Such other provisions as the Board may determine to be consistent with this Chapter and will not materially and adversely affect the financial position of the Board and the marketing of the bonds or notes at a reasonable interest cost to the Board.

(d) Notes shall mature at such time or times and bonds shall mature, not exceeding 40 years from their date or dates, as may be determined by the Board. The Board shall determine the form and manner of execution of the bonds or notes, including any interest coupons to be attached thereto, and shall fix the denomination or denominations and the place or places of payment of principal and interest, which may be any bank or trust company within or without the United States. In case any officer whose signature or a facsimile of whose signature shall appear on any bonds or notes or coupons, if any, shall cease to be this officer before the delivery thereof, this signature or the facsimile shall nevertheless be valid and sufficient for all purposes the same as if the officer had remained in office until the delivery and any bond or note or coupon may bear the facsimile signatures of such persons who at the actual time of the execution thereof shall be the proper officers to sign although at the date of the bond or note or coupon the persons may not have been these officers. The Board may also provide for the authentication of the bonds or notes by a trustee or other authenticating agent. The bonds or notes may be issued as certificated or uncertificated obligations or both, and in coupon or in registered form, or both, as the Board may determine. Provision may be made for the registration of any coupon bonds or notes as to principal alone and also as to both principal and interest, and for the reconversion into coupon bonds or notes of any bonds or notes registered as to both principal and interest, and for the interchange of registered and coupon bonds or notes. Any system for registration may be established as the Board may determine.

(e)   No bonds or notes may be issued by the Board under this Chapter unless the issuance thereof is approved and the bonds or notes are sold by the Local Government Commission as provided in this Chapter. The Board shall file with the Secretary of the Local Government Commission an application requesting approval of the issuance of the bonds or notes which application shall contain any such information and shall have attached to it any such documents concerning the proposed financing as the Secretary of the Local Government Commission may require.

In determining whether a proposed bond or note issue should be approved, the Local Government Commission may consider, to the extent applicable as shall be determined by the Local Government Commission, the criteria set forth in G.S. 159-52 and G.S. 159-86, as well as the effect of the proposed financing upon any scheduled or proposed sale of obligations by the State, by any of its agencies or departments, or by any unit of local government in the State. The Local Government Commission shall approve the issuance of such bonds or notes if, upon the information and evidence it receives, it finds and determines that the proposed financing will satisfy such criteria and will effect the purposes of this Chapter.

Upon the filing with the Local Government Commission of a written request of the Board requesting that its bonds or notes be sold, the bonds or notes may be sold by the Local Government Commission in such manner, either at public or private sale, and for such price or prices as the Local Government Commission shall determine to be in the best interest of the Board and to effect the purposes of this Chapter, provided that the sale shall be approved by the Board.

(f)   The proceeds of any bonds or notes shall be used solely for the purposes for which the bonds or notes were issued and shall be disbursed in such manner and under such restrictions, if any, as the Board may provide in the resolution authorizing the issuance of, or in any trust agreement securing, such bonds or notes.

(g)   Prior to the preparation of definitive bonds, the Board may issue interim receipts or temporary bonds, with or without coupons, exchangeable for definitive bonds when the bonds have been executed and are available for delivery. The Board may also provide for the replacement of any bonds or notes which shall become mutilated or shall be destroyed or lost.

(h) Bonds or notes may be issued under the provision of this Chapter without obtaining, except as otherwise expressly provided in this Chapter, the consent of any department, division, commission, board, body, bureau, or agency of the State and without any other proceedings or the happening of any conditions or things other than those proceedings, conditions, or things that are specifically required by this Chapter and the provisions of the resolution authorizing the issuance of, or any trust agreement securing, such bonds or notes. (1989, c. 756, s. 1; 1989 (Reg. Sess., 1990), c. 1004, ss. 22, 23; c. 1024, s. 38(a), (b); 2011-266, s. 1.26(c).)

§ 159I-16. Trust agreement or resolution.

(a) In the discretion of the Board, any bonds and notes issued under the provisions of this Chapter may be secured by a trust agreement by and between the Board and a corporate trustee or by a resolution providing for the appointment of a corporate trustee. The corporate trustee may be, in either case, any trust company or bank having the powers of a trust company within or without the State. Such trust agreement or resolution may pledge or assign all or part of the revenues or assets of the Board, including, without limitation, loan agreements, agreements or commitments to enter into loan agreements, contracts, agreements and other security or investment obligations, any fees or charges made or received by the Board, the moneys received in payment of loans and interest thereon, and any other moneys received by the Board. The trust agreement or resolution may contain such provisions for protecting and enforcing the rights and remedies of the owners of any bonds or notes issued thereunder as may be reasonable and proper and not in violation of law, including covenants setting forth the duties of the Board in respect of the purposes to which bond or note proceeds may be applied, the disposition and application of the revenues or assets of the Board, the duties of the Board with respect to the acquisition and disposition of any project and the purchase, acceptance and disposition of any loan agreement, the charges and collection of any revenues and administrative charges, the terms and conditions for the issuance of additional bonds and notes, and the custody, safeguarding, investment, and application of all moneys. All bonds and notes issued under this Chapter shall be equally and ratably secured by a pledge, charge, and lien upon the revenues or assets provided in such trust agreement or resolution, without priority by reason of number, or dates of bonds or notes, execution, or delivery, in accordance with the provision of this Chapter and of such trust agreement or resolution; except that the Board may provide in such trust agreement or resolution that bonds or notes issued pursuant thereto shall, to the extent and in the manner prescribed in such trust agreement or resolution, be subordinated and junior in standing, with respect to the payment of principal and interest and to the security thereof, to any other bonds or notes. It shall be lawful for any bank or trust company that may act as depositary of the proceeds of bonds or notes, revenues, assets, or other money hereunder to furnish such indemnifying bonds or to pledge such securities as may be required by the Board. Any trust agreement or resolution may set out the rights and remedies of the owners of any bonds or notes and of any trustee, and may restrict the individual rights of action by any such owners. In addition to the foregoing, any trust agreement or resolution may contain such other provisions as the Board may deem reasonable and proper for the security of the owners of any bonds or notes. Expenses incurred in carrying out the provisions of any trust agreement or resolution may be treated as a part of the cost of any project or as an administrative charge and may be paid from the revenues or assets pledged or assigned to the payment of the principal of and the interest on bonds and notes or from any other funds available to the Board.

(b) The Board may set the terms and conditions of loan agreements, including, without limitation, the repayment terms, so as to provide a fund sufficient, with such other funds as may be made available therefor, including, without limitation, investment income and the proceeds of administrative charges to the extent determined by the Board:

(1) To pay the costs of operation of the Board,

(2) To pay the principal of and the interest on all bonds and notes as the same shall become due and payable, and

(3) To create and maintain any reserves provided for in the trust agreement or resolution securing such bonds or notes.

(c) All pledges of any assets or revenues of the Board as authorized by this Chapter shall be valid and binding from the time when such pledges are made. All such assets or revenues so pledged and thereafter received by the Board shall immediately be subject to the lien of such pledge without any physical delivery thereof or further act, and the lien of any such pledge shall be valid and binding as against all parties having claims of any kind in tort, contract, or otherwise against the Board, irrespective of whether such parties have notice thereof. The trust agreement or resolution by which a pledge is created or any loan obligation need not be filed or recorded except in the records of the Board.

(d) The State does pledge to and agree with the holders of any bonds or notes issued by the Board that so long as any of such bonds or notes are outstanding and unpaid the State will not limit or alter the rights vested in the Board at the time of issuance of the bonds or notes to set the terms and conditions of loan agreements in connection with which the bonds or notes were issued, so as to provide a fund sufficient, with such other funds as may be made available therefor, including without limitation, investment income and the proceeds of administrative charges to the extent determined by the Board, to pay the costs of operation of the Board, to pay the principal of and the interest on all bonds and notes as the same shall become due and payable, and to create and maintain any reserves provided therefor, and to fulfill the terms of any agreements made with the bondholders or noteholders. The State shall in no way impair the rights and remedies of the bondholders or noteholders until the bonds or notes and all costs and expenses in connection with any action or proceedings by or on behalf of the bondholders or noteholders, are fully paid, met, and discharged. (1989, c. 756, s. 1; 1989 (Reg. Sess., 1990), c. 1004, ss. 24, 25; c. 1024, s. 38(c), (d); 2011-266, s. 1.26(c).)

§ 159I-17. Trust funds.

Notwithstanding any other provisions of law to the contrary, all moneys received pursuant to this Chapter, including, without limitation, payments made under and the proceeds received from the sale or other disposition of loan agreement, proceeds received from the disposition by the Board of any project and any other revenues and funds received by the Board, (except any portion, as designated by the Board, representing administrative charges), shall be deemed to be trust funds to be held and applied solely as provided in this Chapter. The resolution authorizing the issuance of, or any trust agreement securing, any bonds or notes may provide that any of such moneys may be invested temporarily pending the disbursement thereof and shall provide that any officer with whom or any bank or trust company with which such moneys shall be deposited, shall act as trustee of such moneys and shall hold and apply the same for the purposes of this Chapter subject to such regulations as this Chapter or such resolution or trust agreement may provide. Any such moneys may be deposited and invested as provided in G.S. 159-30 and G.S. 147-69.1, as either section may be amended from time to time, provided, however that:

(1) Any deposit or investment authorized by G.S. 159-30 or G.S. 147-69.1 may be deposited or invested with any bank located inside or outside the State, including outside the United States of America, provided that any such bank is a

bank whose unsecured obligations are rated in either of the two highest rating categories by either Moody's Investors Service or Standard & Poor's Corporation; and

(2) Any deposit or investment may be made pursuant to either G.S. 159-30 or G.S. 147-69.1. If one section is less restrictive or the other section authorizes additional deposit and investment options, the Board may proceed under either section in order that the Board shall have the broadest deposit and investment options available under either section. (1989, c. 756, s. 1; 2011-266, s. 1.26(c).)

§ 159I-18. Remedies.

Any owner of bonds or notes issued under the provisions of this Chapter or any coupons appertaining thereto, and the trustee under any trust agreement securing or resolution authorizing the issuance of such bonds or notes, except to the extent the rights herein given may be restricted by such trust agreement or resolution, may either at law or in equity, by suit, action, mandamus, or other proceeding, protect and enforce any and all rights under the laws of the State or granted hereunder or under such trust agreement or resolution, or under any other contract executed by the Board pursuant to this Chapter; and may enforce and compel the performance of all duties required by this Chapter or by such trust agreement or resolution by the Board or by any officer thereof. (1989, c. 756, s. 1; 2011-266, s. 1.26(c).)

§ 159I-19. Status of bonds and notes under Uniform Commercial Code.

All bonds and notes and interest coupons, if any, issued under this Chapter are hereby made investment securities within the meaning of and for all the purposes of Article 8 of the Uniform Commercial Code, as enacted in Chapter 25 of the General Statutes. (1989, c. 756, s. 1.)

§ 159I-20. Bonds and notes eligible for investment.

Bonds and notes issued under the provisions of this Chapter are hereby made securities in which all public offices, agencies, and public bodies of the State and its political subdivisions, all insurance companies, trust companies, investment companies, banks, savings banks, building and loan associations, credit unions, pension or retirement funds, other financial institutions engaged in business in the State, executors, administrators, trustees, and other fiduciaries may properly and legally invest funds, including capital in their control or belonging to them. Such bonds or notes are hereby made securities, which may properly and legally be deposited with and received by any officer or agency of the State or political subdivision of the State for any purpose for which the deposit of bonds, notes, or obligations of the State or any political subdivision is now or may hereafter be authorized by law. (1989, c. 756, s. 1.)

§ 159I-21. Refunding bonds and notes.

(a) The Board may issue bonds and notes for the purposes of refunding any bonds or notes issued pursuant to this Chapter, including the payment of any redemption premium thereon and any interest accrued or to accrue to the date of redemption or maturity of such bonds or notes, and, if deemed advisable by the Board, for any additional corporate purposes of the Board.

Any such refunding bonds or notes may bear interest at rates, including variable rates as authorized in G.S. 159I-15, lower, the same as, or higher than and have maturities shorter than, the same as, or longer than the bonds or notes being refunded. The proceeds of any such refunding bonds or notes may be applied:

(1) To the payment and retirement of the bonds or notes being refunded by direct application to such payment and retirement;

(2) To the payment and retirement of the bonds or notes being refunded by the deposit in trust of such proceeds;

(3) To the payment of any expenses incurred in connection with such refunding; and

(4) For any other uses not inconsistent with such refunding.

(b) Any money so held in trust may be invested in:

(1) Direct obligations of the United States of America.

(2) Obligations, the principal of and the interest on which are guaranteed by the United States of America.

(3) Evidences of ownership of a proportionate interest in specified obligations described in subdivision (1) and (2) of this subsection, which obligations are held by a bank or trust company organized and existing under the laws of the United States of America or any state thereof in the capacity of custodian.

(4) Obligations of the State or local governments of the State, provision for the payment of the principal of and interest on which obligations shall have been made by deposit with a trustee or escrow agent of obligations described in subdivisions (1), (2) or (3) of this subsection, the maturing principal of any interest on which, when due and payable, shall provide sufficient money with any other money held in trust for such purpose to pay the principal of, premium, if any, and interest on such obligations of the State or units of local government and which are rated in the highest category by Standard & Poor's Corporation and Moody's Investors Service.

(5) Obligations of the State or local governments of the State, the principal of and interest on which, when due and payable, have been insured by a bond insurance company which is rated in the highest category by Standard & Poor's Corporation and Moody's Investors Service.

(6) Full faith and credit obligations of the State or local governments of the State, which are rated in the highest category by Standard & Poor's Corporation and Moody's Investors Service.

(7) Any obligations or investments in which the State Treasurer is authorized, at the time of such investment, to invest funds of the State.

The proceedings providing for the issuance of any refunding bonds or notes may limit the investments in which the proceeds of a particular refunding issue may be invested.

(c) Nothing in this section shall be construed as a limitation on:

(1) The duration of any deposit in trust for the retirement of bonds or notes being refunded, but which shall not have matured and which shall not be then redeemable or, if then redeemable, shall not have been called for redemption; or

(2) The power to issue bonds or notes for the combined purpose of refunding bonds or notes and providing moneys for any corporate purpose as provided in this Chapter. (1989, c. 756, s. 1; 2011-266, s. 1.26(c).)

§ 159I-22. Officers not liable.

No member or officer of the Board shall be subject to any personal liability or accountability by reason of his execution of any bonds or notes or the issuance thereof. (1989, c. 756, s. 1; 2011-266, s. 1.26(c).)

§ 159I-23. Tax exemption.

All of the bonds and notes authorized by this Chapter shall be exempt from all State, county, and municipal taxation or assessment, direct or indirect, general or special, whether imposed for the purpose of general revenue or otherwise, excluding inheritance and gift taxes, income taxes on the gain from the transfer of the bonds and notes, and franchise taxes. The interest on the bonds and notes shall not be subject to taxation as income. (1989, c. 756, s. 1; 1995, c. 46, s. 19.)

§ 159I-24. Conflicts of interest.

If any member, officer, or employee of the Board shall be interested either directly or indirectly, or shall be an officer or employee of or have an ownership interest in any firm or corporation, not including units of local government interested directly or indirectly, in any contract with the Board, such interest shall be disclosed to the Board and shall be set forth in the minutes of the Board. The member, officer, or employee having an interest therein shall not participate on behalf of the Board in the authorization of any such contract. Other provisions of law notwithstanding, failure to take any or all actions necessary to carry out the purposes of this section may not affect the validity of any bonds, notes, or loan agreements issued pursuant to the provisions of this Chapter. (1989, c. 756, s. 1; 2011-266, s. 1.26(c).)

§ 159I-25. Disbursement.

(a) The proceeds of any bonds or notes to be used to make loans shall be disbursed by, or pursuant to the direction of, the Office of State Budget and Management. No such proceeds shall be disbursed until the Office of State Budget and Management has received from the Division a certificate of eligibility that states that the applicant meets all eligibility criteria, and that all procedural requirements of this Chapter have been met.

(b) Once the prerequisites for disbursement have been satisfied pursuant to subsection (a) of this section, the proceeds shall be disbursed as the Board may provide. (1989, c. 756, s. 1; 2000-140, s. 93.1(a); 2001-424, s. 12.2(b).)

§ 159I-26. Withdrawal of commitment.

Failure of an applicant, within one year of the date of acceptance of a loan application to arrange for necessary financing of the proposed project, shall constitute sufficient cause for withdrawal of the commitment. Prior to withdrawal of a commitment, the Division shall give due consideration to any extenuating circumstances presented by the applicant as reasons for its failure to arrange necessary financing. The commitment may be extended for an additional period of time if, in the judgment of the Division, an extension is justified. (1989, c. 756, s. 1.)

§ 159I-27. Inspection.

(a) The Division shall perform one or more inspections of each project and shall monitor its progress. If the Division determines that the project is not in substantial compliance with the approved schedule of implementation, the Division may revoke its approval of the project, further disbursement of loan proceeds may be rescinded, and the outstanding loan, together with accrued interest, may immediately become due and payable.

(b) Inspection of a project for which a loan has been made under this Chapter may be performed by qualified personnel of the Division or by qualified professional engineers, registered in this State, who have been approved by the Division. No person may be approved to perform inspections who is an officer or employee of the unit of local government to which the loan was made or who is an owner, officer, employee or agent of a contractor or subcontractor engaged in the construction of any project for which the loan was made. (1989, c. 756, s. 1.)

§ 159I-28. Rules.

(a) The Office of State Budget and Management and the Commission for Public Health may adopt, modify and repeal rules establishing the procedures to be followed in the administration of this Chapter and regulations interpreting and applying the provisions of this Chapter, as provided in the Administrative Procedure Act. Uniform rules may be jointly adopted where feasible and desirable, and no rule jointly adopted may be modified or revoked except upon the concurrence of both agencies involved.

(b) A copy of the rules adopted to implement the provisions of this Chapter shall be furnished free of charge by the Division and the Office of State Budget and Management to any unit of local government. (1989, c. 756, s. 1; 1997-443, s. 11A.114; 2000-140, s. 93.1(a); 2001-424, s. 12.2(b); 2007-182, s. 2.)

§ 159I-29. Annual reports to Joint Legislative Commission on Governmental Operations.

(a) If the General Assembly appropriates funds for loans authorized by this Chapter in any fiscal year, the Office of State Budget and Management and the Division shall prepare and file on or before July 31 of the following fiscal year with the Joint Legislative Commission on Governmental Operations a consolidated report for the preceding fiscal year concerning the allocation of loans authorized by this Chapter. No report shall be filed for fiscal years in which no funds are appropriated or otherwise available for loans authorized by this Chapter.

(b) The portion of the report prepared by the Office of State Budget and Management shall set forth for the preceding fiscal year itemized and total allocations for loans authorized by the Division. The Office of State Budget and Management shall also prepare a summary report of all allocations for each fiscal year; the total funds received and allocations made; and the total unallocated funds as of the end of the preceding fiscal year.

(c) The portion of the report prepared by the Division shall include:

(1) Identification of each loan made during the preceding fiscal year; the total amount of the loan commitments; the sums actually paid during the preceding fiscal year to each loan disbursed and to each loan previously

committed but unpaid; and the total loan funds paid during the preceding fiscal year;

(2) A summary for all preceding years of the total number of loans made; the total funds committed to these loans; the total sum actually paid to loans; and

(3) Assessment and evaluation of the effects that approved projects have had upon solid waste management within the purposes of this Chapter.

(d) The report shall be signed by each of the chief executive officers of the two State agencies preparing the report. (1989, c. 756, s. 1; 1993, c. 553, s. 57; 2000-140, s. 93.1(a); 2001-424, s. 12.2(b); 2012-200, s. 26.)

§ 159I-30. Additional powers of units of local government; issuance of special obligation bonds and notes.

(a) Authorization. - Any unit of local government may borrow money for the purpose of financing or refinancing its cost of the acquisition or construction of a project and may issue special obligation bonds and notes, including bond anticipation notes and renewal notes, pursuant to the provisions of this section and the applicable provisions of this Chapter for this purpose.

(b) Pledge. - Each unit of local government may pledge for the payment of a special obligation bond or note any available source or sources of revenues of the unit and, to the extent the generation of the revenues is within the power of the unit, may enter into covenants to take action in order to generate the revenues, as long as the pledge of these sources for payments or the covenant to generate revenues does not constitute a pledge of the unit's taxing power.

No agreement or covenant shall contain a nonsubstitution clause which restricts the right of a unit of local government to replace or provide a substitute for any project financed pursuant to this section.

The sources of payment pledged by a unit of local government shall be specifically identified in the proceedings of the governing body authorizing the unit to issue the special obligation bonds or notes.

After the issuance of special obligation bonds or notes, the governing body of the issuing unit may identify one or more additional sources of payment for the bonds or notes and pledge these sources, as long as the pledge of the sources does not constitute a pledge of the taxing power of the unit. Each source of additional payment pledged shall be specifically identified in the proceedings of the governing body of the unit pledging the source. The governing body of the unit may not pledge an additional source of revenue pursuant to this paragraph unless the pledge is first approved by the Local Government Commission pursuant to the procedures provided in subsection (i) of this section.

The sources of payment so pledged and then held or thereafter received by a unit or any fiduciary thereof shall immediately be subject to the lien of the pledge without any physical delivery of the sources or further act. The lien shall be valid and binding as against all parties having claims of any kind in tort, contract, or otherwise against a unit without regard to whether the parties have notice thereof. The proceedings or any other document or action by which the lien on a source of payment is created need not be filed or recorded in any manner other than as provided in this Chapter.

(b1) Security Interest. - In connection with issuing its special obligation bonds or special obligation bond anticipation notes under this Chapter, a unit of local government may grant a security interest in the project financed, or in all or some portion of the property on which the project is located, or in both. If a unit of local government determines to provide additional security as authorized by this subsection, the following conditions apply:

(1) No bond order may contain a nonsubstitution clause that restricts the right of a unit of local government to:

a. Continue to provide a service or activity; or

b. Replace or provide a substitute for any municipal purpose financed pursuant to the bond order.

(2) A bond order is subject to approval by the Commission under Article 8 of Chapter 159 of the General Statutes if it:

a. Meets the standards set out in G.S. 159-148(a)(1), 159-148(a)(2), and 159-148(a)(3), or involves the construction or repair of fixtures or improvements on real property; and

b. Is not exempted from the provisions of that Article by one of the exemptions contained in G.S. 159-148(b)(1) and (2).

The Commission approval required by this subdivision is in addition to the Commission approval required by subsection (i) of this section.

(3) No deficiency judgment may be rendered against any unit of local government in any action for breach of a bond order authorized by this section, and the taxing power of a unit of local government is not and may not be pledged directly or indirectly to secure any moneys due under a bond order authorized by this section. This prohibition does not impair the right of the holder of a bond or note to exercise a remedy with respect to the revenues pledged to secure the bond or note, as provided in the bond order, resolution, or trust agreement under which the bond or note is authorized and secured. A unit of local government may, in its sole discretion, use tax proceeds to pay the principal of or interest or premium on bonds or notes, but shall not pledge or agree to do so.

(4) Before granting a security interest under this subsection, a unit of local government shall hold a public hearing on the proposed security interest. A notice of the public hearing shall be published once at least 10 days before the date fixed for the hearing.

(c) Payment; Call. - Any bond anticipation notes may be made payable from the proceeds of bonds or renewal notes or, in the event bond or renewal note proceeds are not available, the notes may be paid from any sources available under G.S. 159I-30(b). Bonds or notes may also be paid from the proceeds of any credit facility. The bonds and notes of each issue shall be dated and may be made redeemable prior to maturity at the option of the unit of local government or otherwise, at such price or prices, on such date or dates, and upon such terms and conditions as may be determined by the unit. The bonds or notes may also be made payable from time to time on demand or tender for purchase by the owner, upon terms and conditions determined by the unit.

(d) Interest. - The interest payable by a unit on any special obligation bonds or notes may be at such rate or rates, including variable rates as authorized in this section, as may be determined by the Local Government Commission with the approval of the governing body of the unit. This approval may be given as the governing body of the unit may direct, including, without limitation, a certificate signed by a representative of the unit designated by the governing body of the unit.

(e) Nature of Obligation. - Special obligation bonds and notes shall be special obligations of the unit of local government issuing them. The principal of, and interest and any premium on, special obligation bonds and notes shall be secured solely by any one or more of the sources of payment authorized by this section as may be pledged in the proceedings, resolution, or trust agreement under which they are authorized or secured. Neither the faith and credit nor the taxing power of the unit of local government are pledged for the payment of the principal of, or interest or any premium on, any special obligation bonds or notes, and no owner of special obligation bonds or notes has the right to compel the exercise of the taxing power by the unit in connection with any default thereon. Every special obligation bond and note shall recite in substance that the principal and interest and any premium on the bond or note are secured solely by the sources of payment pledged in the bond order, resolution, or trust agreement under which it is authorized or secured. The following limitations apply to payment from the specified sources:

(1) Any such use of these sources will not constitute a pledge of the unit's taxing power; and

(2) The unit is not obligated to pay the principal or interest or premium except from these sources.

(f) Details. - In fixing the details of bonds or notes, the unit of local government may provide that any of the bonds or notes may:

(1) Be made payable from time to time on demand or tender for purchase by the owner thereof as long as a credit facility supports the bonds or notes, unless the Local Government Commission specifically determines that a credit facility is not required upon a finding and determination by the Local Government Commission that the absence of a credit facility will not materially and adversely affect the financial position of the unit and the marketing of the bonds or notes at a reasonable interest cost to the unit;

(2) Be additionally supported by a credit facility;

(3) Be made subject to redemption or a mandatory tender for purchase prior to maturity;

(4) Bear interest at a rate or rates that may vary for such period or periods of time, all as may be provided in the proceedings providing for the issuance of

the bonds or notes including, without limitation, such variations as may be permitted pursuant to a par formula; and

(5) Be made the subject of a remarketing agreement whereby an attempt is made to remarket the bonds or notes to new purchasers prior to their presentment for payment to the provider of the credit facility or to the unit.

(g) Definitions. - The following definitions apply in this section:

(1) Credit facility. - An agreement entered into by the unit with a bank, a savings and loan association, or another banking institution; an insurance company, a reinsurance company, a surety company, or another insurance institution; a corporation, an investment banking firm, or another investment institution; or any financial institution, providing for prompt payment of all or any part of the principal, or purchase price (whether at maturity, presentment, or tender for purchase, redemption, or acceleration), redemption premium, if any, and interest on any bonds or notes payable on demand or tender by the owner, in consideration of the unit agreeing to repay the provider of the credit facility in accordance with the terms and provisions of the agreement; the provider of any credit facility may be located either within or without the United States of America.

(2) Par formula. - Any provision or formula adopted by the unit to provide for the adjustment, from time to time of the interest rate or rates borne by any bonds or notes including:

a. A provision providing for such adjustment so that the purchase price of such bonds or notes in the open market would be as close to par as possible;

b. A provision providing for such adjustment based upon a percentage or percentages of a prime rate or base rate, which percentage or percentages may vary or be applied for different periods of time; or

c. Any other provision as the unit may determine to be consistent with this section and the applicable provisions of this Chapter and does not materially and adversely affect the financial position of the unit and the marketing of the bonds or notes at a reasonable interest cost to the unit.

(3) Project. - Any of the following:

a. A project as defined in G.S. 159I-3.

b. Any of the following as defined in S.L. 1998-132: water supply systems, water conservation projects, water reuse projects, wastewater collection systems, and wastewater treatment works.

c. With respect to a city, any service or facility authorized by G.S. 160A-536 and provided in a municipal service district.

(g1) Credit Facility. - The obligation of a unit of local government under a credit facility to repay any drawing thereunder may be made payable and otherwise secured, to the extent applicable, as provided in this section.

(h) Term; Form. - Notes shall mature at such time or times and bonds shall mature, not exceeding 40 years from their date or dates, as may be determined by the unit of local government, except that no such maturity dates may exceed the maximum maturity periods prescribed by the Local Government Commission pursuant to G.S. 159-122, as it may be amended from time to time. The unit shall determine the form and manner of execution of the bonds or notes, including any interest coupons to be attached thereto, and shall fix the denomination or denominations and the place or places of payment of principal and interest, which may be any bank or trust company within or without the United States. In case any officer of the unit whose signature, or a facsimile of whose signature, appears on any bonds or notes or coupons, if any, ceases to be the officer before delivery thereof, the signature or facsimile shall nevertheless be valid and sufficient for all purposes the same as if the officer had remained in office until the delivery. Any bond or note or coupon may bear the facsimile signatures of such persons who at the actual time or the execution thereof were the proper officers to sign although at the date of the bond or note or coupon these persons may not have been the proper officers. The unit may also provide for the authentication of the bonds or notes by a trustee or other authenticating agent. The bonds or notes may be issued as certificated or uncertificated obligations or both, and in coupon or in registered form, or both, as the unit may determine, and provision may be made for the registration of any coupon bonds or notes as to principal alone and also as to both principal and interest, and for the reconversion into coupon bonds or notes of any bonds or notes registered as to both principal and interest, and for the interchange of registered and coupon bonds or notes. Any system for registration may be established as the unit may determine.

(i) Local Government Commission Approval. - No bonds or notes may be issued by a unit of local government under this section unless the issuance is approved and the bonds or notes are sold by the Local Government

Commission as provided in this section and the applicable provisions of this Chapter. The unit shall file with the Secretary of the Local Government Commission an application requesting approval of the issuance of the bonds or notes, which application shall contain such information and shall have attached to it such documents concerning the proposed financing as the Secretary of the Local Government Commission may require. The Commission may prescribe the form of the application. Before the Secretary accepts the application, the Secretary may require the governing body of the unit or its representatives to attend a preliminary conference, at which time the Secretary or the deputies of the Secretary may informally discuss the proposed issue and the timing of the steps taken in issuing the special obligation bonds or notes.

In determining whether a proposed bond or note issue should be approved, the Local Government Commission may consider, to the extent applicable as shall be determined by the Local Government Commission, the criteria set forth in G.S. 159-52 and G.S. 159-86, as either may be amended from time to time, as well as the effect of the proposed financing upon any scheduled or proposed sale of obligations by the State or by any of its agencies or departments or by any unit of local government in the State. The Local Government Commission shall approve the issuance of the bonds or notes if, upon the information and evidence it receives, it finds and determines that the proposed financing will satisfy such criteria and will effect the purposes of this section and the applicable provisions of this Chapter. An approval of an issue shall not be regarded as an approval of the legality of the issue in any respect. A decision by the Local Government Commission denying an application is final.

Upon the filing with the Local Government Commission of a written request of the unit requesting that its bonds or notes be sold, the bonds or notes may be sold by the Local Government Commission in such manner, either at public or private sale, and for such price or prices as the Local Government Commission shall determine to be in the best interests of the unit and to effect the purposes of this section and the applicable provisions of this Chapter, if the sale is approved by the unit.

(j) Proceeds. - The proceeds of any bonds or notes shall be used solely for the purposes for which the bonds or notes were issued and shall be disbursed in such manner and under such restrictions, if any, as the unit may provide in the resolution authorizing the issuance of, or in any trust agreement securing, the bonds or notes.

(k) Interim Documents; Replacement. - Prior to the preparation of definitive bonds, the unit may issue interim receipts or temporary bonds, with or without coupons, exchangeable for definitive bonds when definitive bonds have been executed and are available for delivery. The unit may also provide for the replacement of any bonds or notes which shall become mutilated or shall be destroyed or lost.

(l) No Other Conditions. - Bonds or notes may be issued under the provisions of this section and the applicable provisions of this Chapter without obtaining, except as otherwise expressly provided in this section and the applicable provisions of this Chapter, the consent of any department, division, commission, board, body, bureau, or agency of the State and without any other proceedings or the happening of any conditions or things other than those proceedings, conditions, or things that are specifically required by this section, the applicable provisions of this Chapter, and the provisions of the resolution authorizing the issuance of, or any trust agreement securing, the bonds or notes.

(m) Trust. - In the discretion of the unit of local government, any bonds and notes issued under the provisions of this section may be secured by a trust agreement by and between the unit and a corporate trustee or by a resolution providing for the appointment of a corporate trustee. Bonds and notes may also be issued under an order or resolution without a corporate trustee. The corporate trustee may be, in either case any trust company or bank having the powers of a trust company within or without the State. The trust agreement or resolution may pledge or assign such sources of revenue as may be permitted under this section. The trust agreement or resolution may contain such provisions for protecting and enforcing the rights and remedies of the owners of any bonds or notes issued thereunder as may be reasonable and proper and not in violation of law, including covenants setting forth the duties of the unit in respect of the purposes to which bond or note proceeds may be applied, the disposition and application of the revenues of the unit, the duties of the unit with respect to the project, the disposition of any charges and collection of any revenues and administrative charges, the terms and conditions of the issuance of additional bonds and notes, and the custody, safeguarding, investment, and application of all moneys. All bonds and notes issued under this section shall be equally and ratably secured by a lien upon the revenues pledged in the trust agreement or resolution, without priority by reasons of number, or dates of bonds or notes, execution, or delivery, in accordance with the provision of this section and of the trust agreement or resolution, except that the unit may provide in the trust agreement or resolution that bonds or notes issued pursuant thereto shall, to the extent and in the manner prescribed in the trust agreement or resolution, be subordinated and junior in standing, with respect to the payment of principal and interest and to the security thereof, to any other bonds or notes. It shall be lawful for any bank or trust company that may act as depository of the proceeds of bonds or notes, revenues, or any other money hereunder to furnish such indemnifying bonds or to pledge such securities as may be required by the unit. Any trust agreement or resolution may set out the rights and remedies of the owners of any bonds or notes and of any trustee, and may restrict the individual rights of action by the owners. In addition to the foregoing, any trust agreement or resolution may contain such other provisions as the unit may deem reasonable and proper for the security of the owners of any bonds or notes. Expenses incurred in carrying out the provisions of any trust agreement or resolution may be treated as a part of the cost of any project or as an administrative charge and may be paid from the revenues or from any other funds available.

The State does pledge to, and agree with, the holders of any bonds or notes issued by any unit that so long as any of the bonds or notes are outstanding and unpaid the State will not limit or alter the rights vested in the unit at the time of issuance of the bonds or notes to set the terms and conditions of the bonds or notes and to fulfill the terms of any agreements made with the bondholders or noteholders. The State shall in no way impair the rights and remedies of the bondholders or noteholders until the bonds or notes and all costs and expenses in connection with any action or proceedings by or on behalf of the bondholders or noteholders, are fully paid, met, and discharged.

(n)   Applicable Provisions. - The provisions of G.S. 159I-15(a), (d), and (e) relating to the Board and its bonds and notes shall apply to a unit of local government and its bonds and notes issued under this section and the applicable provisions of this Chapter, except that the source or sources of revenue pledged to pay bonds and notes of a unit of local government shall be limited as provided in this section.

The provisions of G.S. 159I-17 relating to the Board and its trust funds and investments shall apply to a unit of local government and its trust funds and investments, except that any such moneys of a unit shall be deposited and invested only as provided in G.S. 159-30, as it may be amended from time to time.

The provisions of G.S. 159I-18, 159I-19, 159I-20, and 159I-23 relating to remedies, the Uniform Commercial Code, investment eligibility, and tax exemption, as they relate to the Board's bonds and notes, shall apply to a unit of local government and its bonds and notes. (1989, c. 756, s. 1; 1989 (Reg. Sess., 1990), c. 1004, s. 26; c. 1024, s. 38(e); 1995 (Reg. Sess., 1996), c. 742, s. 39; c. 743, s. 26; 1997-6, s. 20; 1997-307, s. 1; 2001-238, s. 1; 2004-151, ss. 2, 3; 2011-266, s. 1.26(c).)

Chapter 160.

Municipal Corporations.

§§ 160-1 through 160-521: Repealed and Transferred.

Vision Books Order Form

Fax Orders:	1-980-299-5965
Phone Orders:	1-704-898-0770
E-mail Orders:	www.visionbooks.org
Mail Orders:	Vision Books, LLC P.O. Box 42406 Charlotte, NC 28215

Shipp To:
Name_____
Address_____
City_____State_____Zip_____
Phone_____Fax_____
Email_____@_____

Bill To: We can bill a third party on your behalf.
Name_____
Address_____
City_____State_____Zip_____
Phone____(_____)_____Fax_____
Email_____@_____

Pamphlet Number ($15.00 Each)	Qty	Total Cost
_____	_____	_____
_____	_____	_____
_____	_____	_____
_____	_____	_____
_____	_____	_____
_____	_____	_____
_____	_____	_____
Full Volume Set 1-92	**92 Pamphlets**	**1,380.00**

Free Shipping & Handling on Full Volume Orders
Add $1.00 Shipping & Handling Per Pamphlet $_____

Total Cost $_____

Thank you for your support. Management!

DID YOU ENJOY THIS BOOK?

Vision Books, LLC would like to hear from you! If you or someone you know has been fasely imprisoned, we would like to hear your story. If the 'North Carolina Criminal Law and Procedure' has had an effect in your life or if you have suggestions, we would like to hear from you. Send your letters to:

Vision Books, LLC
Attn: Staff Writers
P.O. Box 42406
Charlotte, NC 28215
Email: staff@visionbooks.org

Order Additional Copies:

Fax Orders:	1-980-299-5965
Phone Orders:	1-704-898-0770
E-mail Orders:	www.visionbooks.org
Mail Orders:	Vision Books, LLC P.O. Box 42406 Charlotte, NC 28215